C000044490

Embodied Narratives

Embodied Narratives

Connecting stories, bodies, cultures and ecologies

Edited by

Laura Formenti, Linden West and Marianne Horsdal

European Society for Research on the Education of Adults (ESREA)

Life History and Biography Network and

the University of Southern Denmark Press.

EMBODIED NARRATIVES
Connecting stories, bodies, cultures and ecologies

Edited by Laura Formenti, Linden West and Marianne Horsdal

European Society for Research on the Education of Adults (ESREA) Life History and Biography Network and the University of Southern Denmark Press.

© The authors and University Press of Southern Denmark 2014
Printed by Specialtrykkeriet Viborg
Cover Design by Donald Jensen

ISBN 978 87 7674 747 3

University Press of Southern Denmark
Campusvej 55
DK-5230 Odense M
www.universitypress.dk

Distribution in the United States and Canada:
International Specialized Book Services
5804 NE Hassalo Street
Portland, OR 97213-3644 USA
www.isbs.com

Distribution in the United Kingdom:
Gazelle
White Cross Mills
Hightown
Lancaster
LA1 4 XS
U.K.
www.gazellebookservices.co.uk

Contents

Editors' notes and ackowledgements

This book derives from an intense collaboration among colleagues from various countries under the auspices of the European Society for Research on the Education of Adults (ESREA) Biography and Life History Network. As is described in the opening chapter, the Network has been meeting over many years, with an especial focus on processes of adult and lifelong learning, interrogated through the lens of auto/biographical and narrative studies. The Network brings together researchers from many and diverse countries across Europe – North, South, East and West – and the wider world, as evidenced in this present collection. Auto/biographical and narrative methods, we suggest, generate rich and deep insights into the lived experience of learners, and encourage many and varied connections in thinking about and interpreting them. This includes an interdisciplinary imagination, and challenge to an overly cognitivist, disembodied, and dis-connected view of learners and learning.

This is the third publication emanating from the Network, alongside many and diverse research collaborations. What is so important about the work is how different language communities and academic traditions combine together to challenge the solipsism and isolationism that can too often bedevil academic writing, especially when English has become the dominant language of exchange and debate; and where writing can draw on a relatively narrow, Anglo-Saxon dominated literature. This book, and ESREA more generally, is a challenge to what easily confines the intellectual imagination.

There are a number of people we would like to thank in helping us with the project and the 'challenging' processes of editing: not least Helen Reynolds who has been a tower of strength in working through, with us, various draft chapters and sensitively and carefully negotiating with particular authors around questions of meaning and English usage. And there is Roselina Peneva, who helped with the formatting alongside countless others who have assisted with the organisation of various conferences, of which this work is an important expression.

Laura Formenti, Linden West and Marianne Horsdal
April, 2013

About the editors and contributors

Laura Formenti

Laura Formenti, PhD, is a Professor of General Pedagogy at the Department of Human Sciences for Education "Riccardo Massa", Università degli Studi di Milano Bicocca, Italy, where she teaches Family Pedagogy and Pedagogical Counselling. After a degree in Psychology and a training as a systemic psychotherapist, she had a PhD in Pedagogy, in the field of Adult Education. She is interested in researching adult learning from a systemic, autobiographical, co-operative and interdisciplinary perspective. She published papers and books on autobiographic methods in education and research, on the narrative development of identity, on vocational training for social workers, adult educators and teachers, and on processes of family education. She coordinates (with Linden West) the Life History and Biography Network of ESREA (European Society for Research in the Education of Adults), and is a member of the Steering Committee of ESREA. Her publications are mainly in Italian: La formazione autobiografica (Guerini), La famiglia si racconta (San Paolo); Dare voce al cambiamento (Unicopli); On english: "Families in a Changing Society: how Biographies Inspire Education", in Herzberg, Kammler (eds.) Biographie und Gesellschaft, 2011.

Linden West

Linden West, PhD, FRSA is a Professor and Director of Research Development in the Faculty of Education at Canterbury Christ Church University, Kent, UK and Visiting Professor at the University of Paris Ouest, La Défence. His books include the highly acclaimed Psychoanalysis and Education: Minding a gap (Karnac), which he co-edited with Alan Bainbridge; and Beyond fragments, (Taylor and Francis), Doctors on the edge, (FABooks) and Using life history and biographical approaches in the study of adult and lifelong learning, (Peter Lang). He is co-author, with Barbara Merrill, of Using biographical methods in social research published by Sage. He has been co-editor of the journal Cliopsy and is author of diverse articles and chapters on themes such as managing change and transitions, on narrative methods in careers counselling; on learning in families, communities and professional contexts, and on psychosocial perspectives and how these can inform understanding of the construction and experience of selfhood. He has written widely on the use of auto/biographical methods in research. His writing is translated in many languages, including French, Italian, Spanish, Chinese and Polish. Linden co-coordinates the European Life History and Biographical Research Network and is also a qualified psychoanalytical psychotherapist.

Marianne Horsdal

Dr. Marianne Horsdal is Professor in Educational Research at the University of Southern Denmark. She has collected and researched life story narratives for more than twenty years, and written a number of books and lots of chapters and articles on the subject of life story narratives, methodology, analysis, narrative theory, and the educational impact of narrative competence, the latest being Telling Lives. Exploring dimensions of narratives. (Routledge). She is seen as a key international specialist in the study of narratives, and her writings are translated into several languages. Horsdal's theoretical view of narrative combines phenomenology, hermeneutics, cultural theory and social neuroscience. A full approach to narrative is conceived to encompass both culture, cognition and the body. She has been involved in several Nordic and European research projects in the context of adult education, active citizenship and democracy.

Rob Evans

Rob Evans was born in London, lives in Duisburg and is a lecturer for Academic English/EAP at the University of Magdeburg, Germany. He studied Russian and History in Leeds and Tübingen. After working for many years as a freelance language teacher in adult, further and higher education and in international companies, he gained an MA Ed and Doctorate in Education from the Open University, UK. Since 1977 he has lived and worked outside the UK, in Germany, Italy and Egypt. His main research interests include biography research methods and discourses of learning, and the close analysis of the language of narrated multilingual learning biographies. His focus is on the qualitative narrative interview and his interests also include the use of digital language corpora (CAQDAS). His publications in these fields have appeared in edited books and journals and he writes in English, German, Italian and French. Recently he has begun work on biographical narratives in Polish and Portuguese. Publications include Learning Discourse. Learning Biographies, Embedded Speech and Discourse Identity (Peter Lang), L'entretien auto/biographique et les paroles, (Université Paris 8), Learning and knowing. Narratives, memory and biographical knowledge (RELA 2013). Rob co-ordinates the ESREA Research Network on Adult Learning, Development and Community.

Peter Alheit

Professor em. Dr Dr Peter Alheit, educationalist and sociologist and former holder of the Chair of General Pedagogy at the Georg August University of Goettingen, Germany, is considered a world expert on biographical

13

research and lifelong learning. He was one of the founders of the European Society for Research in the Education of Adults (ESREA), held numerous guest professorships, recently in South Korea and Brazil, and has been involved in a number of European research projects. Peter Alheit is a member of the editorial board of various international research journals. His publications include more than 50 books, an abundance of articles in sociology and education with selected examples of translations into 15 languages.

Juan Carlos Pita Castro

Juan Carlos Pita Castro, PhD, is Maitre-Assistant in the Adult Education Department (Education Sciences) at the University of Geneva. His researches investigate the training of the artists, contemporary identities, the passage from initial training to the world of work and the use of biographical methods in research. He is author of diverse articles and chapters on themes such as the interpretation of narratives of life, on recognition and identity. He coordinated with Janette Friedrich a book Un dialogue entre concept et réalité (Raison et Passion) on the main used concepts in the research on adult education.

Andrea Galimberti

Andrea Galimberti is Ph.D. student at Università degli studi di Milano-Bicocca (Italy), faculty of Educational Sciences. He works as a professional counsellor in different contexts related with intercultural issues and family conflicts. His research interests focus on adult education and the relationships between (self) representations and learning from a systemic and socio-constructionist perspective. He is exploring the wide "landscape of qualitative inquiry", in particular auto/biographical methods in social research.

Christopher Parson

Chris Parson is a lecturer in adult education at the faculty of Psychology and Educational Sciences of Geneva University in Switzerland. His teaching and research interests are centred on issues arising from basic adult education, literacies as social practice, and the role of adult education and training in systems of social and economic integration. His background is in adult literacies provision and he is a member of several regional committees and commissions dealing with political and strategic issues in adult education in French-speaking Switzerland. He has published articles and presented papers on a variety of issues to do with basic adult education provision and literacies.

Samra Tabbal Amella

Samra Tabbal Amella is an assistant and doctoral student in the Adult Education Department (Education Sciences) at the University of Geneva since September 2010. Her PhD thesis investigates how adult immigrants, who have received no formal schooling in their country of origin, learn to read and write for the first time in French as part of "French as a foreign language" programmes in Western Switzerland. Her approach is in the tradition of biographical research and life histories in adult education. In addition to her academic research, she also teaches French to adult immigrants at the Workers' University in Geneva. Two articles are currently under development: the first presents the first results of her research and the second focuses on the difficulties encountered by researchers investigating the socially deprived public. Presently, in collaboration with Professor Jean-Michel Baudouin (thesis supervisor), she is preparing an article (forthcoming) based on the analysis of literacy courses such as "biographical bifurcation".

Maria Francesca Freda

Maria Francesca Freda is an Associated Professor in Clinical Psychology at the Faculty of Philosophy and Literature of the Naples University "Federico II", she is president of the Master Degree Course in Dynamic, Clinical and Community Psychology. She works on the psychosocial intervention in institutions, with particular attention towards educational and health institutions. Many of her studies are on narrations as a methodology for the elaboration of experience's meaning. Her current interests are for the study of narration as a device of psychological clinical intervention, an area of study in which she published Narrazione e Intervento in Psicologia Clinica [Narration and Intervention in Clinical Psychology] (Liguori, Napoli, 2009). E-mail: fmfreda@unina.it

Giovanna Esposito

Giovanna Esposito, PhD, Research Fellow, Department of Humanistic Studies, University of Naples Federico II. Her research interests are centered around the promotion of reflective competences within educational contexts and around intervention for the prevention of psycho-social risk with university students. She currently works with the European Project INSTALL as a trainer of Narrative Mediation Path (NMP)

Maria Luisa Martino

Maria Luisa Martino, PhD, Department of Humanistic Studies, University of Naples Federico II. Her research interests are focused around the use and evaluation, within institutional setting, of different narrative devices addressed to the promotion of processing and integration of traumatic events. She is a researcher on the European Project INSTALL.

José González-Monteagudo

José González-Monteagudo is a Senior Lecturer in Educational Theories at the University of Seville, Spain. He has written and researched in these areas: contemporary educational theories; qualitative research and Ethnography; life-history and narrative approaches related to research and education, specially auto/biographical narratives; non-traditional and international students. Last books published: (2010): Educational Journeys and Changing Lives. Adult Student Experiences. Seville: Digital@Tres (co-edited with Barbara Merrill); (2011) (Ed.): Les Histoires de vie en Espagne. Entre formation, identité et mémoire. Paris: L'Harmattan.

Myriam Graber

Myriam Graber, is a doctoral student in educational sciences at the University of Geneva, where she is an associate member of the Mimèsis et formation research team. She is also Professor and researcher at the health school of The University of Applied Sciences, Western Switzerland. She is co-editor with Gakuba, T. and Mégard Mutezintare, CL. of a book: Les représentations et les discours des acteurs des Hautes écoles de la santé et du social sur les processus et les conditions d'apprentissage des étudiants d'Afrique subsaharienne, and has participated with Lioba Howatson-Jones on Biographical learning: a process for promoting person centredness in nursing, which will be published later this year. Her research activities and teaching focus on questions of intercultural communication, interaction processes and identity processes in intercultural situations, questions of identity and professionalization. She is particularly interested in auto/biographical research as a methodology for exploring these topics.

Lioba Howatson-Jones

Lioba Howatson-Jones, Ph.D, RGN, is a Senior Lecturer in the Department of Nursing and Applied Clinical Studies at Canterbury Christ Church University. Her books include Reflective Practice in Nursing (Sage) which has just been published as a second edition; Patient Assessment and Care Planning in Nursing (Sage) with co-authors Dr. Mooi Standing and Susan Roberts; Outpatient, Day Surgery and Ambulatory Care (Wiley-Blackwell) which she co-edited with Peter Ellis. She is the author of diverse articles and chapters on the themes of learning and teaching, making sense of subjective experience, using auto/biographical methods for researching in nursing, clinical supervision and servant leadership. She is also a reviewer for Sage Publications, the International Practice Development Journal and Nurse Education in Practice. As a qualified nurse she also still works in nursing practice.

Claire Thurgate

Claire Thurgate, MSc, RSCN, RGN is a Principal Lecturer in the Department of Health, Well-being and Family at Canterbury Christ Church University. She has co-edited a book Workplace learning in health and social care: a student's guide (McGraw-Hill) with Carolyn Jackson. She is the author of articles and chapters on the themes of workplace learning, children with disabilities and workforce development. She is on the Editorial Advisory Board for the Journal of Further and Higher Education and a reviewer for Journal of Nursing Management and the International Practice Development.

Catherine Karen Roy

Catherine Karen Roy, PhD, is a Sessional Instructor of German in the Faculty of Central, Eastern, and Northern European Studies at the University of British Columbia, Vancouver, Canada. Her research interests include autobiography, photography, as well as language teaching and learning.

Rebecca Corfield

Rebecca Corfield is a Senior Lecturer in the Centre for Career and Personal Development, part of the Faculty of Education at Canterbury Christ Church University, Kent UK. She has studied Management up to MBA level and is a qualified careers counsellor. She is a past elected President of the national Institute of Career Guidance, the professional body for careers counsellors in the UK. Rebecca has written many best-selling careers titles published by Kogan Page including Successful Interview Skills; Preparing Your Own CV; Knockout Job Interview Presentations and The Redundancy Survival Guide, three of which are now in their fifth editions. Managing Your Career published by Dorling Kindersley came out in 2002. Her writing is translated into many languages, including Czech, Dutch, Latvian, Polish, Portugese, Spanish and Thai. She is currently studying for a doctorate using auto/biographical narrative methods to explore the motivation of school governors.

Nora Bateson

Nora Bateson is a filmmaker, lecturer, writer, as well as director & producer of the award-winning documentary film "An Ecology of Mind" (CA/USA 2010), a portrait of her father Gregory Bateson's way of thinking. She has developed educational curricula for schools in Northern California, and produced and directed award winning multimedia projects on intercultural and ecological understanding.

Chapter 1

Introduction: only connect, the parts and the whole: the role of biographical and narrative research?

◊ LAURA FORMENTI, LINDEN WEST AND MARIANNE HORSDAL

What pattern connects the crab to the lobster and the orchid to the primrose and all the four of them to me? And me to you? And all the six of us to the amoeba in one direction and to the backward schizophrenic in another? (Bateson, 1979:8).

This book focuses on neglected issues in adult and lifelong learning, and education more generally: surrounding the body and emotionality, and their relationship to thinking and the imagination; and the neglect of the idea of learning as fundamentally to do with relationship, both to other human beings but also to symbolic, socio-cultural and ecological worlds. Why and how such neglect has happened lies at the heart of the writing: and these issues are addressed from many points of view, historical, cultural, psychological, and sociological. Our aim has been to build a new, more holistic ecology of learning, and in interdisciplinary ways. Fundamentally, we seek to make and expand connections, and a consciousness of how everything interconnects, beyond an overly individualised, disembodied cognition: our learning and selves, we suggest, are always and inevitably situated, part of a broader nexus of dynamic interactions.

Hannah Arendt (1988) taught how thinking, and resistance to it, for instance, is culturally embedded: when the neighbour goes missing, in a totalitarian society, other neighbours may not want to know, or to think, and memory itself gets lost. At a psychological level, Freud observed how the censor operates in analogous ways: some thoughts, particular desires, may be unacceptable to the conscious mind and have to be repressed, obliterated even, partly because of our absolute dependence on the other in early life, and the fear of being rejected, found wanting and or of being abandoned (Bainbridge and West, 2012; Honneth, 2009). These cultural and psychological dynamics may be more pervasive than we often think: learning might be encouraged or discouraged within many relationships and cultures. Dis-connection is both a socio-cultural and psychological phenomenon: psychoanalysis teaches that anti-learning or resistance to understanding may be stronger than the desire to know and learn from experience (Bainbridge and West, 2012). Resistance to thinking may also be at work in relation to the environment and ecological fragility, in which we, as human beings, are deeply implicated. Thinking about what we do, and why, may, at times, seem unbearable and the difficulties of thinking need to be better understood.

At the end of the twentieth century, notions of the "linguistic" or "narrative" turn also became influential in academic contexts, encompassing writing and research in education as well as most other social sciences: which has implications for our theme. The turn has shaped the book, and the development of auto/biographical and narrative research, as a whole, in that the increased focus on language and discourse, and the idea of a linguistic construction of reality, illuminates the significant impact of discursive worlds on ways of being and knowing; yet, at the same time, the role of the body seems to have been downplayed or to have been reduced in discourse to simply 'text'. In the history of the humanities, as Horsdal (this volume; 2012) notes, the body is the underprivileged stepchild of academic enquiry. This may be deep rooted: divisions between nature and culture, body and soul, emotions and rationality, have framed dominant discourses, creating a distinctive idea of true humanity being the self-reflective rational individual, distant and distinct from the body. There has been a tendency, shaped, in part, by Christian theology, and Western metaphysical traditions, of the body, and feelings and even subjectivity, as something to be overcome and transcended. The disembodied logos of traditional philosophy has prized semantics over voice, mind over body, men over women (Cavarero, 2005).

Modern philosophy, in its search for epistemological certainty and clarity, tends, still, following Descartes, to split mind from body, while transcendence is presumed to lie in escape from our animal, corporeal base. The deep suspicion of the body, and of feeling and subjectivity, is embedded in many contemporary notions, including of transformative learning, where epistemic shifts, rather than in feelings, or subjective dynamics, has been regarded as fundamental (see West, this volume). Moreover, if the body is frequently absent from discussions and consciousness, then the interactions of the whole human being, the *sentio* as well as *cogito*, in relation to others, and the environment, has been pervasively neglected in an overly individualised, narrowly psychologised, decontextualised view of the human subject. Such limited perspectives on learning and the subject are damaging: they exclude or implicitly denigrate other ways of knowing, whether heart-felt, spiritual, and or experiential. There is a triumph of a kind of disembodied cognition, which can be profoundly alienating from self and experience. In the twentieth century, the establishment of empirical research and an overly scientistic view of human and social research have progressively marginalised informal, tacit, and emotional ways of knowing (Illeris, 2002).

Our book challenges the above and is energised by the desire to chronicle and understand experiences of learning and change processes through the frame of life history and or auto/biographical narrative research. When we engage in in-depth research, of this kind – in a care-full chronicling and analysis of learner narratives – we can become more aware of the whole people and wider ecologies implicated in learning and its antithesis. The biographical and narrative turn (Chamberalyne et al, 2000; West el al, 2007; Merrill and West, 2009) has spawned more holistic ways of understanding the human subject, and her learning, as well as struggles for reflexivity: indeed how creating more personal meaning, in relationship, enhances the potential for reflexivity, and agency, and thus may be dynamically constitutive of who we are and might be in potentially life enhancing ways. Our book, in these terms, is a contribution to forging greater connectedness in understanding learners and learning, in a world and at a moment of history, where this is much needed. At the heart of the writing lies a fundamental aspiration: the desire to better understand and theorise how the body and relationships, both to immediate and wider worlds, find expression in learning biographies, and how such experiences can be enhanced.

Alongside such an aspiration, or implicit in it, is doing research using a particular family of methods, and, we suggest, the powerful contribution these bring to building knowledge of learners and learning, derived from the generation of rich stories of lived experience and sophisticated modes of analysis. Yet, this family of biographic and narrative methods has differences as well as commonalities, which we want to celebrate: researchers may have more of a sociological orientation and be preoccupied, for instance, with how cultures or their discourses structure how we think and feel; those of a more psychological, and especially psychoanalytic orientation, may be more attuned to the nuance of individual difference, including in groups, that seem, on the surface, to be made up of people who are much alike. The narrative theorist, drawing on literary ideas, or neuroscience, can insist that we examine the pervasive role of language and how it works in relation to the body: discourse may, in quite a basic sense, as Damasio suggests, become the word made flesh via our relationships and the stories that pervade these (Hunt and West, 2009). Or to put it slightly differently, we are our stories, or are storied, as well as storytellers. Our brain is an organ of adaptation, within particular cultures and sets of relationship from which we develop our narrative repertoires (Horsdal, 2012).

There are other differences in the family: researchers in education from the south of Europe tend to pose more philosophical questions and/or are interested in educational practice as well as in research, while some northern, especially Anglo-Saxon researchers, can be more empirically oriented and/or use critical theory and feminism to interrogate their data. Sub-cultures of research may adopt their own perspectives and core concepts. Our aim is to create connections, to build dialogue between these differences, instead of warring against the other, in what too often is typical academic competitiveness, a kind of symbolic cannibalism. We suggest that the challenge of creating more inclusive understanding of humans and their potential for learning and change is too complex to be solved by one member of a family, alone, or, for that matter, even within whole families. The methodologies at the heart of the book represent an important contribution, but one among many, to illuminating the human condition: although we consider them to be particularly powerful in chronicling the human condition, and as a basis for developing more nuanced and interdisciplinary theories.

The Network and the conference: a cosmopolitan community

The dialogue at the heart of the book is a product of the work of the ESREA (European Society for Research on the Education of Adults) Life History and Biography Research Network. This is a strong community of researchers, which has met every March, at a conference, for 20 years, with the aim of sharing insights, exhilarations and frustrations, and to engage in methodological and epistemological debate. It has provided the basis for a number of books (Alheit et al, 1995; West et al, 2007), and has been a focus for European-wide research, such as a study of retention and drop-out among non-traditional learners in universities (Merrill, et al., forthcoming). It was central to the publication of a special issue of the French journal *Pratiques de formation/Analyses*, n. 55/2008, edited by José Gonzalez Monteagudo, which mapped the "non-francophone approaches" to life history in Europe. Despite a common interest in "stories" of adult and lifelong learning – their generation, analysis and representation – the Network remains, as noted, a heterogeneous family: geographically, linguistically, and disciplinarily. In this historical moment, the geographical heterogeneity of the family might be crucial in an attempt to avoid forms of linguistic and cultural colonialism in scientific communities, predicated on the dominance of the English language. The effort towards respecting different views and ways of making meaning, and for learning from each other was there from the outset of the Network, as was an ambition to create a safe place for Ph.D. students and their presentations. The first conference, held in Geneva, in 1993, addressed the interplay between "structures and subjectivity" in learners' lives. It was clear, from that beginning, that there were different positions, as represented, for instance, by the work of the first two conveners, Peter Alheit, from Germany and Pierre Dominicé, from the Francophone Switzerland.

Peter Alheit has developed a distinct life history approach in sociological research, with an emphasis on how lives are structured as well as potential sites for what he terms 'biographical learning', or 'biographicity' (Alheit, 1995; Alheit and Dausien, 2002). Dominicé's preoccupation has been with generating "histoires de vie", with a strongly practical, professional dimension. He was concerned with how to cultivate deeper reflexivity and critical knowledge of self and culture among various professionals (Dominicé, 1990, 2000, 2007). Alheit emphasised the importance of rigour and objectivity in research, exercised as he was by a need to establish the legitimacy of such methods in a somewhat sceptical German scientific community. Pierre Dominicé came from adult education, as a field of intervention; he sought to cultivate a better understanding of self and reflexivity in adult learners: encompassing self and other, individuals and cultures, one background and another. He created space in the university to build educational biographies in small collaborative groups, learning from each other's experience by employing oral and written methods, iteratively. He addressed the ethical and political engagement of the biographic researcher, as well as the cultivation of a culturally sensitive reflexivity, from the beginning (Dominicé in Alheit et al., 1995). Alongside all this, many scholars (most of them women, and maybe this matters) brought in the Network a strong social and relational sensibility, through their studies, and were active in enhancing relationships and keeping alive a spirit of community. Among them, from the outset, were Agnieszka Bron, Barbara Merrill, Gunilla Härnsten, and Marie Christine Josso.

The Network, however, struggled, for many years, to sustain the dialogue between what could seem very different preoccupations: on the one hand, with subjectivity, and educative aspirations; on the other, with objectivity, and using learners' lives to ground sociological theorising in complex terrain. All of which co-existed with different, sometimes neglected, traditions in south and even the north of Europe, where storytelling was often seen as more of a collective process in struggles for social justice.

Over time, interest in subjectivity, intersubjectivity and structure, as well as their interplay, came to encompass questions of the detachment and objectivity of the researcher herself, as against her potential role as co-enquirer, working empathically and dialogically with learners, to make mutual sense of experience. These differences found expression, in varying ways, as the Network addressed different yet overlapping themes, over many years, in a developing conversation:

- In 2008, in Canterbury, England, the topic was the *"Emotions and learning, a neglected species"*. To tell a story, it was stated, might be about expressing or disguising one's emotions, and/or sharing them with the person who is listening, or not; conventional distinctions between self and other, memory and immediacy, one biography and another, were problematized as was the myth of the rational, information processing subject that seemed to dominate, unreflexively, much conventional social science research. Biographical research itself could also be trapped in simplistic binaries: of rationality/irrationality, consciousness/false consciousness, rather than more sophisticated, psychosocial acknowledgement of the defended as well as social subject, whose stories might change, depending on the context and the quality of the interaction with the researcher (Hollway and Jefferson, 2000).

- In 2009, in Milan, Italy, the theme was "*Wisdom and knowledge in researching and learning lives: diversity, differences, and commonalities*". Researchers sought, it was suggested, to build knowledge of adult learning, but left, to the shadows, fundamental issues in adult life, to do with what we might call quests for wisdom (Josso, 2011). The conference also explored – thanks to Josso, Baracchi, Giannini, and others, who contributed to plenaries and workshops – the relationship of such quests to spirituality, ethics, philosophy, and other ways of meaning making. However, it was noted that wisdom as an idea can sometimes sit uncomfortably in the academy, although Aristotle placed it at the apex of sense making: the search for Sophia, or transcendental forms of knowing, was fundamental to composing the meaningful life.

- In 2010, at Växjö, Sweden, the theme was "*Representing lives and learning. The science and poetics of our work*". We strive, it was suggested, to chronicle human lives and to understand them, but how do we guarantee that our representations are respectful of the complexity of life? How can art and science find a purposeful and creative relationship in understanding learning lives? Clearly, we were searching, again, for dialogue across difference. Between, for instance, a more feminist and literary inspired desire to convey lives more authentically, vibrantly and auto/biographically, alongside the wish for some analytic detachment as well as theoretical rigour: for science and poetry, logos and mythos, perhaps. Logos emanates from rationality and precision, from taking care and bringing order into knowing. Mythos searches for meaning as well as the feeling of lives. The biographical research family needed to manage difference creatively, it was concluded, because there was a place for both science and artistry, if only to do full justice to lives, learners and learning.

- In 2011, in Geneva, Switzerland, we focused on the theme of "*Human agency and biographical transformations. Adult learning, education and life paths*". We drew attention to the difficult, even distressing situation in many societies and the rapid, sometimes disturbing transformation of lives that globalisation brings in its train. There is, in biographical research, a wish to chronicle and theorise moments of significant agency and personal transformation, including the way individuals think and talk about their experience in different ways, after significant learning. The whole debate was fuelled by anxiety in a runaway world, as Giddens (1999) termed it, where individuals can feel their lives are out of control, and powerless in turn. They can turn to fundamentalist solutions, to anti-learning rather than cosmopolitanism, in desperation.

- Finally, there was the conference in 2012, at Odense, Denmark, the birthplace of Hans Christian Andersen, from which our book stems. The theme was "*Expanding Connections. Learning, the body and the environment*". We wanted to engage with the interplay of different levels of experience: the embodied mind, the situated self, and selves within complex ecologies. We sought to celebrate the complexity of life and to recognize potentially deep connections between life stories, bodies and whole contexts. This preoccupation was rooted in concerns about human, social and ecological well-being: by listening to the stories people tell, it was suggested, we can sketch potential interconnections between human flourishing, environmental as well as financial fragility.

To repeat, ours is a community of researchers who share the 'same' or similar methods but who do not necessarily have the same presuppositions or ways of thinking. However, we have sought to build a cosmopolitan and inclusive dialogue around learning and its role in creating a more sustainable, less greedy, narcissistically obsessed world: this is a community that is epistemologically relativistic and polyphonic, yet politically and ethically engaged too. It is a community where stories are valued and regarded as essential for generating better understanding of one another, of whole selves, and of our interconnectedness; and of what inhibits or enhances human reflexivity, compassion, and the desire to know and engage with troubles, however difficult, and to create new possibilities for human flourishing.

Only connect

Stories are one starting point, but do not stand by themselves. They draw on a 'material' base, namely the interacting bodies of teller and listener, of voices, gestures and unconscious communication, and of the artefacts employed, including the recording device. Stories are generated in a physical as well as imaginal space, shaped by cultures, and their interplay with inner worlds: whether the home, office, the university and the like. Culture intrudes in storytelling in diverse ways: around the time that can be taken in the increasingly frenetic work place; or in the need to deliver 'chunks' of research in more 'efficient' ways. Materialities and cultures matter, in these terms, including cultures of the academy. This includes the ubiquitous pressure to produce answers, with the danger of reducing stories, and human beings, and experience, to overly reductive categories or simplistic causal relationships. The telling of a story, and its interpreta- tion, is a creative and generative process, with multiple implications and dynamics, to be interpreted from different angles. What we can do is to explore this irreducible complexity, imaginatively, with a diverse reper- toire, and within a community of scholars; and make learning, learners and life a little more comprehensible, in respectful rather than reductive ways. But we require openness and imagination, alongside intelligence and method, to this end.

Gregory Bateson attempted such a task, in his work, and he was an influ- ential symbolic presence at the Conference. Here was a man who sought, more than most, to illuminate the connections between evolution and learning, Mind and Nature (1979), in systematic and imaginative ways. His daughter, Nora Bateson, was a literal presence, with her film *An Ecology of Mind* – a documentary premièred at the Vancouver International Film Festival, and honoured with many awards, (including the *Morton Marcus Documentary Feature Award* (2011, Santa Cruz Film Festival), and the *John Culkin Award for Outstanding Praxis in the Field of Media Ecology* (2011)). Nora introduced the film and reflected with us, at the conference, on her father's idea of learning, and his own way of thinking and learning: whether from the symmetry of a starfish or a crab, or from observing play in wolves and dolphins; or from mothers, babies and their interactions in Bali; or, not least, from his own daughter. A basic point, in Bateson's work, is to realize how limited our grasp is of what we may term the circuitry to which we belong. This is a system of relationships that are hierarchically organized in levels, each one interdependent on the other. He applied cybernetics and information theory to the field of relational ecological anthropology, using complementary concepts such as homoeostasis and schismogenesis, positive and negative feedback, change and stability, to understand what is happening in what he called Creatura. He saw the world as a tangle of hierarchically ordered systems: individuals, societies, and ecosystems. At each of these levels, learning happens when an exchange of information brings new configurations, new structures, or frameworks, in the system, while interdependency (i.e. mutual adaptation) is maintained, both within the living system, and in its relation to other systems, and a whole context.

A system, then, undergoes adaptive changes, which depend upon feedback loops, always maintaining some balance or identity, and an enduring relationship with the environment. Something, paradoxically, that is changing all the time, yet coherently within a whole. The key unit of survival in evolution is the organism *and* its environment (or context): they need to be connected, and to co-evolve, to sustain life. The way to understand this is by seeing and honouring this complex interrelation. The natural ecological system is not good or bad in itself: if life goes on, it is by maintaining an identity through relative stability *and* change, fuelled by information, i.e. 'any difference which makes a difference in some later event' (1972:381).

The individual, society and ecosystem, then, may be seen as different levels of the 'same' immanent structure, 'the pattern which connects' (1979:8). However, a delicate balance was disrupted by the dominating epistemology, which separated Mind and Nature, using lineal notions of causality to force change into the system without understanding it. Ecological disasters and many sorts of crises are then caused, in Bateson's view, by "pathologies of epistemology" (1972:478), i.e. wrong assumptions rooted in a kind of scientific hubris or arrogance, driven by narrow purpose and diminished sensibility. In 1967, years ahead of current ecological preoccupations, he wrote: "The ecology and population dynamics of the species has been disrupted; parasites have been made immune to antibiotics; the relationship between mother and neonate has been almost destroyed" (Bateson, 1972:145). When we allow purpose and consciousness to control our lives, we reduce our perceptiveness and responsiveness. In this way, we limit our potential for wisdom. This is an educational problem, of course, and brings consequence for the way we do research.

The human being has learned to exert power – a potentially autocratic regime – over all kinds and levels of the system, not least the environment; hence, ecological (and other) crises are not provoked by one cause, but by "the *combined* action of (a) technological advance; (b) population increase; and (c) conventional (but wrong) ideas about the nature of man and his relation to the environment" (1972:488). This carries the potential to do irrevocable damage and destroy the system. To overcome this, or at least reduce its impact, new forms of understanding, of complex and interconnected knowledge, are needed.

These positions entail remarkable consequences for biographical research. Forms of "disconnected knowledge' and 'bad stories' will influence many phenomena at a global scale, as well as individual lives, and research. Yet, we know from Bateson's work, that 'real life" does not work in a disconnected way, and people suffer from the lack of harmony between their lives and the way these are told. The diabolic effects (*dia-ballein* in Ancient Greek means 'to separate', 'to divide') in disconnected knowledge can be overcome by symbolic actions (*syn-ballein*, 'to unify'), where connectivity, 'the real stuff of life', is actively represented. Hence, the relevance of stories, and of "thinking in terms of stories" (Bateson 1979:14). Narration is a crucial way to symbolize our complexity (in fact, a part of it, as the totality never is totally achieved), in a physical and symbolic space, e.g. a narrative interview, that allows the development of a 'good story'.

To honour, or celebrate, connectedness involves a class of actions and relations, a "style" (Bateson, 1971). It means that, when doing research, we act in such a way to symbolize and represent "the pattern which connects". This has ethical and epistemological implications for our action as researchers; a story tells of the constraints and structures involved in human becoming, at the different levels cited above: individual, relational, socio-systemic, and even planetary. Among these, there are also the constraints and structures built into the process of researching. The best that we can do is to be aware that what we are seeing is but a small component of a larger circuitry, as researches show in the second half of this book. In an 'ecology of ideas', thought, emotion and imaginative empathy combine, to build knowledge not separated from wisdom (as the Network explored in the 2009 conference). Spirituality and art have an important role to play in cultivating a greater and necessary consciousness and interconnectivity (as explored in 2010).

At the Odense conference, there were diverse calls to build better, interconnected understanding: in the desire for new forms of interdisciplinary, psychosocial understanding, for instance, surrounding the dynamics of inner and outer worlds (see West, this volume). Such understanding might enable us to better appreciate the complexity of experience – for adults, young people and children – of selves struggling to be; and of the need to re-imagine education as more than a rational exercise of mind but rather a deeply embodied, interconnected, difficult, emotional process; one alive with the play of fantasy, desire and resistance, new and older ways of knowing, sensibilities as well as denial and illusion. Psychoanalysis, broadly defined, has encouraged us to delve beneath surface appearances, and to challenge overly sanitised, emotionally deadened and ultimately unsustainable accounts of learning. A core preoccupation in this work is to understand the whole human being, the defended as well as social subject, the meaning maker and potentially resistant soul, at the heart of education; and, essential to such a task, is to straddle old tribal boundaries between psychology and sociology. Axel Honneth's (2007; 2009) concept of 'recognition' reminds us, for instance, of the role of love and good enough relationships in human flourishing; but also how self-respect and self-esteem are products of wider institutional and socio-cultural dynamics. If we feel recognised within a group, as a legitimate member with rights and responsibilities, we can become more alive and agentic; if we feel valued and are considered important to wider well-being, then we can experience stronger self-esteem and a capacity to think and act, more agentically, with others to challenge oppressive forces. From such interacting, inter-dependent micro, meso and macro dynamics, serious thinking can grow, alongside greater mutual loyalty, solidarity and potentially healthier, more sustainable, cultures. It is, as Bateson taught, all of a piece.

There was also, within the conference, preoccupations with narrative theory and how theoretical understanding is deeply bound up with the methods of biographical narrative research. Neurophysiology, philosophical perspectives, literary theory, research and methodology can be brought together to formulate deeper, more connected understanding of narrative, its analysis and material, as well as relational origins. Marianne Horsdal, for example, in a lecture at the conference, explored the influence of cultural and social environments on our narrative memories, and the development of competencies, including as thoughtful, potentially political agents. Of how such competencies get embodied, in the perspectives of contemporary neuroscience. Rob Evans, in his contribution, built a further connection with the idea of the embodied production of language, in varying social space. He cites Bourdieu on language, as "a dimension of an individual's physical hexis in which the social world in all its relationships and the world in all its socially instructed relationships are given expression" (Bourdieu, 2001). Participants in biographical research are communicating, "talking bodies", deploying the "interactional qualities and language of the body" (Evans, this volume). Making meaning, in this view, is physically situated between the historical and cultural grounding of the self, and the construction of the self and the world in new ways. This creates tension, anchored in the life-worlds of participants. There are many connections here, as language shapes and determines the interaction out of which the life history is narrated. Yet the telling shapes, in turn, the language used, opening new possibilities. In examining the business of learning by individuals in our research, we are examining, too, a search for new forms of language in which to express and embody learning more authentically.

Connecting the chapters: multiple views of life and learning

In our efforts to 'expand connections', we are aware of the necessity of building good, satisfying theory: including of body and selfhood, and of the context(s) of auto/biographical research. We are mindful of the range of factors – psychic, unconscious, social, cultural, linguistic, emotional and practical – that shape stories, and sustain or hinder learning and potential transformation. We also feel it important to know more about processes of co-construction in research, as people inhabit contexts where psychosocial and cultural forces, not least power and unconscious processes, are in play. We are storied as well as storytellers, whether at work, in our intimacies, and or in our aspirations; in our use of words and how discourse inhibits or liberates us. Research itself is a narrative with varying dimensions in play.

The first set of chapters offers a developing theoretical repertoire, to make sense of such dynamics. They provide a rationale for placing the body in context, of embodied cultures and particular relationships, when theorising auto/biographical research. They offer a panoply of perspectives, using different disciplines, but also seeking to build interdisciplinarity, in developing their case. As often happens within the Life History and Biography Network, authors draw on heterogeneous sources and points of reference, rather than from one tradition, or even paradigm, or methodological orientation. This variety obliges the reader to reflect on and to engage with the chapters as a whole: their composition, contradictions, and possible complementarities. They offer, in fact, various windows into the body, and thus mind, in context, and of the cultural situatedness of people and storytelling.

At the conference in Odense, as stated, there was a heterogeneous community of researchers who presented but also listened to and discussed differing perspectives, impelled by a conviction that learning itself emanates from making connections across differences. Now, at this moment of writing, something new and additional is woven, in the effort to create an overall frame by bringing together the different threads to create more of a patchwork or mosaic that transcends the fragments. Each piece of research, in every chapter, involves an effort to create more embodied, contextualised, and complex understanding of adult learning. What unites them all is an anti-reductionist spirit, and a desire to challenge separation and polarity: of mind and body, psyche and society, the person and nature, one biography and another, the individual and collective, learning and sustainability, narrative and personhood.

Marianne Horsdal, in Chapter 2, begins the process with a deceptively simple statement: "Our stories are embodied", challenging mind/body dualism still pervading educational research. Stories are written in, with and about the body. This means, for Horsdal, that we must be aware of the connections between findings from social and affective neuroscience, from the narrative cultures we inhabit, and the phenomenology of our interactions and journeys in space and time. Our stories connect the "here and now" of a sentient body, and the "there and then" of autobiographic memory. Interactions and emotions work through the body, and are constitutive parts of the researcher's endeavour to chronicle and celebrate the complexity of human lives. The researcher needs to be bodily aware in order to do her work effectively. Being stuck in the head is a kind of denial of humanity, of the capacity for empathy, and of the interplay of here and now, there and then.

In Chapter 3, Linden West asks us to focus on a further complexity: the need for more nuanced interdisciplinary understanding of the experiences of non-traditional students in universities. Much too often, the researcher stays at one level of explanation, within one discipline, he suggests. Learners' stories are, by their nature, interdisciplinary: there are always and inevitably fragments of the social, the psychic, the cultural, the economic, and of being storied as well as of agency in narrative. A way to manage this multiplicity is by bringing into play some interdisciplinary "sensitising concepts", connecting macro, meso and micro-levels. Thus, Bourdieu's theory of "social reproduction" can be aligned with Winnicott's play of subjectivity, in "transitional space"; and Honneth's concept of "recognition" in human flourishing, with both, to build understanding of how systems may reproduce themselves but also get challenged and changed. They offer, together, a richer frame of understanding how concrete interactions in groups and across whole cultures matter, as does the most intimate of experience, in creating agency, individual and collective, and in challenging oppression; or succumbing to its power.

In Chapter 4, Rob Evans takes us into the materiality of stories, i.e. words. Sense making always comes from acts of communication and interactions, where words are in play, but following specific rules. A good theory and good method for biographical research entail the possibility of investigating such complexities in meaning-full ways. In biographical interviews, language shapes and determines the interactions, and the quality of the telling itself shapes in turn the language that is used. Evans proposes a way of examining what happens in the here and now of the research space, and the language used to express learning. Spoken words should not be treated as "de-contextualised games", or the simple effect of neurones firing at will.

Peter Alheit, in Chapter 5, straddles the sociological and historical. Dominant images of subjectivity, as well as the technologies of the self, change in relation to the nature of our work and intimacy, in different historical times and within different social groups and cultures. Alheit demonstrates the richness and variety of representations of the subject, in modernity: in bourgeois, post-bourgeois, and post-modernist cultures. He shows us a way of connecting history, class and particularities. The evolution of configurations of the subject, over the last few centuries, can be understood, he suggests, by using metaphors and images: such as the cycle, the arch (or stairs), the line, and, more recently, the patchwork or perpetual puzzle. The last two metaphors fit well with our idea of connectivity in learning and knowledge: perhaps we too are being shaped by cultural metaphor, as well as creating such an image, in our time.

Parts of the whole: how biographical research honours interactions and interdependences

> We live in a life in which our percepts are perhaps always the perception of parts, and our guesses about wholes are continually being verified or contradicted by the latter presentation of other parts. It is perhaps so, that wholes can never be presented; for that would involve direct communication. (Bateson, 1979:126)

The second part of the book offers diverse examples of auto/biographical and life history research. Each chapter has a different focus: the authors' backgrounds are contrasting, from different countries, using different languages, disciplines, pursuing varying research questions, and methodological choices. Threads, however, are to be found if we read these pieces as multiple examples of a common effort to engage with complexity and interdependence in human lives and learning. These researchers have made a moral choice to honour stories, as such, while also having in mind specific questions about the content or context of learning. The focus, in each chapter, is on an aspect of human experience; but each chapter says something too about general questions, and how we might research them.

For example, in Chapter 6, "*The Myth of Birth: Autobiography and Family Memory*", Laura Formenti uses a specific aspect of autobiography – the story of one's birth – to illuminate a general feature of autobiographic research: the interplay of three levels of relationship, that are always in-volved in shaping the telling of stories, and their understanding. These are the micro, the meso and the macro-level. At the micro-level, in the here-and-now of narration, an individual and his/her audience participate in the co-construction of that story, defining what is possible, in short, to narrate in those circumstances. The meso-level encompasses how someone's birth has been constructed as shared stories (a lasting myth) by the people who are part of the same 'us' (in this case, a 'family'). The macro-level involves an overall context and its dominant narrations and practices: birth can be better understood as a socially, culturally, and historically determined practice that influences the way things are talked about at the other levels. The meso-level is usually under-represented in auto/biographical research, where psychology and subjectivity (the mi-cro) or sociology, culture, and history (the macro) tend to dominate the scene. However, in education and learning, our proximal relationships, communities, and enduring contexts, at the meso-level, are remarkably involved in both stabilizing *and* changing our personal myths.

Chapter 7, *"Interrelations between narration, identity and place"*, by Juan Carlos Pita Castro, examines how identity and place are linked, when biographic interviews, narratives of place, and self-portraits are used to investigate the transformation of young artists' identities. Since places are reminders of life's episodes, the researcher involves participants in revisiting such places. What we call 'place narratives' help to complete the subjective dimension, alongside biography and self-portrait; all are part of a quest for individuality but also for belonging and recognition in making identities. In a world of mobile and networked identity, and no apparent attachment to place, the study illuminates how solitude, loss of creativity, lack of col-lectivity, feelings of emptiness, propel subjects to search for constants, by attaching to places notions of landmarks, symbolic homes, or pillars; even of *lost paradises*. A "law of proximity" is formulated, where places close in time appear to facilitate a story of *what* the subject is, while the place that is far away, temporally, in narrative terms, becomes more autobiographic. Closeness of place to current experience also brings with it more of a collective dimension, of shared worlds. This chapter illuminates the affective identification with place; and of the collective energy attached to it; and of the impossibility of living free of any bounds, in heightened mobility. Identity becomes more contextual and territorial in consequence.

Chapter 8, "*Non-traditional students and imagined social capital: the resources of an embodied mind*", written by Andrea Galimberti, examines stories of non-traditional learners in auto/biographic workshops. His aim is to gain better understanding of student experience and relationship within the university. Embodied stories, evoked in personal and meaningful ways, during the workshops, were helpful in making sense of experience; "satisfying theory" was built by the students, using metaphors of space and time: "empty space", "huge mechanisms", a "university bubble", "time to walk", "we get to our expiry date". Storytelling and metaphor build bridges between past and present, and between student's diverse experiences and strategies, explored, in a constellation of possibilities created in narrative play. According to Arendt, a "political space" is made when freedom and action bring something new and unpredictable. Can university be such a space?

In Chapter 9, "*Literacy and the social environment: when the context sets the agenda for learning*", Christopher Parson and Samra Tabbal Amella employ biographical interviews to interrogate how adult migrants, who never attended formal schooling, "enter the world of written language"; and the forms of support they find when trying to improve basic literacy skills. The ultimate aim of the research is to identify experiences that have helped people to find a "breakthrough". The authors conclude that the narrator is dependent on the social context, at any given time. The availability of support and resources varies in relation to this context; access to such things affects the development of agency. Among forms of support, there are special relationships with third parties – a friend, for instance – that may help integrate a person in a context, and learning becomes more possible. Learning might also be energised by interactions with native speakers and the development of linguistic capacities. Other forms of support derive from structural elements of the environment, in the university, for instance, which combine with individual resources, generated by experiential capital, forged in challenging structural constraints. Such notions as 'poietic agenc' and 'mobility capita' are introduced, and we become aware of how learning provides a new field of tension. The authors pose ethical questions in relation to this: who and what are shaping a person's learning, for better but also worse?

In Chapter 10, Maria Francesca Freda, Giovanna Esposito, Maria Luisa Martino, and José González-Monteagudo illuminate how auto/biographical narrative methods are used in preparation for studying at university. They use ideas about narrative mediation with four dynamic elements: metaphor, icons, forms of writing, and collective sculpting of the body to explore the actual and potential meanings of the university. As a research instrument, written narratives offer first-hand biographical materials to do with recent history, society, culture, the family and education. These materials make it possible to connect historical and socio-cultural worlds with the subjective and experiential perspective of the subjects. As a training instrument, autobiographical narratives encourage the production and appropriation of knowledge, and facilitate the learning of basic techniques about the application of disciplinary knowledge to social and very personal contexts. They can, as a result, be highly motivating.

In Chapter 11, *"Struggles for identity: students from sub Saharan Africa and vocational training courses for nurses in Switzerland"*, Myriam Graber illuminates experiences of learning among students from sub Saharan Africa, taking a bachelor's degree in nursing. When they arrive in the host country and begin training, they suffer from the impact of a different context, and struggle with limited knowledge of the codes and rules of the country, and of the training system, whose methods and values seem very different from previous experience. This challenges their values, and perceptions of health and disease: since, for instance, they have to take care of patients who carry cultural taboos in relation to body contact; or different ways of representation of disease and death. Moreover, they are expected to learn from reflexive, discursive, and symbolic work, while their experience of ways of knowing can be more traditional. This evokes a more or less acknowledged identity crisis, and a need to de-construct and reconstruct meanings, values and symbolic systems. Their stories reveal strategies of adaptation, through processes of self-reconstruction, re-contextualisation, and managing opposites. Cultural innovation, states the author, does not happen in an obvious or linear way: some parts of a past identity are rejected, yet the subject also strives to keep some coherence with the past at the same time.

Lioba Howatson-Jones and Claire Thurgate, in Chapter 12, *"Biographical learning: a process for recovering the soul in nursing"*, also enter the world of nurses and their biographical narrative learning. They argue that the body can be perceived in quite impersonal ways within healthcare systems and practices, thus diminishing the potential for compassionate relationship. The whole system of learning in health can be overly technocratic and the authors seek to stimulate new ways of thinking, where change and learning can foster more of what they term "the soul of nursing". They draw on the narrated experiences and reflections of students and teaching staff (including the researchers themselves) on a new nursing degree programme. The biographical narrative approach offers an opportunity for people to make sense of their lives and to integrate learning from personal and professional experience. In the process, they become more connected with and attentive to the narratives of others, and to the complex subjectivities of those for whom they care.

In Chapter 13, *"Interaction between body and environment in Steveston recollected"*, Catherine Karen Roy reflects on transformative learning in individual, collective, and global terms, in the context of a Japanese fishing community in British Columbia. Japanese migrants went there during the Second World War, following enforced evacuation from other areas of Canada. Roy focuses on learning as the engagement of the learner with the world, and how immigrants learn from their relationship with the environment, through concrete interactions of body and nature. In the book to which she refers, images of the living environment become metaphors of human experience, illustrating how embodied learning and memory of places are constitutive of identity. Autobiographic poetry connects too with adult education: people are described as "flowing with the river", "navigating through life changes"; words such as "roots" and "routes" are used to address the ambivalent process of "starting new lives", and being cut off from roots "just like the salmon that they catch for a living". Through dialogue, reflection, and questioning assumptions, people experience a sense of collectivity, beyond seperateness.

In the final chapter, we are taken to the different world of inner London to consider the motivations of a different group of people. Rebecca Tee uses auto/biographical narrative research to chronicle and interpret the motivations of school governors. School governors form one of the largest groups of volunteers in the UK: all state-funded schools and colleges in the UK have a governing body, to which a Head teacher reports. A typical governing body is made up of staff representatives, community governors and the parents of students. The role of the school governor is voluntary and unpaid, while their duties include setting strategic direction, establishing policies and objectives, approving the budget, reviewing progress against the budget and objectives as well as challenging and supporting senior staff. Drawing on Goffman and others, Rebecca plays with the life as theatre metaphor; and in her interviews she has become more sensitive to the totality of the interview experience, in an 'encyclopaedic sense': what is happening between the 'here and now' and the 'there and then'. In this final chapter, we return to a central feature of the whole book: how particulars connect to more general issues, of people in distinct interaction, yet shaped by cultural settings.

In conclusion, these pieces of research illustrate the power and potential of life history and biographic research to honour the complexity of human life, by giving space to interrelations and interdependencies in many aspects and at different levels of experience. None of them can be excluded in the development of a more satisfying theory of adult learning, and the challenges and possibilities of undertaking such a project. In every chapter, reference to place, body, physical and social environment, language and action, the individual and the collective, psyche and society, are omnipresent, and have to be respected in theorising learning. There is:

–   specific attention to the generation of "good stories", i.e. stories that are not only a collection of words, but rooted in the body, in living experience, in concrete places and landscapes, and in research settings where these aspects are actively engaged with: the chapters illustrate innovative ways of doing auto/biographic research, beyond the use of words;

–   the use of concepts in stories themselves, as they help to give meaning to life and learning, for example when they become part of the story – in narratives of "my relationship with my body, and its changes", or "the different landscapes of my life, and how I integrate them", etc. These are directly addressed by subjects and enter into their personal theory; this always happens, of course, when doing biographical research, but it can be underestimated by researchers who may fail to recognise the theory making subject, and the importance of creating narrative truth in a life;

–   the role of these concepts in opening possibilities for new theory; how life, learning and human interdependency are theorized, as we said at the outset, can be reductionist and overly individualised. It can also be overly rational, functional, and logo-centric. The choice of life history methods in adult education is itself an effort to break free of such stultification by getting back to participants' views and how adults experience their worlds. There is an insistence, across the chapters, on the importance of engaging with concrete aspects of life and the role these play in telling stories. This can open now possibilities for researchers, and for people concerned with education, not least because we better recognise the interconnections between all aspects of life, and also imagine how the world, and human beings within it, may develop in less fragmented, less destructive, more connected, satisfying and life enhancing ways.

As Heinz von Foerster wrote in his (interconnected) Aesthetical and Ethical Imperatives:

If you desire to see, learn how to act.
Act always so as to increase the number of choices (1981:308).

The book closes with a story. We asked Nora Bateson, a guest at our conference in Odense, to write a post-script, and she did what many adults in our research do: she decided to tell a story, one that celebrates, in her case, knowledge and wisdom without separating them, as stories often do. It develops an embodied theory of life, love, and inter-generational learning. Today, as an adult, she is able to return to her beginnings and to explore the origins of her view of education. A father can teach you a lot, and her father also learned a lot from her, as she shows in her touching film "An ecology of mind". A father can be worried about his daughter's future, and the non-sense of some institutional practices. But Gregory Bateson did something that only a few fathers dare to do: he showed his thoughts and feelings openly, hence teaching her – paradoxically – some hope for herself, and for the future, and for her lifelong ability to learn.

References

Alheit, P. (1995). Biographical learning. In Alheit et al. *The Biographical Approach in European Adult Education*. Vienna: Verband Wiener Volksbildung.

Alheit, P., Bron-Wojciechowska, A., Brugger, E., and Dominicé, P., (Eds) 1995, *The Biographical Approach in European Adult Education*. Vienna: Verner Wiener Volksbildung.

Alheit, P. and Dausien, B. (2002). Lifelong Learning and Biographicity. In Bron, A. and Schemman, N. (Eds.), *Social Science Theories in Adult Education Research*. Bochum: Studies in International Adult Education, pp. 211-241.

Arendt, H. (1988). *The Human Condition*. Chicago: University Press.

Bainbridge, A. and West, L. (2012). *Psychoanalysis and Education, minding a gap*. London: Karnac.

Bateson, G. (1972). *Steps to an Ecology of Mind.* New York, NY: Ballantine Books.

Bateson, G. (1979). *Mind and Nature. A Necessary Unit.* New York, NY: Bantam Books.

Cavarero, A. (2005). *For more than one voice. Toward a Philosophy of Vocal Expression.* Stanford: Stanford University Press.

Chamberlayne, P., Bornat, J. & Wengraf, T. (2000). *The Turn to Biographical Methods in Social Science.* London: Routledge.

Dominicé, P. (1990). *L'histoire de vie comme processus de formation.* Paris: L'Harmattan.

Dominicé, P. (1995) in Alheit, P. et al., *The Biographical Approach in European Adult Education.* Vienna: Verner Wiener Volksbildung.

Dominicé, P. (2000). *Learning from Our Lives: Using Educational Biographies with Adults.* San Francisco, CA: Jossey Bass.

Dominicé, P. (2007). *La formation biographique.* Paris: L'Harmattan.

Foerster, H. von (1981) *Observing Systems. Seaside.* Cal.: Intersystems Publications.

Giddens, A. (1999). *Runaway World.* London: Profile Books

Hollway W., and Jefferson, T. (2000) *Doing Qualitative Research Differently.* London: Sage. Honneth, A. (2007). Disrespect, the normative foundations of critical theory. Polity Press. Honneth, A. (2009). Pathologies of Reason. Columbia University Press.

Horsdal, M. (2012). *Telling Lives; exploring dimensions of narratives.* London: Routledge

Hunt, C. and West, L. (2009). Salvaging the Self in Adult Learning. *Studies in the Education of Adults,* 41 (1): 68-82.

Illeris, K. (2002). *The Three Dimensions of Learning. Malabar FL: Krieger.*

Josso, M.-C. (2011). *Expériences de vie et formation.* Paris: L'Harmattan.

Merrill, B. and West, L. (2009). *Using biographical methods in social research.* London: Sage.

Merrill, B., Thurnborg, C., and Finnegan, F., (2013, forthcoming), *Student voices on inequalities in European higher education.* London: Routledge.

Monteagudo, J. (2008) (Ed) Pratiques de Formation Analyses, Approches non-francaphones.

Monteagudo, J.G. (Ed) 2008, Pratiques de Formation/Analyse nr. 55/2008.

West, L., Alheit, P., Siig Andersen, A. & Merrill, B. (2007). *Using Biographical and Life History Approaches in the study of adult and lifelong learning.* Frankfurt am Main: Peter Lang.

Chapter 2

The body and the environment in autobiographical narratives and in autobiographical narrative research

◊   MARIANNE HORSDAL, UNIVERSITY OF SOUTHERN DENMARK, DENMARK

Our stories are embodied. A life story is, of course, like all other narratives, whether fictive or autobiographical, a form of discourse. A life story may be represented in writing, orally told, performed in drama, or pictured in a film; or we may even silently travel in time and space within ourselves. No matter what medium or kind of communication the autobiographical narrative is a symbolic representation of lived experience. Its meanings and characteristics cannot, however, be fully captured within a discursive approach. I suggest that autobiographical stories reflect our physical movements and journeys in time and space and the accompanied emotions, and that our cognitive abilities for mental time travelling inhabit our narratives. We need, in my opinion, a theoretical approach which combines the cultural, cognitive, and corporeal elements of autobiographical narratives.

At the end of the last century, terms like "the linguistic turn", or "the narrative turn" were particularly influential in the academic context. The increased focus on language and discourse and the social construction of reality shed light on the significant cultural impact on our worlds but, at the same time, designated an academic environment in which the role of the body was downplayed or had completely disappeared from the discourses. In the history of the humanities the body often was an underprivileged stepchild apart from the theoretical approach of phenomenology. Divisions between nature and culture, body and soul, emotions and rationality, culturally framed many discourses creating a picture of the distinctive traits of our true humanity – the self-reflective rational being – as something quite distant from the body. So we may tell lots of grand narratives that exclude the body. Nevertheless, to fully understand the notion of narratives we have to take the body and the environment into account in narrative research.

My approach to narrative theory and research as it is developed in my book: *Telling Lives. Exploring Dimensions of Narratives* (Horsdal, 2012) has its focus on bodies, minds, and stories in interaction. The book demonstrates how the theoretical understanding of narrative is bound up with methods for biographical narrative research. Neurophysiology, philosophical perspectives and research data and methodology are brought together to formulate a new understanding of narrative analysis. The book also outlines the influence cultural and social environments have upon our own narrative memories, and development of narrative competences. To represent this interconnected theoretical approach would take up much more space than a small chapter in an anthology allows. Therefore, in this chapter I intend to develop and explain the crucial role of the body in interaction with the environment in autobiographical narratives and briefly discuss some consequences for narrative autobiographical research.

Life is a journey

From the beginning of life human infants are carried around in the environment from place to place. They observe a changing environment as they are moved around and, at the same time, they observe how other beings, not least their care-givers, move around, come and go, appear and disappear. Quite soon, infants themselves initiate little journeys by self-propelled motion, crawling, walking, and running onto new adventures. Life IS a journey, in the sense of an embodied metaphor as noted by Lakoff and Johnson (1999), but also literally and physically we move our bodies from place to place, from context to context throughout our lives (although our mobility varies considerably, also in a historical sense (Alheit, this volume)). Never did two individuals follow exactly the same path in time and space– apart from Siamese twins. In spite of all the relationships everybody's journey in time and space is different because of our individual bodies.

Our bodies are individual, but we are always related to the environment with which we are interacting. And the quality and character of the interactions with and relationships to the environment evoke emotions. Interactions are never completely neutral; briefly speaking, we want to approach what feels delightful and to avoid, if possible, and distance ourselves from unpleasant encounters (Watt, 2003, Damasio, 2000).

Throughout the journey of life we interact with and relate to various communities of practice (Lave and Wenger, 1991), the first of which, normally, is the infant's family. The baby enters as a newcomer with a remarkable impact on the social life of the existing community. In most contexts we start as newcomers, entering a stage on which the play has been going on long before our arrival. In a few cases, in intimate relationships or entrepreneurial contexts, we initially form the community. Some communities are given, others are freely chosen. But we are always embedded in the culture. Some communities succeed or replace one another (such as kindergarten, primary school, secondary school), some are simultaneous contexts in which we may participate at different times of the day during the same period (e.g. representing work life, family life, leisure activities, friendships etc.). We form affiliations through our interactions, but the quality and character of the relationships vary a lot. In some contexts we remain in peripheral positions or even get excluded, in others we are welcomed and thrive. Some result in lasting affiliations while others are brief encounters, and soon we move on along the journey of life. The contexts change and so do we along the way. We learn from all our interactions with the environment. Our physical journeys are journeys of formation and transformation. And this happens so much more as we develop the cognitive ability to remember our journeys in time and space and the interactions and emotions they involved.

Mental time travelling

Human infants implicitly learn from their interactions and from the emotional feed-back of the interactions from the very beginning of life. And infants form models of repeated interactions (Nelson 1996). At the end of the second year small children begin to remember explicitly what happened. Cognitively, children exceed the here and now of the present existence, and develop the capacity for autonoetic awareness (Wheeler, Stuss & Tulving 1997). They begin to experience themselves and the present situation as a continuation of the past and as a prelude to the future. They develop the ability to mental time travelling aided and guided by the development of autobiographical memory and, probably, the cultural introduction to narratives. So, the infant may mentally repeat the path she just travelled in time and space – a good thing that helps us not to get lost – or imagine future expeditions and explorations of the environment. The ability for mental time travelling makes it possible to learn from experience, not just by automatically upgrading the implicit learning or our semantic knowledge of the world, but it is now possible to be aware of changes, transformations as well as similarities, and to dream of new possible options.

It is this remarkable ability that we use in autobiographical narratives, when we tell about our journeys of the past or imagine the future colored by the frame of the present. But mental time travelling and its symbolic tool narrative contain more treasures: the potential for making sense of temporality (Horsdal 2009). Narratives make our temporal world inhabitable as Ricoeur puts it (1984).

Here, demarcations are indispensable. We have to put brackets, set frames, to demarcate beginnings and endings in order to see the patterns in space and in time. We know from writers like Samuel Beckett how the meaning of a narrative breaks down without beginnings and endings (see also Kermode 1966). Just like demarcations are indispensable to make sense of the time-span within a narrative, we are also acquainted with the provisional placement of demarcations in other areas of our perception of our environment. We experience the internal relationship in a painting because of the frame, and we experience music due to the beginnings, endings and pauses in the sequence of sounds. We perceive, for example, the landscape that surrounds us framed by the horizon, a demarcation which is only there in our perception, dissolving and changing as we move. As Lakoff and Johnson showed us (1999), the cognitive experience of demarcations is part of primary metaphors, developed from bodily experience of movement in space.[1] In my interpretation, this cognitive development that allows for mental time-travelling and autonoetic awareness based on the embodied and emotional experience in an always already cultural environment of relationships, provides us with the significant format of narrative, necessary in order to make sense of the transformations of temporality.

Narrative and vicarious experience

The narrative format, a time space with a beginning and an end, thus enables our endeavors to make sense of the course of interactions in a changing environment and of our transformed selves as we move along the path of life. But one more significant feature of narrative must be mentioned before we move on: narratives have a perspective ultimately based on our embodied physical being in time and space. We interpret the world and ourselves in it from our contextually situated position, and we are as embodied beings not able to float high above and beyond the cultural limits of time and space and speak out the final and ultimate truth from there. This particularity of perspective is true in spite of the recognition of the omniscient narrator as a typical figure in some types of literature[2]. We aim to achieve authenticity and meaning through our narrative endeavors, but sense-making is culturally situated. We see the world and ourselves from where we are at the present, but we have a variety of cultural plotlines at our disposal. All narratives are configured. The narrative configuration transcends the simple list or enumeration of actions. Ricoeur (1984) employs the term "emplotment" in order to underscore the configuring act. The plot gives us an interpretation of the course of action, a suggestion of the meaning of what happens (and what has happened). Ricoeur speaks of a threefold mimesis. I largely agree with his distinctions as my slightly adapted paraphrase will show: Mimesis1 refers to the world of action, the spontaneous, pre-narrative conception and organization of action. Mimesis2 represents the configuring act, the act of emplotment in a narrative, a symbolic expression of happenings and actions. Mimesis2 is rooted in our physically and culturally situated perspective and shows the configuration of meaning we pick out among the culturally available models for a plot, according to what we find to be the most authentic and true version of what happened, for the time being. Sense-making is a provisional and never ending endeavor exactly because of the embodied origin of the narrative perspective. Mimesis3 "marks the intersection of the world of the text and the world of the hearer or reader" (1984:71). Here the situated perspective of the interpreter is at work in negotiation with the potential otherness of the narrative.

As stated in the beginning, narratives are symbolic expressions. We are immersed in stories long before we learn to tell about what happened to us or what we dream of doing in the time to come. This implies that stories can – and should be – shared. Meaning is not an individual act but is constructed in a potential space between interlocutors telling and listening and negotiating what makes sense. This negotiation also takes place in the encounter between a reader and a text. The narrative culture in our environment has a great impact on our own narrative capabilities, on how and when we tell what to whom, or not, and even on the development of our autobiographical memory, our identity and sense-making skills.

Listening to stories is fascinating, as well as watching movies, drama, or reading. We often identify with the protagonist of the story, sympathize with her joys and sorrows, and follow the course of actions. We use stories as vicarious experience. Through this fabulous medium that narrative is we are able vicariously to set out and follow an immense variety of journeys in time and space. We can vicariously follow different perspectives and negotiate meaning between them. We can attach ourselves to stories of our families, ancestors, and fellow citizens and make them part of our identity construction. And we may learn from the life experience of others through their stories. Through the stories we share we may transcend the limits of our own perspective and limited horizon of experience towards a wider potential for human understanding, naturally depending on the type and genres of the narratives with which we are confronted. What kind of narrative culture we inhabit is of great significance: how our stories are responded to and how we respond to others and it is important which kind of stories we identify with.

A possible cause of this potentially intense identification may be the existence of mirror neurons. The mirror neuron system, our mimetic capability may provide some answers regarding the issue of identification; answers which have implications for autobiographical, narrative research, but also for the type, content and range of the narratives to which we are exposed (e.g. in computer games). A.O. Rizzolatti, Craighero, Gallese, and Iacoboni, (2001,2004 and 2005) have researched and written about the mirror neuron systems in monkeys and in humans and expanded our knowledge of how we imitate, how we learn from and through others, of the source of empathy, and of cultural communication.

The mirror neuron system is a motor simulation system that allows us spontaneously to get an idea of social actions in our environment in order that we quickly catch an idea of what our fellow creatures are up to. Action simulation does not mean that we physically repeat or copy the actions of others as in echolalia; we mirror the actions, movements and emotions AS IF we were performing the actions themselves[3]. The researchers suggest that the mirror neuron system in humans is active in connection to perceived, imagined, planned, and communicated actions in contexts. And it is not only visual perceptions. The sound of action itself stimulates motor simulation, and an echo neuron system enables identification with and simulation of action sentences. This is exactly the point at which we may explain our identification with the stories we listen to or read. We perceive the narrated interactions and emotions almost as if we experienced the actions and emotions ourselves.

Gallese says: "we do not just perceive…someone to be broadly speaking, similar to us. We are implicitly aware of this similarity because we literally embody it" (2005:104), and he continues by mentioning a "shared manifold of intersubjectivity", "and initial we-ness". Carr et al. (2003) underscore the emotional implications:

> Taken together, these data suggest that we understand the feeling of others via a mechanism of action representation shaping emotional content, such that we ground our empathic resonance in the experience of our acting body and the emotions associated with specific movement. As Lipps noted, "When I observe a circus performer hanging on a wire, I feel I am inside him" (2003:5502).

And Cozolino adds:

> Mirror neurons and the neural networks they coordinate work together to allow us to automatically react to, move with, and generate a theory of what is on the mind of others. Thus mirror neurons not only link networks within us but link us to each other. They appear to be an essential component of the social brain and an important mechanism of communication across the social synapse (2006:198).

Cozolino's expression "the social synapse" is interesting. He emphasizes the significance of what goes on in the space between individuals[4]. What is significant here is not the single neuron, nor the single individual but the connections between them. The interactions and the emotional environment in the space between people determine the synaptic connections created in the brains. But part of our reactions happens very spontaneously without conscious or rational reflections.

At this point it is worth emphasizing that narratives are very viable tools for negotiation of meaning (Bruner 1990) because they are symbolic and aesthetic representations of experience and interactions. Identification and action simulation take place spontaneously; they appear to be implicitly functioning according to the character of previous experience, but in a narrative symbolic expression, the perspective and meaning of what happened may be negotiated between interlocutors.

Research implications

The theory of the mirror neuron system and the research on affective neuroscience once again underscores the crucial role of the body and the environment. The significant focus on interactions and emotions has implications not only for theories of experience, and of narrated experience, but for theories of education and learning. Research on mind, brain and education shows how emotions and cognition are intertwined in our social interactions with the environment. Traditional views that separated cognition and emotion and neglected the body are seriously challenged:

> Put simply, what affective neuroscience is revealing is that the mind is influenced by an interdependency of the body and brain; both the body and brain are involved, therefore, in learning. (Immordino-Yang & Damasio, 2007)

"Neuroscientific evidence suggests that we can no longer justify learning theories that dissociate the mind from the body, the self from social context" (Immordino-Yang, 2011).

Another aspect of traditional epistemology, with consequences for humanistic and sociological research, is also challenged: the division between subject and object, and the point of departure in the individual subject. Cozolino, who recalls the thoughts of Gregory Bateson, put forward this suggestion concerning a potential bias in Western thought:

> Trying to understand human experience by studying words and behaviors of an individual may be like analyzing a film by counting the pixels in a tiny corner of a screen. We may come to know the flickers of light in that corner quite well but completely miss the meaning of the film (Cozolino 2006:300).

Also Lakoff & Johnson join the critique of the subject-object dichotomy:

> The environment is not an "other" to us. It is not a collection of things that we encounter. Rather, it is part of our being. It is the locus of our existence and identity. We cannot and do not exist apart from it. It is through empathic projection that we come to know our environment, understand how we are part of it and how it is part of us (Lakoff & Johnson, 1999:566).

Acknowledgements of these thoughts will have an impact on narrative theory and narrative autobiographical research. Though filtered through our physical and emotional experiences the stories we share may transcend the limited horizon of own physical existence. Instead of being confined to implicit models of the world we may collect a narrative repertoire that allows us to negotiate meaning between multiple perspectives, and vicariously and empathically set out on so many journeys with our fellow human beings. Here, the impact of the narrative culture must be emphasized. The vast difference between the character, quality and scope of the narrative repertoire children may acquire in different environments and accordingly different acquisition of narrative competences plays a considerable role regarding the possibility for an understanding of other people and the development of identity.

The theoretical assumptions sketched out in this chapter will clearly influence the methodologies in autobiographical narrative research. However, the methodological issues regarding the collection and the analysis of life story narratives cannot be elaborated within the limits of this chapter, which is why I must refer the reader to *Telling Lives* for a detailed account. But a few main points must be sketched out here.

The process of collecting a life story through a narrative interview is a collaborative process taking place in a potential space between teller and listener. They follow the same path, activating their capability for mental time travelling and personal repertoire of activated experiences and emotions.

As an interviewer I ask the narrator to tell about her life from the beginning until we are here today with no interruptions on my side in order not to lead the configurational act astray by my preferences of choice. And I ask her to tell her story in a slow rhythm that I can write down every single word she is saying without missing anything and, thus, by a rhythmic collaboration in telling and writing perform the transition from oral narrative to text attentively mirroring and embodying everything which is told. The symbolization and reification of experience that takes place in this potential space is significant as an act of sense-making. Collecting an autobiographical narrative is equivalent to receiving a gift due to the fact of our individual bodies and individual journeys in time and space. Every single narrative widens the horizon of the attentive listener.

The analysis of a life story narrative is an inquiry into the interpretations of selves and existence, from the context of the present. The analysis of the interview encompasses much more than the issue of themes. An examination of the order of what is told, the configuration, the voices, the duration of narrated episodes, the metaphors, and not least, the narrated experience of interactions, participation and affiliations in the various communities of practice, may open the text for a much more careful interpretation, acknowledging the complexity of a life story narrative.

The narrated experience of the interactions and relationships in the different contexts show us significant features of formal, non-formal and informal learning. Autobiographical research may enlighten our view of the scope and quality of biographical learning which, always, involves the body, the emotions, and the environment.

Notes

1 Lakoff and Johnson 1999 talk about a container metaphor and a source-path-goal metaphor as primary metaphors. A cognitive blending of the two provides us with the narrative format: a demarcated sequence from a beginning to an end.

2 Even in this case, the Olympic view must be regarded as a perspective an author (of fiction) may chose among the available cultural plots at the time of writing.

3 The spontaneous interpretation of action through the mirror neuron system may correspond to Mimesis1 mentioned above.

4 Synapse is Greek and means "connection". "The social synapse" corresponds in a sense to the terms "potential space", and "transitional space" (see West, this volume).

References

Bruner, J. (1990). *Acts of meaning*. Cambridge, M.A.: Harvard University Press.

Carr, L., Iacobini, M., Dubeau, M., Mazziotta, J.& Lenzi, G. (2003). Neural mechanisms of emphathy in humans: A relay from neural systems for imitation to limbic areas. In *Proceedings of the National Academy of Sciences, 100 (9)*, 5497-5502.

Cozolino, L. (2006). *The neuroscience of human relationships*. New York: W.W. Norton.

Gadamer, H.G. (1965) *Wahrheit und Methode*. Tübingen: J.C.B. Mohr.

Gallese, V. (2005). "Embodied simulation: From neurons to phenomenal experience. In *Phenomenology and the cognitive sciences*. Berlin: Springer.

Horsdal, M. (2012). *Telling lives. Exploring dimensions of narratives.* London: Routledge.

Horsdal, M. (2009). The Wonders of Narrative. In B. Fraser & K. Turner (Eds.). *Language in Life, and Life in Language: Jacob Mey – A Festschrift.* United Kingdom: Emerald.

Iacobini, M., Molnar-Szakacs, I., Gallese, V., Mazziotta, J. & Rizzolatti, G. (2005). Grasping the intention of others with one's own mirror neuron system. *PLoS Biology, 3 (3), 79.*

Immordino-Yang, M. & Damasio, A. (2007). We feel, therefore we learn: The relevance of affective and social neuroscience to education. *Mind, Brain, and Education, 1 (1),* 3-10.

Immordino-Yang, M. (2011) Implication of affective and social neuroscience for educational theory. In *Educational Philosophy and Theory. Vol 43, No. 1.*

Kermode, F. (1966). *The sense of an ending.* Oxford: Oxford University Press.

Lakoff, G. & Johnson, M. (1999). *Philosophy in the flesh.* New York: Basic Books.

Lave, J. & Wenger, E. (1991) *Situated Learning: Situated peripheral participation.* Cambridge: Cambridge University Press.

Nelson, K. (1996). *Language in cognitive development: The emergence of the mediated mind.* Cambridge: Cambridge University Press.

Ricoeur, P. (1984 [1983]). *Time and narrative.* Chicago: University of Chicago Press.

Rizzolatti, G. & Craighero, L. (2004) The mirror-neuron system. *Annual Review of neuroscience, 27,* 169-192.

Rizzolatti, G. Fogassi, L & Gallese, V. (2001). Neurophysiological mechanisms underlying the understanding and imitation of action. *Nature Reviews Neuroscience, 2 (9),* 661-670.

Watt, D. (2003). Psychotherapy in an age of neuroscience. Bridges to affective neuroscience. In Corrigall, J. & Wilkingson, H. (Eds.) *Revolutionary connections: Psychotherapy and neuroscience.* London: Karnac.

Wheeler, M., Stuss, D. & Tulving, E. (1997). Toward a theory of episodic memory: The frontal lobes and autonoetic consciousness. *Psychological Bulletin, 121 (3),* 331-354.

Chapter 3

When Bourdieu met Winnicott, and Honneth: bodily matters in the experiences of non-traditional learners

◊   LINDEN WEST, CANTERBURY CHRIST CHURCH UNIVERSITY, ENGLAND

Introduction

In this chapter, Pierre Bourdieu's sociological understanding of student experience in higher education – in particular his notions of habitus, disposition and capital – is connected with a more interdisciplinary, psychosocial appreciation of the place of recognition and selfhood in human interaction, learning and transformative processes. Reference is made, especially, to the work of the psychoanalyst Donald Winnicott but also to the critical theorist Axel Honneth when interpreting the narratives of samples of 'non-traditional learners' in higher education. These narratives were generated as part of a European Union financed research study of such learners in 8 European countries (RANLHE Lifelong Learning Project: http://www.ranlhe.dsw.edu.pl.) We worked with samples of students and staff from different types of universities (mainly elite (or older) and reform (relatively new)) in each country. The term 'non-traditional' encompassed students from backgrounds normally under-represented in universities: from minority communities, and or working class backgrounds, from migrant populations, to the disabled etc. The research included younger and older learners. For present purposes, the focus is on the narratives of particular students who were interviewed, using auto/biographical narrative research, at the beginning, the middle and the end of three years at university in England. The basic question we asked was what enabled learners to keep on keeping on at university, or not, by reference to whole lifeworlds and life histories.

Bourdieu coined the phrase of students either being 'fish in or out of water' in the varying habitus of different universities: some survived and thrived, others might not, especially those lacking particular forms of social and educational capital (Bourdieu, 1990). We sought to understand this phenomenon in greater depth, which required more holistic, embodied, interdisciplinary and dynamic understanding than Bourdieu provides. Learners can, for instance, be seen as more agentic in their social interactions at university, and notions of capital might need to be broadened to include psychological and family dimensions. This could encompass, in the case of older learners, resilience forged in diverse forms of lifelong learning, including surviving various life crises, such as divorce or unemployment. In building this more dynamic, and agentic understanding, (while recognising the continuing pervasiveness of processes of social reproduction), Bourdieu's concept of embodied cultures – shaping and scripting the inner world – is connected to Winnicott's understanding of changing experiences of selfhood in transitional space, and its potentially radical implications for challenging norms. The preoccupation here is on the complex business of negotiating who we are – an established preoccupation in biographical narrative enquiry – and the resources we may draw in self-negotiation and challenging how we may have been scripted (West, 1996).

The ideas of Bourdieu and Winnicott are in turn linked to Honneth's work on recognition in human interactions, and its fundamental importance to human well-being. Honneth straddles micro, mezzo and macro-levels: from the importance of feeling loved by others, in intimate relationships; to the central place of feeling accepted and legitimate within particular sub-cultures and thence to becoming valued within a wider social order. This conceptual, interdisciplinary theoretical repertoire provided a sensitising if always provisional frame with which to engage with and think about our narrative material.

Some background

Working on the RANLHE study raised many difficult questions of how to conceptualise non-traditional learners in universities, but also to make sense of adaptation, change, transitional and even transformative processes. Notions of transformative learning, for instance – of profound changes in perspectives among learners – have tended to be conceptualised in overly cognitivist terms, as shifts in mental or epistemic frames or modes of understanding, reflecting, perhaps, the continuing dominance of a sort of disembodied cognition in theorising learning more widely (Illeris, 2002). We easily neglect the embodied, felt, as well as unconscious aspects of transitional and transformational processes (West, 2011a). This of course reflects an old Western epistemology problem: Saul Frampton (2011) notes the continuing and pervasive tendency, shaped, in part, by Christian theology, of separating mind and body; and of viewing the body, feelings and subjectivity as things to be overcome and transcended; as feminine and other, to state it provocatively. (Although there are alternative if neglected pre-Cartesian traditions in Western philosophy, as with Montaigne, which bring us back to the sensual, to feeling and the body, alongside more immediate experience, as a basis for philosophical enquiry and grounded ways of knowing. There may be links here with philosophical pragmatism as developed in the early part of the twentieth century).

Modern philosophy, however, in its search for epistemological certainty and clarity, tends, still, following Descartes, to split mind from body and transcendence can be seen to lie in an escape from our animal, corporeal base. The deep suspicion of the body, and of feeling and subjectivity needing to be transcended, via thinking, is deeply embedded in some contemporary notions of transformative learning. At the heart of Jack Mezirow's ideas, for instance, (Mezirow, 2000; Dirkx, Mezirow and Cranton, 2006) is a metacognitive application of critical thinking (this despite some acknowledgment, for instance, of psychoanalytic perspectives in Mezirow's work, but these tend to get marginalised in theorising (Hunt, 2013)). Critical thinking transforms an acquired frame of reference, a mind-set, with potentially radical consequences. Critical rationality involves an old mind-set being replaced by a different world view. While any mind-set consists of values, beliefs and feelings as well as concepts, transformation, fundamentally, has to do with changing epistemic assumptions. However, John Dirkx perceives this to be worryingly reductionist (Dirkx, Mezirow and Cranton, 2006). He takes the debate on transformative learning into deeper, more embodied territory: of the search for meaning, even for self and soul. It is persons in relationship, including to the symbolic order, he argues, which lies at the heart of epistemic shifts. While Dirkx recognises changes in cognition, he places these in shifting experiences of self in relation to others, and the symbolic order. In my own earlier work on diverse learners managing change, using auto/biographical narrative research, I chronicled how people are in effect re-negotiating selfhood, in new qualities of relationship and storytelling, including with other learners, teachers and via a developing narrative repertoire. Students may find new narrative resources, and people who value them in new ways, which can change their understanding of self in the world. Such research illuminates the complexity of change processes, including what may be deep ambivalence and ambiguity towards the new and unfamiliar – like a challenging idea – often rooted in primitive (that is early) experience, and fear of being vulnerable and unable to cope.

Axel Honneth (2009) would understand such processes by reference to Freud's anthropological idea: the notion that humans, in comparison with other mammals, are born prematurely, and are deeply dependent on a protective environment and the other, from the very beginning. Any hint of being left alone, and helpless, evokes anxiety and a potential repression of desire. This is a fundamentally affective and relational dynamic, the traces of which are embodied in what Melanie Klein famously termed 'memory in feeling'. Such memories can re-emerge at times of change and new possibility, in largely unconscious ways. We may also hold on to aspects of existing ways of seeing and being, for fear of what is repressed, and or of being abandoned and helpless, which mirrors early dynamics (West, 2009; 1996). Past and present are constant companions.

An auto/biographical imagination

In the RANLHE study, we encouraged learners to tell their stories, over time, as openly and honestly as they could. Learners engaged reflexively with their material, using transcripts and recordings to identify themes and to think about them with the researchers. It should be noted that there were different methodological orientations among the different teams of researchers, despite a common 'biographical research' label. One orientation may be categorised as more 'scientistic' and objectivist, as against a more relational auto/biographical understanding (in the former, attempts are made to minimise the presence of the researcher, for instance, in order to build greater reliability in generating interviews; in the latter, the researcher's presence is seen as a resource in creating good enough space, in Winnicott's language, for more open, exploratory and reflexive storytelling (West, 2011b)). In my work, I emphasise the importance of attentiveness and respectfulness, and of the need to take time to build a relationship of trust and mutual understanding; and of the necessity of managing anxieties and to build a secure, collaborative space for storytelling and interpretative work, especially when working with unconfident people. There is a focus on the emotional qualities of the relationship between researcher and her subject, as part of making sense of narrative material (Merrill and West, 2009). Participants are also involved in the analysis of their material, by being given transcripts and recordings; and given the longitudinal nature of the process, this includes thinking about what may be difficult to say and or may be missing from the account. Such narrative interviewing can be described as being in a more clinical style, reflecting good practice in therapeutic settings (West, 1996, 2001; Merrill and West, 2009). Attention is paid, for instance, to exploring complex and or emotionally charged material. The clinical style, mirrors, in certain respects, some characteristics of an analytic session, which is proving fruitful in psychosocial research more generally (Bainbridge and West, 2012). It can illuminate struggles to change, and moments of transformation, as well as the complex interplay of desire and resistance in learning of any significant kind.

A proforma is used to identify themes but also to consider the quality of the process, including the transference (what the researcher may represent, unconsciously, to the interviewee), and the counter-transference, which has to do with what this may evoke in the researcher (another way of describing this is the auto/biographical dynamics). These processes can be a source of rich insight into the meanings and emotions being communicated (Merrill and West 2009). Each proforma is developed iteratively over time, and consists of standard biographical data, emerging themes, reference to relevant literatures, including fiction, but also reflection on the fantasies of the researchers, which might provide clues as to what is happening beneath surface appearances. There is an analytic openness and eclecticism in the process, beginning with a thorough immersion in recordings and transcripts: time and space are given for the emergence of any gestalt or overall pattern and form in the material, which can help in making better sense of detail. (This is a quite different approach to grounded theory, for instance, which tends to work in the opposite way (West, 2011b)). Members of the Canterbury research team, it should be emphasised, each completed a proforma, independently, and then compared and contrasted their interpretations, as well as noting what seemed illusive and difficult to understand in stories. This was a way of building a critical reflexivity into the whole process.

Sensitising concepts: Bourdieu

Bourdieu, as indicated, offers a sociological, social reproduction framework for considering learner narratives. His work encompasses the concept of the habitus, which can be understood as a kind of embodied culture, in which ideas but also diverse practices and ways of being are in play (Bourdieu, 1990). Such cultures shape how people behave, speak, think and communicate one with another, and even how they deport themselves, as in studies of doctors and the medical training habitus (Sinclair, 1997). Bourdieu's notion of disposition has to do with how people internalise an idea of what is expected of them in a particular habitus, in a particular kind of university, for instance. They will be more or less confident with the rituals of communication and language, for example, and with what is expected of them in writing, in presentations, and assessment; and even in self-deportment, as in seminars or a range of professional practice-based settings. Such expectations and ways of being in the world, for some, may have been unconsciously internalised, in a previous education or social milieu, while the habitus of particular middle class homes may be close to the habitus of specific universities. People may understand, intuitively, what is expected of them, of what counts as academic writing or discussion; and or how to engage in the diverse rituals that university may involve, including rites of passage or ways of managing anxiety (experiment with drugs, drink and or sex among the young come to mind). Mature working class students can struggle in particular universities, because their social and educational 'capital' may be someway removed from what is valued, understood or practised in a new habitus; or they bring informal psychological capital, such as resilience, derived from wider experience, which may initially go unrecognised. They may feel, in effect, in Bourdieu's terms, "fish out of water" (Bourdieu, 1990).

However, Chapman Hoult (2009; 2012) has observed that Bourdieu fails sufficiently to engage with how some students, from a non-traditional habitus, with apparently limited educational and social capital, nonetheless survive and prosper. These are 'les miraculés', 'an uncharacteristically metaphysical turn', as Chapman Hoult puts it, 'for a materialist such as him' (Chapman Hoult, 2012: 9). How in fact they might prosper, even in a culturally exclusive habitus of an elite institution, is glossed over by Bourdieu, who never really engages with the dynamics of inner and outer worlds. Of course he was aware of this phenomenon and argued, structurally, that these learners serve to mask systemic inequalities, as institutions proclaim "look, we are open to all the talents!" Yet he fails to engage with "the subjective experience of objective possibilities" among les miraculés: with those learners who may buck the trend and prosper. It may be that Bourdieu's view of capital is overly constrained – with neglect of psychological or experiential capital (such as lifelong learning) – because his gaze is too deterministic. We need, it is suggested, more fine grained, psychosocial analysis.

Winnicott and Honneth

Donald Winnicott's (1971) provides one way of engaging with subjective experiences of objective possibilities. Winnicott meticulously observed the qualities of relationship in which infants were embedded and the interplay of objective and subjective worlds, self and other. He was initially concerned with transitional processes in early experience, not least how a child psychologically separates from a prime caregiver, in healthy ways, moving, developmentally, towards greater individuation and openness to experience. He placed the capacity for play and creativity, within the context of relationship, to be at the core of healthy development, where a child can let go of anxiety and absorb herself in the moment, rather than being unduly preoccupied with what a prime caregiver thinks. Winnicott argued that early experiences of recognition provide templates for life: good enough early relationships, in which the putative self feels loved and secure, offer a means simply to be, and a sense of the world as satisfying where desire can be expressed in relatively straightforward ways. On the other hand, a less satisfactory relationship, and the anxieties this provokes, may evoke more false or compliant responses: a need to appease or please, for fear, for instance, of not being good enough or acceptable in the eyes of the other. An obsession may develop with pleasing others and doing what they want: such patterns can find later expression in education, in relationships with teachers and professors, for instance, in the seminar room (West, 1996).

Winnicott (1971) clearly suggested that these ideas could be applied to adult development; and particular writers have used his concept of transitional space, when thinking, for example, of storytelling as a kind of transitional activity, a process of self negotiation, more or less productive of selfhood (Sclater, 2004). We can think too of university, as a space where a self is in negotiation, and where struggles around separation and individuation – letting go of past ideas and relationships – take place. Like the child, the adult, or rather the infant and child in the adult, might be riddled with anxiety about her capacity to cope, and or whether s/he can be good enough in the eyes of significant others. S/he may cling to an existing identity or idea, and or be overly preoccupied with what others think: with getting it right, perhaps, for the teacher, which can denude experience of emotional vibrancy. Learning may feel deadened in consequence. The stories people tell – including to researchers – may, on the other hand, become vehicles for renegotiation of self, for a kind of narrative embodiment of selfhood, which can be legitimised in the eyes and responses of important others.

We may feel recognised and more legitimate, in short, connecting us to Axel Honneth's writings. Recognition, in his view, is simultaneously an individual as well as wider socio-cultural phenomenon. It requires love in the family or interpersonal sphere in order for the child to develop basic self-confidence. Recognition of the autonomous person, bearing rights in law, provides a basis for self-respect, in a broader social frame. And the formation of a co-operative member of society whose efforts are socially valued and important can lead to what he terms self-esteem (Honneth, 2007). Honneth was influenced, among others, by the object relations theories of Donald Winnicott (Honneth, 2009). The first form of relating, in Honneth's schema, is, as noted, to do with self-confidence, born in relationships of love and of feeling seen and valued. If one experiences love, an ability to love one's self and others, is developed. An identity (or selfhood) is being forged by receiving recognition from others. Without such a special relationship with another, it is impossible to become aware of one's own uniqueness and thus experience a basic and positive sense of one's abilities. Only by being recognized can we achieve a vibrant identity (Fleming, 2010).

The second type of relationship to self has, as stated, to do with self-respect, when a person belongs to a community of rights and is recognized as a legally mature person. Through this comes the ability to participate in discussions and rituals of the institution concerned. Respect is shown to others by acknowledging their rights. This form of self-relation is, as observed, self-respect. Without rights there is no respect, to put it slightly differently. It is not just having a good opinion of self but a sense of possessing a kind of shared dignity of persons as morally responsible agents and as capable of participating in public deliberations. The experience of being honoured by a community for contributions leads to the form of self-relation which Honneth labels self-esteem. People with high self-esteem will reciprocate a mutual acknowledgement of each other's contribution to the community. From this grow loyalty and greater social solidarity (Fleming, 2011; Honneth, 2007: 139).

In a recent article (West, Fleming and Finnegan, 2013) note is made of how Honneth (2007, 2009) re-visited Freud's work and critiqued a contemporary trend to move away from any imperative to understand ourselves by reference to a deep engagement with our past, and proposes, instead, that psychoanalysis makes an important link between freedom and biographical work (Honneth, 2009, pp. 126-156). Autobiographical work involves an ability through reflexive activity to overcome 'the rupturedness of each individual' and 'only by a critical appropriation of her own process of formation does the human seize the opportunity provided to her for freedom of will' (p. 127). In asking how freedom is attainable at all Honneth asserts that we can re-appropriate our own will by means of recollective work. For Freud, according to Honneth, the individual is 'less a self-interpreting being than one who critically scrutinizes its own past to see whether traces of compulsions that have remained unconscious can be found in it' (2009, p. 139). As the desire for freedom resides within, we can turn to our life-histories as valid expressions of our possibilities as humans. In his remarkable departure from Marxism in general and most of early critical theory, and even, to some extent, from Habermas, Honneth attempts to reimagine the emancipatory project of critical social theory. His solution is to forefront a theory of intersubjectivity and the "struggle for recognition" (West, Fleming and Finnegan, 2013).

Two cases in point

I want to use the narratives of two non-traditional learners, from the RANLHE study, to illustrate and interrogate these processes. Adults often frame their narratives of returning to education by reference to increased self-confidence, however fragile. Except university can clearly be a problematic habitus for working class students; yet becoming more of a fish in water is possible too. Self-confidence can be enhanced, (perhaps more fundamentally, experiences of selfhood strengthened, as Winnicott would have understood it), in being accepted by lecturers and significant others: the feeling that we can legitimately and meaningfully play in this space – play with ideas, for instance – and feel valued in doing so. Self-respect may be forged by feeling accepted as part of a wider community of rights: of being a student with a status and things to give as well as receive. And self-esteem, and greater freedom of the will, may be an outcome of being honoured in a university and a broader community: perhaps via success in the practical rituals of professional placements or in advocacy work. Take the case of someone we have called Sue, a working class student in the habitus of an elite university law faculty, somewhere near the pinnacle of esteem in higher education, at least in terms of Bourdieu's framing of the French academy of the 1960s (Bourdieu, 1988).

A passion for law

Sue was a serious and passionate student of Law. Divorced with two children, she had lived for a while on welfare benefits and had been a carer for her father till his death. She returned to a childhood ambition to practice law. Her biographical narrative material embodies a determination to overcome difficulties, which include poverty and emotional vulnerability. She persevered with the challenge of learning in higher education. Whilst deeply disturbed by class and its manifestations in the academy, she also kept on. We noted with interest that issues of gender were relatively unimportant for Sue; rather it was class that troubled her. She looked for recognition in the academy, feeling awkward in lectures and in the world of the London Inns of Court, where students were expected to spend at least some of their time. In her first interview (10.8.2009), she said:

> I mean it's getting used to…the gap with the education you know it's so different going back into that environment you know comparing with younger students, you know, but it's a natural progression for them and they're up to speed with everything…well I would need to complete my degree and do the bar…a year at bar school … I don't doubt I will do it, I don't doubt myself, I really don't. I worry about how good I will be… sorry… (upset)

She talked of her relative 'lack of education' and constantly asked in seminars what words meant. She said she had learned 'the confidence to speak up and say 'oh what's that then….and I'll look it up later'. Sue talked at length about her background, in all the interviews: the law was 'just part of your everyday life' in the working class area of London where she was born: arrests and even murder, she said, were "frequent companions". She also mentioned feeling an outsider in the community, at times, of "not wanting to push buggies down the High Street":

> You know I wanted to make something of my life and always believed that you could do whatever you wanted to do, and…. that that wasn't all there was you know there was a lot more to it than that and you could bring up children and have children and ideally you know in a situation where you've got a husband or stuff like that and if it doesn't work out like that then you just get up and

get on with it but it was never going to stop me from doing what I wanted to do, be a success in my own business or you know to do this, what I wanted to do since I was about 11 years old.

Sue agonised, once at university, about moving between the different cultures (or habitus) of the university and the street, and over what others might think of her. Negotiating the space was hard, for example in terms of her accent:

> I've really agonised over the way I speak and stuff I think you know I'm just not going to be able to speak how I would wish to speak and I've got to be comfortable with that and if make slips so be it. I've got to say this is me and here we go…. but it sounds really naive but I didn't know how a university worked, I really never and I just sort of oh right, this is what you do because nobody has ever been to university. I had never spoken to anyone about a university and none of my family has ever been so I had no idea what it was going to be, it is a shock.

In the classroom, an accent like hers could be associated, she said painfully, with very negative qualities:

> … to ignorance and bad manners and you know all of that and lack of intelligence…I've got to understand that it is natural and just think and overcome that with my own abilities. It's like an inner turmoil almost every walk of life comes with prejudice and you know discrimination and I put it akin to racial discrimination, it's no different really from social discrimination you know but that's not recognised, it doesn't really.

She had been fearful of "messing it up and then you've humiliated yourself because you've pretended to be something you're not…" She was, she said, past trying to speak in a particular way; and if she changed, "then I would have all my family ridicule me." Moreover, she thought of the law as a "kind of close knit community", a space that was difficult to enter. In a second and third interview, Sue talked more of her Dad and his heroic struggles against legal authorities, including the police. He was, she said, an important influence, inspiration even, whose struggle continued to inspire her against injustice. There may be a kind of imaginal capital at play, as Jossey Quinn (2011) terms it, consisting of people and events that provide some inspiration from the past. She had been a successful business woman too, underlining the danger of reducing Sue simply to deficit capital status. She had also begun to subscribe to *The Times* newspaper for 2 years (with its extensive, daily law reports). She talked positively of experiences in some of the practical rituals of the legal training, including the Moot and of advising marginalized people in a free law clinic:

> ...I got involved in a lot of university like mooting, I became a mooting officer
>
> ... they call it a mock trial but it's not, it's at appeal level so it's a mock appeal... that's really interesting...and I volunteered in the law clinic which has been really good which I actually won an award... and you know you do get I mean when I've been in many courts and listened to advocates and you get sort of international words of English together. So I think well never mind I can't speak English but neither can you... But in a courtroom I've always felt more comfortable for some strange reason which goes against anything I'd normally feel.... (laughing).....

She was highly commended for her advocacy by an observing magistrate and the experience of being a mooting officer, and of providing good, free legal advice in a law clinic, was very positive. This contrasted with a continuing struggle to feel at home, her-self, in other rituals and the particular habitus of the Inns of Court. She went to an end of term party there, in London, and felt so out of place among the rich and privileged young people and their behaviour. Yet she also felt valued by some of her tutors, and her work in the moot and the law clinic. Self-confidence (expressing selfhood, in Winnicott's terms), self-respect (through feeling accepted in community of rights) but also self-esteem (legitimacy and importance to a wider academic and legal community) were developing, it could be suggested, 'psychosocially'.

Sue remained both vulnerable and tough, at one and the same time, having survived difficult circumstances, including the divorce. Her psychological capital, forged in difficult experiences, and in successful adult learning, including an Access programme, was at times strong yet vulnerable, not least in negotiating a classed habitus. She was no feminist or socialist, she said – values often promulgated by 'radical' members of the law faculty – but she did feel deeply about injustice and negotiated particular habitus rituals rather well. She was managing the overall transition reasonably successfully and the resources drawn on included some of her teachers, her imaginal allies but also the recognition gained in parts of the habitus, as a valued member and contributor to its development. We are presented here with a notion of habitus which is less deterministic, a space in which students in relationship can effect change.

Seeking asylum

Feeling more self-confident can work at an unconscious, emotionally primitive level (reaching back, as explained, to earlier stages of development). Mathew offers a further case in point. He was a black refugee carer/student in his mid-thirties. He struggled with academic work primarily because of limited confidence with English, (this was his fourth language). His narrative material cannot, however, be read, simply, as deficit. Mathew recognised the value of the languages he did know, viewing them as opportunities for better understanding of others' worlds. He was the son of an African Chief and had managed to flee war zones. He had worked as an hourly paid-minimum wage carer since arriving on British soil, seeking asylum. He had initially dropped out of an elite university, where he struggled with writing and with understanding the personal tutor system. He took an Access course and made friends with an English couple working in a college of further education, gaining their support for an asylum status application and to renew his university education. He found a partner with her four sons, creating some psychological/psychosocial resources in his struggle to keep on keeping on.

Mathew, like a number of students, inhabited a world where boundaries between full and part-time study, work and university, family and student life, were blurred:

> I do work...I used to work for agency but agencies shifts are not constant so I joined BUPA as a healthcare assistant. The rate is £5.90 for an hour... my partner is a nurse works shifts... I would be looking after the kids I have four boys... I've given up sleep lost hours of sleep to attend to the family and then education sometimes. I go to bed by three o'clock I get up by four o'clock five o'clock... I get up... prepare whatever I've got to take into [my] school, eat and shower the boys and leave them to dress by themselves and then go pack their bags/ lunch and leave home by 8 o'clock they're supposed to start classes by 8.30 I mean 8.45 I'm supposed to start by 9... I have to drive to drop them to a neighbour who is very close to the school and who can just walk... so it's very much more difficult than people might think.

The two lecturers in the college were significant others in his struggle over self-confidence: he forged a close relationship with them, first as a student struggling with English, and then in the process of making his asylum application. Five years later, he was officially recognised as a British citizen in a citizenship ceremony, and they were there as witnesses. They were like good parent figures, he said, and he felt looked after and understood. He celebrated the ceremony itself, as a moment of transition, a benchmark of achievement in what could be a fragile world. He worked hard to find supportive others in a new (or reform) university in the multi-cultural world of a particular part of London. Finding a good personal tutor, and other sympathetic staff and students, was central to this.

A public healthcare degree appealed because of the shortage of male carers in the NHS. In a second interview, he looked back on his struggles and language issues were important:

> It is difficult because when we started in the first year they said to us OK this first year we give you the opportunity and accept your assignment as is... that has been changed because of the stage of second year so you're now needing proof reading and that makes it difficult for people like me considering my background which I'm always constantly worried about how to translate my thoughts my ideas from one language to another, from Mende/Kissi/Creole languages, to African English, then to British English is something that makes it difficult for me....

Yet cultural diversity, and the recognition this brought, began to be seen by him, more and more, as a resource in negotiating a new identity:

> Well from my languages from the various languages that I've gone through if you look at health for instance you cannot purely have a disease by itself. In that way you look at the medical models instead of looking at the social... or psychosocial aspect of it for the patient...having got some ideas about the um psychosocial aspect of health, taking it back to my past cultures... without making the connection with the social aspect you cannot treat the patient... so I bring in this system where I realise or begin to understand how I can actually help the sick from different cultures.

He became a student advocate and community activist. He served as a representative for overseas students in the university and was a member of important committees. He learned to argue his case within this context, finding greater self-respect, maybe self-esteem too, in the process (and in telling stories about it). He critiqued the neglect of the cultural dimensions of health care and a lack of attention given to minority communities and their experiences in the delivery of health services; and the failure to locate health and dis-ease in a wider socio-political context. He felt recognised in diverse communities. Yet, Mathew's is no simple linear tale. He continued to struggle with written assignments and in both the second and third interviews, the research itself became, for a moment, an explicit transitional space, in which he thought about his options and looked to us for guidance, in an emotionally needy way:

> I don't want it to be a sign of weakness if I ask somebody to help me [proof reading my essay], that might make me a weak person… but there are a lot of resources which they call academic skills…I did it once, I've never done it again…but I have to change that because if I want to succeed I have to do that because the system is set up for that.

He asked what we thought and the boundaries between biographical narrative interviewing and educational counselling, and between past and present, became blurred, and self-confidence, fragile. A colleague researcher (there were two of us interviewing), encouraged him to seek help and to overcome his reluctance. He really wanted to know what she thought and began to talk at length. Admitting vulnerability was a dangerous business, he said, for someone like him, and he valued our meetings. He made the decision to try again with an assignment. By the time of the third interview, he had organised a new pressure group for multi-cultural sensitivities in health care, building on his work as a student advocate at the university. Mathew, in effect, had embraced po-litical agency in different spaces, exploiting aspects of his own biography and experience. We have glimpses in the material of different levels of recognition: at the most intimate, in terms of new relationships, and of feeling seen and valued, including in the research; there is self-respect too, in being accepted as part of a wider community of rights; and self-esteem has found space to breathe, as an effective political activist and advocate. Yet, to repeat, this is no simple, linear progression: after the interviews, Mathew wrote on a number of occasions to us, asking for help with assignments, and he constantly feared 'failure' in the ritual called academic writing. It remained hard to admit vulnerability and the need for help.

Conclusion

There are profound if insufficiently understood psychosocial and embodied dimensions to such transformative learning, in which recognition and selfhood are fundamental. I have brought into the analytic frame a dynamic of self recognition encompassing intimate, mezzo as well as wider cultures, which seems both respectful and illuminating of the material. At core, for students such as these, there is the possibility of existing in the world more openly and spontaneously, despite anxieties, because of feeling seen, understood and valued by people who matter. A self can begin to claim more space for play and experiment, breaking free of potentially crippling anxiety. But we have moved beyond intimate relationships alone to processes of recognition at institutional and wider social levels, as a basis for human flourishing, reciprocity and greater freedom of the will. And have traversed important disciplinary boundaries in the process. If Bourdieu helps us to understand how cultures become embodied in everyday encounters, and how a university habitus often inhibits people from particular backgrounds, the narratives of non-traditional learners, with the help of Honneth and Winnicott, reveal how learners can bring diverse forms of capital into universities, and via good enough recognition, claim space for self, agency, and social justice. Students can also shape the habitus itself, creating new qualities of space, and ways of being, that challenge overly deterministic, rigid views of what a habitus actually is. The research also takes us well beyond a technicist, highly instrumentalist or overly cognitivist understanding of what a university education actually is, or ought to be: we have moved to more of a relational, dynamic and embodied sensibility, where what tutors and others do, matters, greatly: not only in creating space for less inhibited experiments of selfhood, but also for a more egalitarian project of education. Tutors, note, you may be unaware of the importance of what you do but also of whom you are and what you may represent to the other; and also of how the other can make real, in embodied, relational senses, the ideal of a university as a transformative space, rather than one simply reproducing the established order.

References

Bainbridge, A. & West, L. (2012). (Eds). *Psychoanalysis and Education, minding the gap*. London: Karnac.

Bourdieu, P. (1988). *Homus Academicus*. Stamford: University Press.

Bourdieu, P. (1990). *In Other Words: Essays toward a Reflexive Sociology*. Stanford, CN: Stanford University Press.

Bourdieu, P. and Passeron, J. (1977/2000). *Reproduction in Education, Society and Culture*. London, Sage.

Chapman Hoult, E. (2009). *Representations of resilience in adult learning*. PhD Thesis, Canterbury Christ Church University, UK.

Chapman Hoult, E. (2012). *Adult learning and La Recherche Feminine. Reading Resilience and Hélène Cixous*. London: Palgrave Macmillan.

Dirkx, J.M., Mezirow, J & Cranton, P. (2006). Musings and Reflections on the Meaning and Context, and Process of Transformative Learning. *Journal of Transformative Learning*, 4, 123-139.

Fleming, T. (2010). Recognition in the work of Axel Honneth: Implications for Transformative Learning Theory. *Paper to the 9th International Conference on Transformative Learning*. Athens, May.

Frampton, S. (2011). *When I am playing with my cat, how do I know she is not playing with me? Montaigne and being in touch with life*. London: Faber & Faber.

Honneth, A. (2007) *Disrespect; the normative foundations of critical theory*. Cambridge: Polity Press.

Honneth, A. (2009). *Pathologies of Reason: on the legacy of critical theory*. New York: Columbia University Press.

Hunt, C. (2013). *Transformative Learning through Creative Writing*. London: Routledge.

Illeris, K. (2002). *The three dimensions of learning*. Leicester: NIACE and Roskilde University Press.

Mezirow, J. (2000). *Learning as transformation*. San Francisco: Jossey-Bass.

Merrill, B. & West, L. (2009). *Using biographical methods in social research*. London, Sage.

Quin, J. (2011). Imaginal social capital. *Keynote paper to the RANLHE International Conference*. Saville, April.

Sclater, S.D. (2004). What is the subject?. In *Narrative Enquiry*. 13(2): 317-330.

Sinclair, S. (1997). *Making Doctors*. Oxford: Berg.

West, L. (1996). *Beyond Fragments; adults, motivation and higher education*. London, Taylor and Francis.

West, L. (2009). Lifelong learning and the family: an auto/biographical imagination. In P.Jarvis (Ed) *The Routledge International Handbook of Lifelong Learning*. London: Routledge, 67-79.

West, L. (2011a). Crises, ambivalence and ambiguity in transformative learning: challenging perspectives from auto/biographical narrative research. *Paper to the 9th International Conference on Transformative Learning*. Athens, May.

West, L. (2011b). Family disputes: Science, Poetry and Subjectivity in Biographical Narrative Research. In H.Herzberg & E.Kammler (Eds) *Biographie und Gesellschaft*. Frankfurt: Campus Verlag, pp. 415-434.

West, L., Fleming, T. & Finnegan, F. (2013, in press). Connecting Bourdieu, Winnicott, and Honneth: Understanding the experiences of non-traditional learners through an interdisciplinary lens. In *Studies in the Education of Adults*. November.

Winnicott, D. (1971). *Playing and Reality*. London, Routledge.

Chapter 4

A body of words: body, language and meaning in biographical research

◊   ROB EVANS, OTTO-VON-GUERICKE-UNIVERSITÄT, MAGDEBURG

… parler, c'est exister absolument pour l'autre. (Fanon, 1952, p. 13)

Those who read or listen to our stories see everything as through a lens. This lens is the secret of narration, and it is ground anew in every story, ground between the temporal and the timeless. (Berger, 2005, p. 31)

The rest is silence. (Hamlet, Act V, Scene 2)

Infattianche il silenzio può essere considerato un discorso, in quanto rifiuto dell'uso che altri fanno della parola; ma il senso di questo silenzio-discorso sta nelle sue interruzioni, cioè in ciò che di tanto in tanto si dice e che dà un senso a ciò che si tace.

In fact, silence, too, can be considered a discourse, as the refusal of the use that others make of words; but the sense of this silence-discourse is in its interruption, that is, in what one says from time to time and the sense that gives to what one doesn't say. (Calvino, 1983, p. 105)

This chapter will engage with embodied learning in the context of our interactions with each other, and in interdependency with the 'natural' material world. It will examine the potential of language developed in biographical interviews to reveal the construction of embodied meaning. The perspective adopted in this chapter perceives the life told in the interview as flooded with meaning in contested language. To elicit a narrative is embodied activity. This view sees gendered, sexualised, aged bodies and bodies framed by contexts of control, by "inequalities in resources and conditions of life"[1], by regimentation and desire, contesting the research space in the interview. The participants in biographical research are communicating, "talking bodies", deploying the "interactional qualities and language of the body" (Coffey, 1999, p. 270).

Individual biographies are, of course, incomplete stories. Biographical, told experience is worked and reworked into former told versions of a life story (Hoerning, 1989, pp. 153-154). Through the interaction of interviewer and respondent and through the wider out-of-frame interaction of both with their respective social worlds, strong elements of interdiscursivity enrich the work of meaning-making that these learning biographies represent.

Meaning-making, which in its very core sense is always and exclusively a shared act, an act of communication and interaction, in the biographical interview involves the reflexive memory work of drawing on layers of lived experience. Making meaning is, in this view, physically situated between historical and cultural grounding of the self and the construction of the self and the world, in a tension that is "anchored in the life-world" (Dausien, 2001, p. 71) of the participants. Language shapes and determines the interaction out of which the life history is narrated. The telling shapes in turn the language use. Thus, in examining the work of learning carried forward by individuals, in our research spaces we are examining, too, the search for a language in which to express learning.

Importantly, we do well to remember that embodied experience can be lost in biographical research when this is "overly focused on words, content and cognition alone"[2]. This chapter embraces the theoretical standpoint which understands language and the linguistic work in biography research as rooted in bodily learning, bodily perception and interaction. Bourdieu, for example, stresses the individual's consciousness of the 'value' of their linguistic production in a social context. This consciousness determines the "assurance", "authority", as well as the "insecurity" or "timidity" of individuals' respective discourses (Bourdieu, 2001, p. 121). This consciousness empowers or disempowers. In an identical vein, Pennycook, citing Deborah Cameron (1997) suggests that a performative approach to identity – one that sees identity as constituted in interaction – "suggests that people are *who they are* because of (among other things) *the way they talk*" (Cameron 1997 cited in Pennycook, 2008, p. 177- my italics). Seen in this light, the ways in which identity is performed through language use, and language in its own right is performed through acts of identity in interaction (Pennycook, 2008, p. 177), allow us to understand the embodied production of language in each different social space and between individuals as, in Bourdieu's words: "a dimension of an individual's physical hexis in which the social world in all its relationships and the world in all its socially instructed relationships are given expression" (Bourdieu, 2001, p. 126).

Close attention to the way language is shared and exchanged in the biographic interview means here a radical break with widespread notions of cognitive or neurolinguistic 'deep structures' of language and mind which reduce language, spoken words, interaction to research artefacts, to decontextualised 'games', to lifeless codes similar to computer programming languages. Accepting the embodied nature of research in the field and the embodied processes of thought, analysis and communication – a "somatic turn" which is concerned to address any over-emphasis on textuality or meta-discourse (Pennycook, 2008, p. 177) – which make up our work, our being, as researchers interacting with narrators and researcher audiences, reminds us that "words are not the Word", and that there are ultimately "no words for the deepest experience" (Eugene Ionesco cited by Steiner,

1998, p. 194). There is, though, the language of social experience, in all its aesthetic and private and emotional forms, and our commitment to its message. And, before all else, there is language in the space, the void, between I and the Other.[3]

Biography, the everyday and language interaction

The unfolding of life stories is, according to Alheit (1983), essentially occupied with the necessity to synchronise two disparate levels of experienced time: firstly, the dimension of events and experiences which usually have a routine, daily, everyday frame, and secondly, those which operate on the life-time scale/horizon, which "links long past events with past experiences, past with present experience and ultimately present with conceivable future events"[4] (Alheit, 1983, p. 189). Stepping out of the everyday frame to "tell" a story of the past, to recall something, to reminisce, is a trigger to retrospective (self-) analysis. In each such case, Alheit argues, we stand before the problem of showing others and ourselves who we are, what we are becoming, what we have been. This task is rendered incomparably more difficult and more threatening in situations when the everyday and its routines and rites, customs and places are thrown out of kilter and where their realignment seems doubtful or even impossible.[5] Having to step out in this way and sort out life both in its everyday manifestation and even more frighteningly in its overarching 'meaning' (or what served till then for meaning) "go right to the core of our biography because they endanger a reconstructable and already anticipated continuity of our 'self-plan'"[6] (Alheit, 1983, p. 193; see also Fischer-Rosenthal, 1995, p. 50).

> The telling of the "story" of the life-plan, the attempt to reconstruct the life/time dimension of the own biography requires the narrator to "look back", to "experience again" what it felt like, what happened, actions, emotions, worries, decisions, pains etc. The "material" of this account is made up of precisely the everyday details, the particularities and idiosyncrasies of the everyday, not of the larger life/time (Alheit, 1983, p. 195).

Biographical narratives, then, are to a large extent reliant both on the clut-tering details of the everyday and the ambiguous, and partly for that reason therefore claimable and re-cyclable words and 'frames' of layered accounts offered in interaction by others. The field of narrative elicitation, is "personal identity work" (Coffey, 1999, p. 40) and establishing field relations involves working rapports and trust, commitment and personal investment, genui-neness and reciprocity (1999, pp. 39-42). The talk issuing in co-production from the participants in a biographic interview or indeed any situation in which the life-story in some form is told, is not a "head thing", mental and intellectual, but very much embodied and mediated inter-relationally, physically, just as the physical also accompanies, shapes, hinders and filters elements of understanding and recognition (Sieder, 1999, pp. 251-252).[7]

The talk is not a 'head thing', then, the interaction that makes up everyday social relations is seemingly so routine, so accepted that it appears "natu-ral" (Alheit & Dausien, 2000, p. 269) and, it has to be added, singularly personal. Biographical processes of identity construction, then, are situ-ated in language interaction at many, at multiple, levels. Interaction and relations of reciprocity between individual subjects and others provide the framework within which 'selves' are constructed in communication with others. Secondly, the changing relationship of individual subjects to their own and others' words, current or long-past, influence identity construction at every step, providing individuals with the language means to describe themselves and the world. Further, the relationships of mem-bership within (and dissociation from) recognisable groups or with rec-ognisable values or characteristics, identities or stigmas, via the situating power of indexicality ('I', 'you', 'here', 'them', 'there' etc.) construct locally 'situated' embodied identities that intersect constantly in discourse (see De Fina, Schiffrin, & Bamberg, 2006, pp. 9-15; and for a broadly similar view of intersubjectivity see Habermas, 1981, pp. 207-208).

There is clearly a theoretically important tension here at work. Here, on the one hand, we have the shifting subjectivity of the individual engaged in on-going interaction, responding to the multiple forces of reciprocity in dialogue and contact with others and the significance this has for the protean character of interactive language use. There, on the other hand, the unseen, 'hidden' structuring framework of habitus, the excess resources of *biographicity* which we cannot fully access and which operate 'behind the scenes', so to speak, essentially unbeknown to us in our talk and intercourse (Alheit & Dausien, 2000, pp. 276-277). In the following, I shall, of necessity briefly, set out some arguments for seeing language as the essential embodying force shaping biographical experience and the construction of shared biographical knowledge.

A body of words: worded bodies

At the outset of this paper, I referred to 'deep structures' of language and mind which reduce language, spoken words, interaction to research artefacts, to de-contextualised 'games', to lifeless codes similar to computer programming languages. It is currently fashionable in university departments of linguistics (but also in biological sequence analysis: see Chiang, 2012, p. 9) to view language from the point of view of 'generative' or 'transformational grammar'. Very briefly, and at the risk of over-generalizing, this approach asserts that language is 'innate' to every human being and that every human being is competent to produce an unlimited number of correct grammatical realizations of their language (for a classic account of generative grammar see Chomsky, 1964; de Villiers & Roeper, 2011). Further, the true study of linguistic phenomena focuses on the 'I-language' (internal language) rather than on the performed E-language (external *performance* as opposed to essential *competence*). The temptation of 'deep structures'[8] which exert their influence on external performance and external action, for related disciplines, as a kind of over-arching structural framework, has been strong since the 1960s and has made itself felt in social sciences in general and biography research, as well (see for example Habermas, 1981; Schütze, 1975; Silverman, 1998). George Steiner, rejecting Chomskyan notions of innateness and universality of language performance, points out that "No two human beings share an identical social context". He goes on:

Because such a context is made up of the totality of an individual existence, because it comprehends not only the sum of personal memory and experience but also the reservoir of the particular subconscious, it will differ from person to person (Steiner, 1998, p. 178).

At the most basic levels of human speech production[9], language is, he continues, "open to contingencies of memory and of new experience", including historical and cultural factors (Steiner, 1998, pp. 179-180). We speak to others "'at the surface' of ourselves", using, Steiner says, "a shorthand beneath which there lies a wealth of subconscious, deliberately concealed or declared associations so extensive and intricate that they probably equal the sum and uniqueness of our status as an individual person" (Steiner, 1998, p. 181).

These remarks, for all Steiner's tendency to overstatement, are of enormous importance to how we encounter the talk of others and ourselves in our research. For Steiner's 'wealth of associations' is '*intertextuality*' (though I prefer to speak of '*interdiscursivity*') by another name, which, Deborah Tannen remarks "in its many guises, refers to the insight that meaning in language results from a complex of relationships linking items within a discourse and linking current to prior instances of language" (Tannen, 2007, p. 9). Seconding Alheit and Dausien (2000, pp. 268-270), I suggest that we see the creative, 'knitting' effects of shared and sharing interdiscursive involvement in language in the way biographical knowledge is constructed in countless interactive situations. Speaking in particular of the con/struction and re/production of gender codes, Alheit and Dausien write: "The construction process of the binary gender code can be traced right back into the furthest reaches of everyday situations and their "embodiedness"[10] (2000, p. 270). Through language and embodied interaction, gender becomes all-pervading, "omnirelevant", expressing itself, too, in individual speech intonation (2000, p. 270; Günthner, 1997).

Written into the body, written into our lives

Education, learning experience, as well as life-wide conditioning/position-ing and appropriation of socially acceptable and socially sanctioned forms of communication determine the context of each and every language(d) encounter, including the narration of a life history. Talk is thus always prepared, that is, the ground and terrain of talk is prepared by the tacit, understood expectation of what can be said or not said. Human beings, Michael Tomasello argues, "wish to share experience with one another and so, over time, they have created symbolic conventions for doing that". Language is "a form of cognition; it is cognition packaged for purposes of interpersonal communication" (1999, p. 150). Acceptability of the lan-guage used in each and every form of social interaction are for Bourdieu as much bound up to their acquisition in the different stages and stations of a life as in their utilisation once acquired, and through utilisation, their continual adaptation to changing social transactions (Bourdieu, 2001, p. 120). Bourdieu stresses the physical, embodied nature of individuals' expectations and chances. The production and re-production of acquired interactional stances – embedded and realised in variously configured hi-erarchically structured social spaces – is balanced by active use of chances that can be taken. Anticipation of what can or should be communicated in a given situation is, for Bourdieu, something of an "embodied objectivity", a "practical sense, almost physical in nature, of the truth in the objective relationship between a certain linguistic and social competence and a certain market in which this relationship is accomplished" (Bourdieu, 2001, p. 120). Language, he states, "is a technique of the body" embed-ded in all these social relationships (Bourdieu, 2001, p. 126). A similar idea was expressed, in relation to such structured social spaces and the range of social interactional stances people take up, by Raymond Wil-liams. Rules and norms of society "run very deep", he argued, and they "are often materialised, and in inheriting them as institutions we inherit a real environment, which shapes us but which we also change. We learn this environment *in our bodies*, and we are taught the conventions" (Wil-liams, 1965, p. 137 – my italics).

Involvement and animation: the body speaks

Thus, in all interaction, there is an interlocking, an involvement on many levels and taking many forms, all of them languaged. Tannen is convincing when she writes that 'involvement' is "an internal, even emotional connection individuals feel which binds them to other people as well as to places, things, activities, ideas, memories, and words"; it is not a given, but "an achievement in conversational interaction". She follows Bakhtin/Voloshinov in saying that no word can be spoken without echoing how others understand and have used it (Tannen, 2007, pp. 27-28). Yet we are not speaking here of words-as-content, words-as-vessels-of-meaning but rather of the void-filling contact that language brings to embodied encounters in human communication. "Part of the effect of participating in sense-making and of being swept up by the sound and rhythm of language" Tannen says, "is emotional. [...] Understanding is facilitated, even enabled, by an emotional experience of interpersonal involvement" (Tannen, 2007, p. 46). Indeed, this is arguably why people in all cultures tell each other stories, why they "share information, feelings and ways of seeing" (Tomasello, 2011, p. 310). Among the bodily associations and omnirelevant "structures of social encounters" with the aid of which we present ourselves to others (Goffman, 1959), Tannen points out the crucial, and ordinary, role of language in making involvement possible:

- thus, rhythm, rhythmic synchrony in stretches of own talk, self-synchrony and synchrony among speakers emerge in interaction and 'push on', make possible and embroider the articulation of identity;
- patterns of repetition, too, developed in dense outcrops and scattered tellingly across longer stretches of talk create signposts and turnings that can mitigate the distance between speakers; repetition may include variations based on phonemes, morphemes, words, collocations of words, longer sequences of discourse, playing on the ear and 'painting', as it were, in the space bridged by the talk, enchanting, encouraging, threatening, challenging;

- style features and repetitive figures, such as indirectness, ellipsis, tropes, dialogue, imagery create enigma and intimacy, break commonplaces and open new paths for teller and told to go down jointly, create hierarchies of authority and knowledge, narrow the dialogical gap or set up impassable barriers (Tannen, 2007, p. 32).
- The embodiment of talk can with the above textural devices be enhanced, magnified, intensified. Rhythm, repetition, 'synching' of sounds and patterns between interactants (Sacks, 1992; Tannen, 2007, pp. 33-34) can be understood as filling out the negotiated context of talk, whether it be a chance conversation, a structured dialogue or the biographic interview. The co-speakers touch and go in talk, enmeshed in dense layers of language.

Another dimension of the embodying force of language, in which its full ex- and transpositional power unfolds, is played out in space and time, jumping from the 'now' of all "naturally-occurring talk" (for caveats regarding this see Szczepek Reed, 2011, p. 5) seamlessly to other times, other places/spaces (of memory, experience, imagination, regret). Goffman's concept of 'embedding' can be used to describe this aspect of the words spoken in talk. The words we speak, he points out, "are often not our own, at least our current 'own'" for "although who speaks is situationally circumscribed, in whose name words are spoken is certainly not" (Goffman, 1981, p. 3). Thus embedding makes it possible to 'enact' numerous voices over space and time within the interactive frame of the oral narrative and narrative interview (Goffman, 1981, p. 4). This is a central feature of interactive talk in the research interview. Indeed, for the development of 'own' discourses within an emergent learning biography, the 'converted' and 'enacted' words of others or a non-current 'self' – what I have called elsewhere 'embedded speech' (Evans, 2004) – are an almost ubiquitous phenomenon of vivid contextualization of talk.

For speakers do not speak only with their 'own' voice. Their own voice, so critically dependent –syntax, lexis, intonation, accent, volume and so on – on the language context (friendly, congenial, familiar, threatening, dangerous, frightening, incomprehensible) they find themselves in, on the power context, the gender constellation, the cultural unknowns crowding in on them, shifts, changes, surges and gives way. Other voices, othered voices and the voices of others can be adopted. The "creation of voices occasions the imagination of a scene in which characters speak in those voices, and … these scenes occasion the imagination of alternative, distant, or familiar worlds, …" This, says Tannen, is "an important source of emotion in discourse" (Tannen, 2007, p. 39). Tannen argues further that by

> animating the voice of the other, speakers create a rhythm and sound that suggests speech at the same time that they shape the meaning thus presented. […] The representation of the sound of speech is considered essential to the accurate representation of characters and their worlds (2007, p. 41).

The language we use, thus, spans and binds the physical ever-present of interaction, giving it colour, texture and impulse, creating and naming the spaces, opening room for voice, the told and the heard, pacing and measuring real and distant, imagined time and timed time, populating the now and then and the still-to-come with loud and soft voices of the once, hence and never-to-be. The language is volume, breath, exhaustion and melody. Physical, the body's own, personal and yet belonging to more than one.

Telling the body, bodying the telling
– Extracts from 'Carola'

Carola develops a narrative of change accompanied by impressive physical and prosodic presence. Her voice overcomes considerable barriers, and her narrative connects different worlds – the family, teenage sexuality, a sexist work environment, learning accomplishment and knowledge claims.

The transcription is given in both German and English, in order that the richness of the language used to give voice to her sense of transition and to surmount a complex web of narrative problems, starting with the difficulty of telling this story to the interviewer, can be appreciated. The left hand columns of the transcript table provide information regarding her use of modal particles, embedded speech and prosody.

Carola grew up in Düsseldorf in Germany. Her parents, as she related, became increasingly central to her learning biography, and possessed only basic school education: her father was a lathe-operator and her mother, a housewife. Carola was the first in her family (she has one sister) to have any contact with the university. Carola left school at 16 to take an apprenticeship as an office clerk with the chemicals giant Bayer in Leverkusen on the river Rhine near Cologne, where her father was also employed. On completion of the apprenticeship, she stayed on at Bayer for three years.

In the following sample, seamless transitions between narrative and purportedly verbatim speech or internal speeches are given. The "frivolous embedding" Goffman speaks of (Goffman, 1981) seems effortless. Cardinal learning experiences are framed and re-constructed and inserted into an interview narrative, jumping any number of hurdles in time and place. The discourse of learning 'tapped' in each case establishes a sense of continuity of self or of understanding, and can be read as a moment of reflexion on the (narrated) present.

The flow of the narrative, which is prosodically driven by repeated modal devices (èMP) 'eigentlich'/'really', 'einfach'/'just', 'einfach'/'just', 'irgendwie'/'like' and by the affective table-banging (èPro for 'prosody', here a kind of physical prosody), is enriched and warranted by the èESp insertion (where ESp stands for 'embedded speech'). The frame is shifted, Carola's position is asserted.

Extract 1 Carola: "I never thought about it"

1	CO:	ich hatte in der Realschule einen	in the secondary school I had
2		Durchschnitt von drei komma	an average of 3.5 was really
3	èMP	fuenf war egentlich sehr schlecht	pretty bad and I just couldn't
4	èMP	(.) und ich hatte einfach keine Lust	be bothered anymore it was
5		es war so ein Zwang da dass ich	just this pressure there that I
6	èMP	zur Schule gehen musste und ich	had to go to school and I just
7		hab +einfach Nichts gemacht++	did nothing (.) I never thought
8		(.) ich hab dort nicht in Erwaegung	that I wasn't perhaps so stupid
9		gezogen dass ich vielleicht nicht	I thought more like <ESp>I
10	èEsp	dumm bin ich dachte also eher so	can't do so much I'll do an
11		<ESp>ich kann nicht so viel mache	apprenticeship I didn't I never
12		ich meine Lehre ich hab gar nicht	even thought ((bangs on ta-
13	èPro	mir kam es gar nicht in den Sinn	ble)) of going to a museum to
14		((bangs on table)) auch mal ins	the theatre or something like
15	èMP	Museum zu gehen ins Theater zu	read a good book just didn't
16		gehen irgendwie ein gutes Buch zu	think of it
		lesen kam mir nicht in den Sinn	

Tannen argues that "evaluation talk" is regularly performed through prosody and voice quality. Further, shifts in prosody are at often crucial in signalling changes in interaction (Tannen, 2007, pp. 18-19). It is through changes in voice pitch, the volume of the voice, variations in intonation, voice quality, choice of pronouns that speakers "position themselves as another speaker …" (2007, p. 22 – her italics). One passage from the data presents an interesting example of the dramatic staging of the speaker's position vis-à-vis an alternative – and opposed – order of discourse. Carola builds up a powerful frame of prosodic language in recounting the work involved in breaking out of her family's influence:

Extract 2 – Carola: massive problems

1	CO:	ich hatte drei Wochen massive	I had really massive prob-
2		Probleme aber (.) meine Mutter hat	lems for three weeks but (.)
3		nie mit mir darueber gesprochen	my mother never talked to
4		mich nie gefragt <ESp>was ist? sie	me about it never asked me
5	è1	hat gesehen wie ich ausgesehen	<Esp>what's the matter? she
6	è2	habe (.) aber es gab nur halt die	could see what I looked like:::
7	è3	Sorge so (.) immer das Essen und	(.) but all she was worried about
8		weil man irgendwie ueber Gefue-	was (.) always just food and
9		hle und dergleichen nicht ((strikes	because somehow it just wasn't
10		table)) reden konnte (.) auch nicht	possible to speak about feelings
11		((strikes table)) ueber irgendwie	and things like that ((strikes ta-
12		das Befinden (.) gar {nicht	ble)) (.) not even ((strikes table))
13			in any way even about how you
14			feel (.) absolutely nothing
15	R:	mhmm}	
16	CO:	=und deswegen ist es bei meinen	and that's why with my parents
17	è4	Eltern halt so es muss einfach al-	it's just like it is everything has
18	è5	les geordnet sein (.) die Nachbarn	to have its place::: (.) the neigh-
19		((strikes table)) die muessen den-	bours ((strikes table)) they've got
20		ken ((strikes table)) dass alles ok	to think ((strikes table)) that eve-
21		ist (.) man muss gepflegt aussehen	rything's just fine (.) you've got
22		(1.0) und Geld ist sehr wichtig (.)	to look smart (1.0) and money
23		kann man sich Essen kaufen und	is really important (.) you can
24		Kleidung (.) und ein Auto (.) {es	buy yourself food and clothes (.)
25		sehen	and a car (.) {the neighbours see
26			
27	R:	(???)}	
28	CO:	=doch auch die Nachbarn und	everything and uhm uhm it's
29	è6	uhm es ist einfach ein System was	just a system of things that I
30		ich (1.0) eigentlich was ich sekun-	(1.0) I think it's really not im-
31		daer finde	portant

Carola here employs a thick web of modal adverbs ('halt', 'eigentlich'/'kind of', 'actually') and moves through hesitations and an obvious search for the 'texture' of the complaints still in her ears to a damning (and accomplishedly rhetorical) list of commandments punctuated by her peremptory emotional raps on the table top (made loud by a mass of heavy rings) which provide a percussionary accompaniment to the telling (è2-5). She completes this biographized vignette with a personal crescendo of triumph and self-confirmation (è6). Interestingly, atè1 she proposes the parental concern and interest that never came in the form of an imagined utterance, another fascinating employment of voicing imagined talk, creating, so to speak, an alternative possible experience. Context is created and potential discourse is roughed in.

In the next Extract, Carola fills out the negative picture of her home and family life and its role in hindering her development and ultimately its place in her learning and personal achievement with the help of emphatic table banging (è1, è3). More importantly, at è2 Carola searches for a formulation for her own conception of values and aims to confront the affectively difficult one left imprinted in her talk by the home. She finds her way to this at è2 with the long drawn-out resolution ('wie wie wie'/'like like like') of finishing something you start ('durchgezogen wie wie wie man einfach alles zu Ende fuehrt'/'finshed like like like you simply finish things'). Like she will finish her studies, too, she asserts. This is a significant use of affective marking to establish an own – hard-won – learning discourse and she leaves no doubt about its importance for her.

Extract 3 – "you just finish something you started"

1	R:	ja aber wenn man dann Geld	yeah, but if you go and spend
2		fuer Buecher von Sartre oder so	money on books by Sartre or the
3		was ausgibt	like …
4	CO:	das ist Unsinn (.) das ist Unsinn	but that's rubbish (.) that's rub-
5	è1	(.) ich kann mich daran erinnern	bish (.) I can remember (.) when
6		dass (.) wenn ein Buch von mir	a book of mine lay on the floor
7		im Zimmer vor meinem Bett lag	in my bedroom I used to get
8		da wurde ich angeschrieen weil	screamed at because (.) uhm
9		(.) uhm es darf nichts rumliegen	nothing was allowed to lie
10		(.) es darf auch kein Buch [strikes	around on the floor (.) not even a
11		table] vor dem Bett liegen was	book was allowed [bangs table]
12		man liest oder so was (.) weiss	to lie next to the bed if you're
13		ich nicht es war (.) so dass meine	reading it or anything like that (.)
14		Eltern haben auch nicht so viel	I don't know it was (.) my parents
15		gelesen wie es	never really read that much like
16			

17	R:	{ok aber es	ok but that is
18	CO:	wurde also so}	so it was like that
19	CO:	ich hab' das einfach ich hab' das	I just I just (.) did it like like like
20		einfach (.) durchgezogen wie	you just finish something you've
21	è2	wie wie man einfach alles zu	started exactly like the way I go-
22		Ende fuehrt was man angefangen	ing to finish my business admin
23		hat genauso wie ich jetzt mein	degree [bangs table]
24		Wiwistudium auch beende	
25	è3	((strikes table))	

Voice and evoking different selves: the teller and the told

Apart from methodological and analytical problems associated with the presentation of data and the selective illustration from transcripts of this kind, the very plurilingual conduct of the research relationship, casual communications, written data and interviews guarantees a thick layer of linguistic detail enriching and complicating the research description proper. Plurilingual elements are present from the moment the dialogue is taken up, and linguistic routines and lexical-syntactic choices are inevitably influenced by the presence of the other(s). The voice of the researcher, pregnant with intentions and in the process of formulating successive questions mixes with the various timbres of this respondent and others, each one a voice coping with the risk of the unknown in the interview situation.

In its textual form, Carola's pithy, vehement story of achievement in a hostile work environment leaps from the printed page, so full it is with the creative energy of a story unfolding against the normal grain of relationships. The proof of this was experienced shortly after, when she participated in a joint-interview with another student, male, quieter than she, exuding gravitas (Evans, 2004, p. 179). This second time she appeared deflated, her voice reduced, her prosodic energy toned down from table-rapping to indecisive puffing.

The body and the narrative – a body of words

The body is present in the interview used here. Much of the emotion felt is suppressed, controlled, redirected, repaired and deflected. Little or none of the emotion evident in the short extracts I have used here was referred to or acknowledged on its happening. And yet the language employed by Carola as well as her table rapping – all of these evocations of difficulty and trouble are hearable and analysable in their sequential unfolding. Fieldwork, working in the field of narrative elicitation, and establishing field relations involves working rapports and trust, commitment and personal investment, genuineness and reciprocity (Coffey, 1999, pp. 39-42).

As much as we must recognise the presence of talking bodies and their emotions in interview situations, it is equally important to understand their anomalous character, their dangers, even. Certainly, the room for emotion was no less difficult in the field relationship with the student Carola. The interview site was partly neutral, yet invested with institutional authority (a vacant Professor's office). Emotions, or even a suspicion of them, behind closed doors and between a teacher and his student, are threatening, for both parties. The space taken over for the duration of the interview is unwonted, difficult to negotiate, left unsaid.

Embodiment and the subject

To conclude, I wish to say only a few words about one aspect of the embodiment processes of the biographical interview. Interview participants invariably experience the beginning, at least, of a long interview as difficult, threatening, even, and normally adjust to this anomalous situation in the process of 'learning the ropes', one might say. That is, narratives are started, false starts are coped with and sequential turns follow one another. The experience, on the face of it, remains highly individual. Yet the narratives, the talk issuing in co-production from these 'talking bodies', is complex, layered, referential, rich in connotation and inference and invariably plurivocal. Mason found that subjects in biographical

99

narratives are frequently not subjects with relations to others, but rather 'relational subjects' embedded in relations which condition their narratives and meaning-making (Mason, 2004, pp. 177-178). Carola, too, is present, and enacts embodied narratives. Her talk enacts and envisions her social worlds, from the microcosms of her momentary emotions to her embeddedness in the issues confronting her as learner, teller, daughter, worker and stranger.

"... so little is being said, so much is being meant."
(Steiner, 1998, p. 35)

The biography is told – in one way or another. The story or stories contained in a biography can be told in many ways, directly and indirectly. Graphic representation, sculpture, music, song, dance: all can, and massively do, communicate biographical experience. The 'biographicity' of such works is in their re-production, mirroring, repeating, coding and deciphering, translation and transformation of layered experience of the artist, communicator, performer, consciously and intentionally, or unconsciously, implicitly. They are all interventions in the bodied world made up of narratives, dialogues, readings, interpretations.

Yet as I have tried to suggest here, *language* – not words – is the quintessential reality of reciprocity. Signor Palomar, Italo Calvino's affectionately drafted piece of troubled humanity who I quote at the opening of this paper, refrains from the use of words in the way others use them, developing his own dialogue with them through his silence. He finds, however, that he has to "think not only about what he is about to say or not say, but about all the things that if he speaks or not will be said or not said by [himself] or others"[11]. At which point, he bites his tongue again and remains silent (Calvino, 1983, pp. 105-106). As Pineau and Le Grand suggest, however, the relationship between the "immense continent of History" told and the untold "small personal histories" remains staggeringly unequal (Pineau & Le Grand, 2007, p. 6). "Il faut", they assert, "la plupart du temps une crise pour en sortir, pour oser commencer non seulement à parler au "je", mais à réfléchir en la faisant travailler, trier et conjuguer à la première personne du singulier les mots et moments hérités" (2007, p. 6). The authors sum up very aptly the act of transition, of passing from the diffident physical silence of Calvino's Signor Palomar to a physically present narrator across times and spaces, picking up the powerful words of the self and 'conjugating' them audibly and actively outwards.

A cramped concentration on the words-as-content, however, either as the direct equivalences of a narrow 'realism' or the result of hardly describable 'deep' cognitive processes governing the choice, categorization and meta-analysis of words may, I argue, miss something central about language and its physical, embodied implications. The correlation between the complexity of the human organism and that of speech, language in use, is suggested, however opaquely, by Wittgenstein: "The tacit agreements regulating the comprehension of talk" he states, "are enormously complicated" (Wittgenstein, 1980, p. 4.002). This sense of the complexity and richness of the language that is shared and created by individuals as they interact is the note on which I wish to finish. To cite George Steiner once more, he reminds us that when examining the content-matter of narratives, we should recall that

> We communicate motivated images, local frameworks of feeling. [...] We speak less than the truth, we fragment in order to reconstruct desired alternatives, we select and elide. It is not the things which "are" that we say, but those which might be, which we would bring about, which the eye and remembrance compose. The directly informative content of natural speech is small. Information does not come naked except in the schemata of computer languages or the lexicon. It comes attenuated, flexed, coloured, alloyed by intent and the milieu in which the utterance occurs (and 'milieu' here is the total biological, cultural, historical, semantic ambience as it conditions the moment of individual articulation (Steiner, 1998, p. 231).

Notes

1 From the Call to the 2012 Conference of the ESREA Biography and Life history Network held at the Syddansk Universitet Odense, March 1-4 2012.

2 From the Conference Call Odense 2012.

3 Wittgenstein reminds us that spoken language is part of the human organism and not less complex than that is ["Der Umgangssprache ist ein Teil des menschlichen Organismus und nicht weniger kompliziert als dieser."] (1980: 32: 4.002).

4 ["...der vorvergangene mit vergangenen Ereignissen, vergangene mit gegenwärtigen und schließlich gegenwärtige mit zukünftig denkbaren verbindet"]

5 Macbeth, on hearing of the "untimely" death of Lady Macbeth says: "There would have been a time for such a word."

6 [" ... treffen immer die Substanz unserer Biographie, weil sie eine rekonstruierbare und bereits antizipierte Kontinuität unseres 'Selbstplanes' gefährden"]

7 Pineau and Le Grand refer to Le Grand's term "implexité" to describe the complexity of entangled implications at work in the interview situation, in which institutional, affective and cultural dimensions intervene ["Aussi peut-on parler de 'implexité' ... ou complexité des implication enchevetrées, où tant les dimensions institutionelles qu'affectives ou culturelles interviennent"] (Pineau and Le Grand, 1993: 114).

8 In a recent generative approach to language acquisition, the authors, de Villiers and Roeper posit the following language scenario: "At the beginning, linguistic theory in the generative tradition offered to science the promise of a unique form of biological explanation: an explanation of how a child acquired language that began from innate mental assumptions that were given in a mathematical representation. The concepts were so abstract that the set of combinations was inherently unlimited, and therefore the set of possible grammars was infinite ... Two inherent capacities were proposed to govern acquisition, the first being the autonomy of syntax. If syntax is autonomous, then it could possibly be recognized just by observing variation in surface order of words, as a hard skeleton might be revealed to underpin the movements of a soft body. If such "distributional" evidence were the key, and meaning played no role, then one could, in principle, learn grammar by listening to the radio. See de Villiers, Roeper (2011: 2).

9 Steiner suggests that "all phonetic elements above the level of morphemes ... can become carriers of semantic values" (Steiner, 1998: 179). The morpheme is the smallest semantically meaningful unit of a language.

10 [Der Konstruktionsprozeß des binären Geschlechtercodes ist bis hinein in die Verästelungen alltäglicher Handlungssituationen und deren ‚Körperlichkeit' zurückzuverfolgen].

11 ["... devo pensare non solo a quel che sto per dire o non dire, ma a tutto ciò che se io dico o non dico sarà detto o non detto da me o dagli altri"].

References

Alheit, P. (1983). *Alltagsleben. Zur Bedeutung eines gesellschaftlichen "Restphänomens"*. Frankfurt / New York: Campus Verlag.

Alheit, P., & Dausien, B. (2000). Die biographische Konstruktion der Wirklichkeit. Überlegungen zur Biographizität des Sozialen. In E. M. Hoerning (Ed.), *Biographische Sozialisation* (pp. 257-283). Stuttgart: Lucius & Lucius.

Berger, J. (2005). *and our faces, my heart, brief as photos*. London: Bloomsbury.

Bourdieu, P. (2001). *Langage et pouvoir symbolique*. Paris: Editions de Seuil.

Calvino, I. (1983). *Palomar*. Torino: Einaudi.

Chiang, D. (2012). *Grammars for Languages and Genes: Theoretical and Empirical Investigations*. Berlin/Heidelberg: Springer-Verlag.

Chomsky, N. (1964). *Current Issues in Linguistic Theory*. The Hague: Mouton.

Coffey, A. (1999). *The Embodied Self. Fieldwork and the Representation of Identity*. London: Sage.

Dausien, B. (2001). Erzähltes Leben – erzähltes Geschlecht? Aspekte der narrativen Konstruktion von Geschlecht im Kontext der Biographieforschung. *Feministische Studien*(2), 57-73.

De Fina, A., Schiffrin, D., & Bamberg, M. (2006). Introduction. In A. De Fina, D. Schiffrin & M. Bamberg (Eds.), *Discourse and Identity* (pp. 1-23). Cambridge: Cambridge University Press.

de Villiers, J., & Roeper, T. (2011). *Handbook of Generative Approaches to Language Acquisition*. Dordrecht: Springer.

Evans, R. (2004). *Learning discourse. Learning Biographies, Embedded speech and Discourse Identity in Students' Talk*. Frankfurt / Main: Peter Lang.

Fanon, F. (1952). *Peau noire, masques blancs*. Paris: Éditions du Seuil.

Fischer-Rosenthal, W. (1995). Schweigen – Rechtfertigen – Umschreiben. Biographische Arbeit im Umgang mit deutschen Vergangenheiten [Silence – Justification – Re-Writing. Biographical Work Dealing with German Pasts]. In W. Fischer-Rosenthal & P. Alheit (Eds.), *Biographien in Deutschland. Soziologische Rekonstruktionen gelebter Gesellschaftsgeschichte [Biographies in Germany. Sociological Reconstructions of Lived Social History]* (pp. 43-86). Opladen: Westdeutscher Verlag.

Goffman, E. (1959). *The Presentation of Self in Everyday Life*. New York: Doubleday.

Goffman, E. (1981). *Forms of talk*. Oxford: Blackwell.

Günthner, S. (1997). Complaint Stories. Constructing emotional reciprocity among women. In H. Kotthoff & R. Wodak (Eds.), *Communicating Gender in Context*. (Vol. 42, pp. 179-218). Amsterdam: John Benjamins.

Habermas, J. (1981). *Theorie des kommunikativen Handelns. Zweiter Band. Zur Kritik der funktionalistischen Vernunft*. Frankfurt am Main: Suhrkamp.

Hoerning, E. M. (1989). Erfahrungen als biographische Ressourcen. In P. Alheit & E. M. Hoerning (Eds.), *Biographisches Wissen. Beiträge zu einer Theorie lebensgeschichtlicher Erfahrung* (pp. 148-163). Frankfurt/New York: Campus Verlag.

Mason, J. (2004). Personal narratives, relational selves: residential histories in the living and telling. *The Sociological Review, 52*(2), 162-179.

Pennycook, A. (2008). Critical Applied Linguistics and Language Education. In S. May & N. H. Hornberger (Eds.), *Encyclopedia of language and Education* (Vol. 1 Language Policy and Political Issues in Education pp. 169-181).

Pineau, G., & Le Grand, J.-L. (2007). *Les histoires de vie* (4th ed.). Paris: Presses Universitaires de France.

Sacks, H. (1992). *Lectures in Conversation*. Oxford: Blackwell.

Schütze, F. (1975). *Sprache soziologisch gesehen. Band II: Sprache als Indikator für egalitäre und nicht-egalitäre Sozialbeziehungen*. München: Wilhelm Fink Verlag.

Sieder, R. (1999). Gesellschaft und Person: Geschichte und Biographie. Nachschrift. In R. Sieder (Ed.), *Brüchiges Leben. Biographien in sozialen Systemen* (pp. 234-264). Wien: Turia + Kant.

Silverman, D. (1998). *Harvey Sacks. Social Science and Conversation Analysis*. Cambridge: Polity Press.

Steiner, G. (1998). *After Babel. Aspects of language & translation* (3rd ed.). Oxford: Oxford University Press.

Szczepek Reed, B. (2011). *Analyzing Conversation. An Introduction to Prosody*. Basingstoke: Palgrave Macmillan.

Tannen, D. (2007). *Talking Voices. Repetition, Dialogue, and Imagery in Conversational Discourse* (2 ed. Vol. 25). Cambridge: Cambridge University Press.

Tomasello, M. (1999). *The Cultural Origins of Human Cognition*. Cambridge, Massachusetts: Harvard University Press.

Tomasello, M. (2011). *Die Ursprünge der menschlichen Kommunikation*. Frankfurt/Main: Suhrkamp.

Williams, R. (1965). The Long Revolution. Harmondsworth: Penguin Books.

Wittgenstein, L. (1980). Tractatus logico-philosophicus. Logisch-philosophische Abhandlung. Frankfurt/Main: Suhrkamp.

Chapter 5

'Subject figurations' within modernity: the change of autobiographical formats

◊   PETER ALHEIT

I will start this chapter with two preliminary notes: firstly, the data material on which I base my considerations comes from a project finished in 2005 that dealt with autobiographies from three centuries: the late 18th century, the late 19th century and the present. And although two thick volumes have already appeared, the huge material of more than 350 autobiographies is not yet fully evaluated. I therefore discuss here, one must say, *'work in progress'*. That gives me the chance to venture some risky hypotheses and the reader the right to criticize me drastically.

Secondly, Odense (where this discussion was first aired at the ESREA conference in 2012) is an excellent place for looking at this material. Hans Christian Andersen would have been the most interesting person to look at if we could have integrated Danish material. However, the data are – unfortunately – just German. Compare Andersen with Goethe if you would like, to get an adequate example from Germany. I will certainly think about him later.

Moving on from these points I would like present my thesis, that biography and Modernity belong to each other, perhaps even that biographical subjectivity is a 'discovery' of European Modernity. Given the theme of the book, this underlines the importance of culture, language and technologies, and how these shape who we are and the categories we even think with when considering individual biographies (1). Later on, I would like to make clear that Modernity is far from being a process of linear development. The analysis of autobiographies from different historical periods, and here is my second thesis, justifies the identification of different 'subject figurations' (2). Here I use, implicitly, the deliberations of both Norbert Elias (1989) and Andreas Reckwitz (2006, 2007), that refer to interesting differences within Modernity and reject simple contrasts such as 'tradition' vs. 'Modernity'. Finally, (3), I will give a summary and provide an overarching table of the subject configurations.

1. The 'discovery' of biography within Modernity

The idea that people have a biography is certainly older than the modern age, but there are interesting examples showing that our current understanding of biographical identity is astonishingly *young*.[1] One example fascinates me again and again: the reconstruction of a criminal case from the late 16th century which we owe above all to Natalie Zemon Davis (1984).

The plot can be told relatively quickly: a certain *Martin Guerre,* inhabitant of the Pyrenees village *Artigat,* is missing for some time. After five years, a man comes into the village who claims to be Martin Guerre. He looks a bit different, is clearly slimmer (the war, he says, was a hard time), but he knows all about *Martin*. There is no real reason not to believe him, particularly because his wife recognizes him. He does a good job. He is reliable, does his work well and keeps in touch with close relatives. His wife even gives the impression that she is happier than she was before his disappearance.

A dispute with a relative, however, leads to renewed doubt that he is actually Martin Guerre and ends in a court of law. Here the accused Martin, his correct name is *Arnaud du Tilh*, defends himself brilliantly in presenting the most intimate details of Martin Guerre's biography, so that the court was ready to believe him.[2] Unfortunately, the 'real' Martin Guerre came to the court, out of the blue he had been identified by a blood relative, and du Tilh was convicted to death by hanging.

This case disturbed people, as indicated by the fact that the report of one of the leading lawyers involved in the case, the famous French lawyer *Jean de Coras*, became a bestseller. It seems that people react to this case as we do when we watch the French movie *"Le Retour de Martin Guerre"* with Gerard Dépardieu, or, even more sentimental, the Hollywood remake *"Sommersby"* with Richard Gere and Jody Foster. Boldness and tragedy fascinate us, someone who commits the sacrilege of slipping into the identity of another fails in the end of course.

But what do we learn from that? Interestingly enough, the criminal case covers exactly the development from a pre-modern into a modern understanding of 'biography'. For the people in *Artigat* it was crucial that they could see his various roles, that he was a good farmer, a careful husband and family father, that he kept his house in order, perhaps that he went into the church. If he did this, it made no sense to doubt him. 'Biography' was therefore nothing else than a loose set of roles, quite different from modern identity.

Obviously the law court has another, if you like, a *'more modern'*, concept of 'biography' than the people in *Artigat*. And so apparently did Arnaud du Tilh who conforms to this modern understanding of identity by being able to defend himself with admirable knowledge, even of the most intimate details of the supposed biography, which almost led to his acquittal.

The attention of people at the time shows that we have a case which marks the *transition to the modern understanding of biography*. The perception that Arnaud du Tilh's slipping into another person's identity, and living in it for a considerable time, is a scandal, presumes an audience for which the presentation of personal identity and integrity is already the norm.

The historical case study indicates convincingly that we can regard biography as a modern phenomenon. The change is immense, and becomes even more concrete if we consider the works of the British social scientists Gareth Morgan (1986) or Tom Schuller (1997) who draw our interest to the *'metaphors' of life* in different periods. While the medieval picture of life represents a circle, that constantly returns in the same cycle from generation to generation, this circle breaks off in the 16th century and forms itself to an arch or to the stairway.

Fig. 1: The stairway of life (by Matthäus Merian, 1614)

Beginnings of an individual lifestyle become visible. In the end – classically reconstructed in Thomas R. Cole's *"The Journey of Life"* (1992) – a new metaphor enters into the game: that of a climbing career line. One of the most convincing artificial icons of this metaphor is the *"man walking to the sky "*monument built on the occasion of the *Documenta IX* 1992 by Jonathan Borofsky.

Fig. 2: "Man walking to the sky"

Moving from circle to arch and then to the line, possibly at the end to the postmodern 'patchwork' or 'puzzle', we certainly discover different biographical 'formats' or better, 'subject figurations'. However, the start of modern biographical thinking lies in the period between the late 16th and 18th centuries.

2. Differences in the culture of Modernity

Obviously things do not stop with the metaphor of the career line. Puzzles and patchworks of social life, the *fragmented existences* as it were, are often cited as signs of postmodern times. Are we actually confronted today with totally new conditions: the end of Modernity, so to speak?

It seems that the opposition of Modernity and Postmodernity is as useless as the idea of a linear modernization which has been proclaimed by most of the classical sociological theories. Furthermore, the material which I will go on to use suggests another conclusion: much more the idea of *"multiple Modernity"*, to quote Shmuel Eisenstadt (2000).

Saying this, I would like to make an observation. In the project which I am involved with we discovered different *'formats'* of autobiographies within Modernity (cf Alheit 2005; Alheit/Brandt 2006). This is interesting enough, but even more fascinating is that Andreas Reckwitz – from a different perspective in Hamburg – comes to the same conclusion using a less empirically grounded, more theoretically driven, investigation (Reckwitz 2006).

That inspired me to make the attempt here to relate the ideas of both discoveries to each other, and to confront the similar themes of Reckwitz's work with our empirical material. To do this I had to create a category in between our respective categories, to find a fair middle path between Reckwitz's 'subject forms' and our 'biographical formats'. I selected the concept 'subject figuration'.

I know such an action can be annoying. Must we use always incomprehensible invented words in order to be 'new'? Of course, we need not. But sometimes we should *irritate*, or more precisely, as in the German word "verfremden", making strange (entirely in the sense Bertoldt Brecht uses it), in order to discover something which we had not seen previously. As subjects we are not just individuals but rather also expressions of our historical time, the conditions under which we live, the social positions that we hold, the practices that we maintain in everyday life. In short it is what the great sociologist Norbert Elias called a *'figuration'*. The 'subject of Modernity' is a foolish fiction, but different 'subject figurations *within* Modernity' are empirically and theoretically highly interesting. And in this context, I consider the suggestion of Andreas Reckwitz to be extraordinarily helpful: namely to identify *"work, intimacy and even technologies of the self as fields of the modern subjectivation"* (Reckwitz 207: 102f).

To modern biographies, *work* is indispensable, not just in the 20th century, but the practices of work vary markedly from each other. Also the *intimate practices* of personal relations, sexuality, family relationships and friendship differ drastically. Furthermore, *self technologies,* a Foucauldian concept, the practices which link oneself to the things around us, feature Here the *media* play an important role.

A view of the media appears to influence Reckwitz too with respect to his *Trio of 'subject forms'* within Modernity. Firstly, the 'bourgeois subject' (at the beginning of the 19th century), where the writing culture is the central medium of self technology: then the 'employee subject', as he terms it (in the first two decades of the 20th century), where the visual media are important, and finally the 'postmodern subject' (since the 1970s, 1980s) with its link to digital media (cf Reckwitz 2007: 107ff).

I will consider these ideas with care. In our data, the 'bourgeois subject' merits at least two 'subject figurations', an early modern variant and, what could be termed a 'classical bourgeois' version. Here we immediately discover cultural differences in the espoused 'monolith' of Modernity. I will now clarify this with a number of examples.

Ulrich Bräker and Wilhelmine Eberhard represent the subject figuration that I would designate as 'early modern'; Johann Wolfgang von Goethe represents an ideal type of the 'bourgeois' figuration, Adelheid Popp and Emil Nolde stand for the 'post-bourgeois' type; Hanns Josef Ortheil and (Germans would be amused) Dieter Bohlen, a media celebrity, represents contemporary, possibly 'postmodern' variants of subject figurations.

2.1 The early modern 'subject figuration'

Ulrich Bräker provides us with one of the first German-speaking autobiographies from the under classes. He was born in 1735 in the east part of Switzerland and raised on a small family farm.[3] The strong pietism of the family ensures that he is literate. Then, conscription into the Prussian army comes as a major shock which pervades and disturbs his reflexive relationship with his life history. Bräker however finds it difficult to express this in a literary form. The autobiography falls, to a certain extent, into two parts: a remarkable description of childhood development before his recruitment, and a chain of fragmentary reflections from the time of his desertion from the army.

The painful, constantly repeated and, at the end, failed, attempt to write provides no coherence for his life. The autobiography remains a fragment, as it were the *chronicle of incoherence.*

The case of Wilhelmine *Eberhard*[4] is quite different. She was born in the middle of the 18th century and raised up in a highly middle class family full of drama. Her autobiography is also influenced by an *experience of shock*: a child's awareness of sexual violence between her father and mother. This trauma stays with her throughout her life and gains a religious momentum through a permanently enacted duality of body and spirit.[5] She finds her identity though her solution to this dilemma which is the strict condemnation of the physical dimension to the advantage of the higher 'spiritual' sphere; and she is indeed able to publish her autobiography, which acts as a sort of "guidebook for mothers and daughters".

The difference between Eberhard and Bräker must be examined. With the former there is a more consistent life design, which finds its subject in the *ritualised duality of spirit and body,* with the latter there is a broken, fragmented biography that treats its own, inconsistent searching movements as subject-matter.[6] The cultural resources seem to be unequally distributed.

And yet we discover a pattern of similar structures: in both autobiographies the initial stimulus seems to be a sort of '*social shock experience*'. The unexpected ejection from a pre-modern rural lifeworld and confrontation with rigid obedience, war and violence is in Bräker's case the reason for his biographical reflections. For Wilhelmine Eberard the directly experienced violence in the private family context becomes the traumatic occasion to initiate a continuous biographical reflection, and constantly repeated discussion on the conflict between body and spirit.

Both protagonists, however, are unable to find a biographical 'format' to process these contradictory experiences adequately. Both make selective use of the literary 'market'[7], in order to express their own problems. And both are not able to connect their individual life adventures with the *idea of personal development*.

The self technology of reading and writing now begins to be vitally important. This is most unusual for a Swiss farmer at the time, and is just as unorthodox for a woman of these times. Interestingly, it is noticeable that intimacy in both cases is not well developed. Eberhard for instance tolerates sexuality as a marriage duty, while detesting it deeply. Bräker's marriage is conventional and sketchy, a phenomenon which causes him suffering.

It is most interesting empirically that the presentation of *childhood* in both autobiographies show a 'format' of individual development, whereas adult life is described frequently in static, more formal and less lively ways. This reminds us of Norbert Elias' studies on estate organizations in pre-modern societies (cf Elias 1989: 39ff). In those societies both social classes and the various ages (life stages) are interpreted as *estates*. While childhood is seen as an appropriate time for informal learning, it is not appropriate for later life stages.

2.2 The bourgeois 'subject figuration'

It would, of course, be arrogant, looking at the next example, if I tried to say something *new*: Goethe's *Aus meinem Leben. Dichtung und Wahrheit* (Goethe 1998) is world literature. I am very wary of giving the 502nd interpretation (which is not entitled to me scientifically). But, please, permit me to make clear at the introduction to Goethe's century what has changed. In his 1811 to 1814 published autobiography, we can identify a *basic chord*, if at the beginning of the text the moment of his birth is already embedded into a cosmic connection:

The constellation was convenient; the sun stood in the sign of the Virgin, and culminated for the day; Jupiter and Venus looked friendly to it, Mercury not repulsive; Saturn and Mars behaved indifferently: only the moon that became just full, practiced the power of its counter glow as it was in the same time its planet hour. (HA 9, 1998: 10; translation by the author)

What can one say? Could one start one's biography in a better way? The lucky constellation of the stars at the time of birth? We must be fair. Goethe was a universal genius and probably far ahead of his time. However, the relationship he had to the world and to himself cannot be compared with Bräker's or Eberhard's experiences any longer. Even the beginning of *Dichtung und Wahrheit* displays a gesture of the *bourgeois subject figuration,* which is distinct and which distances him from Bräker and Eberhard: that is the gesture of *sovereignty.*

Goethe, at the beginning of his text, describes as a "main task of the biography",

> ... the man in his present circumstances, and to show to what extent the whole reality is against him, or to what extent it favours him, how he formed a world and mankind's meaning out of it, and how he, if he was an artist, poet, writer, reflected back this meaning to the outside world. To do this, however, a hardly won accomplishment is needed, namely, that the individual knows himself and his century, himself – to what extent he has remained under all circumstances the same, the century – as it has determined and formed both the willing and the unwilling, so that you feel able to say, each one, only ten years earlier or later born, would be a completely different one as far as it concerns his own education and the agency outward. (HA 9, 1998: 9; translation by the author)

"A completely different one" becomes man in this interpretation, thus, "as far as it concerns his own education and the agency outward". However, at the same time the possibility of change in changed conditions has a limit. Within all movement of the century, the *subject* should be him- or herself.

The bourgeois subject figuration finds its ideal type in Goethe. Part of this lies in the work around creative self implementation (*"artist, poet, writer"*), more generally, and also including the citizen outside of the arts: the knowledge-based autonomy in other words: early entrepreneurship. However, perhaps the field of intimacy is a stronger feature; with Goethe's *Werthers Leiden* romantic love enters the historical stage, with the developing of privacy within the bourgeois family. If we look at the self technologies and their most important media, then writing is at the centre: diary and autobiography are the media, and this presupposes education, *"Bildung"* in German (cf Reckwitz 2007: 107ff).

At the same time as thinking of Goethe, we should remember *Karl Philipp Moritz*, whom Goethe referred to in a letter to Charlotte von Stein as "a younger brother (in spirit)". He is, as he describes his painful self becoming in his anonymised autobiography *Anton Reiser* (Moritz 2001), also very typical of the bourgeois subject figuration. Perhaps Moritz makes even clearer than Goethe how intimacy and privacy become central aspects of biography: his continuous reflection on his body pain, or, on people connected with him, documents a dimension discovered through this subject form: *inwardness.*

2.3 The post-bourgeois 'subject figuration'

Things change distinctively by the end of the 19th century and I want to try to show that with two very different autobiographies, Adelheid Popp and Emil Nolde.

Adelheid Popp[8] was born in 1869 into a working class family and forced from an early stage to contribute to the small family income. She compensates for the heavy burden of her work experiences in childhood and early youth by the construction of a kind of private 'dream world', which she finds in popular literature of the day, the 'penny novels'. During a later period of working in a factory she comes into contact with the social-democratic movement, begins to engage with it, and finally becomes one of the most important women in the Austrian workers' movement. Her autobiography is written proof of unusual personal development at that time. Her political career only ended with the rise of National Socialism. She died in 1939.

Emil Hansen[9] who calls himself "Nolde", after his home, in 1902 when he began his creative work, was born in 1867 near Tondern at the Danish border. Growing up in an affluent farming household he could not realize his early desire to become a painter, although his father allowed him to take an apprenticeship as a wood carver. Through a long auto-didactical process, which finally leads him to Switzerland, Berlin, Paris and Copenhagen, he is able, relatively successfully, to establish himself as a painter. Although he was involved with the Danish Nazi party some of his work was condemned by them and destroyed. He died in 1956.

Here again two virtually incompatible autobiographical outlines face each other: the politician and the artist. What unites both is the clear contrast with the previously discussed subject figurations: in contrast with the early modern type they present *clear and consistent developments*, even convincing and sustainable life plans which differ from the bourgeois figuration. Both overcome biographical periods of inwardness and move their internal development process *outward*: with Adelheid Popp to the collective identity constructions of the workers' movement[10], with Nolde, to aesthetic investment in his painting.[11] This process is connected to cultural framing of self experiencing: the political culture of the workers' movement in the case of Adelheid Popp, the role of art in self-formation, with Emil Nolde.

If we take these two life reports also as examples of a new subject figuration, then the boundary markings are clear for the bourgeois subject form. It is the *refusal to maintain an introverted concentration* on their own development (as applies for Anton Reiser), and an overcoming of the *excessive subject culture* (as is typical for Goethe). In its place steps an *extraverted culture of the self perception*, which comes with a connection to collectives or to aesthetic movements, which reflects work in modern large organizations, which use new techniques and whose self technologies shift from writing to audiovisual media: radio, the pictorial and increasingly film.

Andreas Reckwitz also includes into this subject culture, developing in the 1920s, the *phase of National Socialism and State Socialism* after the Second World War (cf Reckwitz 2007: 109). While this sounds plausible I would like to investigate the idea further by undertaking more intensive analyses of autobiographical documents (cf here Alheit/Bast-Haider/Drauschke 2004).

2.4 The postmodern 'subject figuration'

There are sound empirical arguments for the notion that we have been confronted with a new formation since the 1970s, 1980s, and it is not important whether we talk about postmodernism or a late modern trend. It is the new elements which belong to this figuration which are relevant. One aspect is clear, the importance of *connection to collective patterns* of the self-manifestation has gone. The drastic transformation of the subject culture before and after the German turn in East Germany may be indicative of this. (cf again Alheit/Bast-Haider/Drauschke 2004).

We can identify two trends: the development of the *'Event Society'* as the Bamberg sociologist Gerhard Schulze (1992) for example describes it, with a subject culture often defined as 'expressive individualism'. And we notice an intensified *'market orientation'* including a consumer oriented aestheticisation which has already become an aspect of the new self technologies, like for instance new body practices, the wellness movement, the meaning of individual sport and above all, of course, the use of the new digital media.

119

In order to test the thesis of a further subject figuration I have selected two, again very contrasting, contemporary autobiographies: Hanns Josef Ortheil's *"Das Element des Elephanten"* (2001 [first published 1994]) and Dieter Bohlen's *"Nichts als die Wahrheit"* (2003 [first published 2001]).

Ortheil was born in Cologne in 1951 and was mute up to the age of six, largely because of the aphasia, resulting from war trauma, of his mother. He maintains an almost dyadic relationship with her throughout the autobiography.

> Through this relationship we became mirrors for each other. My mother identified her muteness in my own silence, I was her image, and I even imitated her in following her speechlessness. (Ortheil 2001: 21; translation by the author)

At the age of six, the protagonist learns, through the substantial intervention of his father, a surveyor, to speak laboriously. He feels tormented through detested school, but successfully studies music, German language and literature, philosophy and art history. He embarks on highly productive writing activity which is acclaimed in the highest literary circles, and which leads him to work in Paris and Rome. Crucially, he feels brought out in his biography and *born through the language*, rather than the language creating the autobiography.

> I was born for the second time in the language, the language has reborn me, and as she has spat out me as a speaking person, writing was there, writing as sealing procedure of the whole world around me, a procedure through which I could fix the world with each syllable, every word and every sentence for ever, never loosing the language as such. (ibid: 20; translation by the author)

Nevertheless, language is for Ortheil actually no communication tool, but always a repeated attempt to write against the muteness of the mother:

Without intending it from the outset, without following a particular plan, I have drafted in five novels variants of my own biography which rotate round about the core cell of my parents' home and my family. In the middle of this cell my mother is seated, silent and closed … […], she is sitting there with the view into the vastness of the landscape, without motions, and I am circling, I am writing and writing against her wordlessness. (ibid: 98; translation by the author)

It almost seems a sacrilege to juxtapose such an autobiography with a most successful current pseudo-biography: *Dieter Bohlen's* irrepressible life shrift *"Nothing but Truth"*. Bohlen was born in 1954 in Oldenburg and grew up in petty bourgeois household. For him too the female characters in his family are formative, above all his grandmother: "The most important person, the greatest love of my life is mama's mama: my grandma Marie. Everything I am, I owe to her." (Bohlen 2003: 11; translation by the author)

She wakes creativity in him. From her he gets, as he expresses it, *"this special sensitivity what a man must have, in order to be a composer"* (ibid). She shepherds and admires him and appears as the basic benchmark for the phalanx of well publicized but constantly failing relationships with women.[12]

Bohlen makes an amazingly uncomplicated ascent: with an above average Abitur, surprisingly successful business studies in Goettingen, entry into music production, creating the well-known 'world hit' *Modern Talking*, "You're my heart, you're my soul", together with an abundance of other compositions and production successes, finally rising to be one of the megastars of German media public. His relationships with the models "Verona", "Naddel" and "Estefania" only add to the glamour.

Is this an autobiography? More than three quarters of the book consists of quasi media reports. Also the sense of authenticity symptomatic of biography is missing. The hired writer[13], a gossip columnist from the red top BILD in Germany, set everything just to *keep the spoken word*. Bohlen stages himself as media event. His autobiography is 'medialised', so to speak. Reflections on certain, internal, developments, any self-communication about contradictions or difficulties across the biography are lacking.

And yet there are surprising parallels between Ortheil and Bohlen. There is the recurring mother-imago: with Ortheil, this is described as a cyclic *return to "the core cell"*; while with Bohlen there is a recognizable structure of macho-like failure in his relationships with women. *'Expressive individualism'* can be identified in both cases: with Ortheil in the regressive metaphor of the continuous 'mother-child-dyad', with Bohlen in the incessant report of his sexual conquests and prowess.

Ortheil certainly selects the medium of language which, within our framework, belongs to the bourgeois subject figuration. When we look more closely we can see more precisely how he uses the language, for him it is an instrument to realize an *unbelievably aestheticized narcissism*. And as Ortheil circles around 'the core cell' and writes and writes, so Bohlen suns himself in his extraverted narcissistic mash as a super juryman with the German talent show, *"Germany looks for the superstar"*.

3. Conclusion

The autobiographical analyses discussed in this chapter illustrate how Modernity is far from being a 'monolith': that it is not the end of history, and that new subject figurations can both arise and dissolve time and again.

As a conclusion to the chapter I have drawn up a provisional tabular overview of the subject figurations and their features. Before this is examined it should perhaps be noted that the central 'subject codes' of the figurations analyzed are: *irritation* for the early modern constellation: *inwardness and expressive subjectivism* for the bourgeois subject culture: *extraversion and collective orientation* for the post-bourgeois figuration, and, finally, *more expressive, almost narcissistic individualism* for the postmodern.

Mode Type	dominant metaphors	dimension of work	dimension of intimacy	dimension of self technologies	hegemonial periods
pre-modern subject figuration	cycle	division of labour according to estates	not yet existing	religious-corporative stereotypes	ca.1200-ca.1600 estate society
early modern subject figuration	arch/ stairs	experiences of break	schwierige Suche nach Intimität	unerreichbare literarische Vorbilder	ca.1600-ca.1800. transition to Modernity
bourgeois subject figuration	(career) line	artistic activity knowledge-based autonomy, early entrepreneurship	the *intimate self*: romantic love and friendship, private space of the family	technology of handwriting: diary, autobiography	ca.1800-ca.1900 beginning industrialisation
post-bourgeois subject figuration	formation	industrial work, employment in large organizations	the *extraverted self*: collective orientations	audio-visual acquirement of the world: radio, pictorial, film	[1870-1980?] industrial society
postmodern subject figuration	patchwork/ puzzle	working entrepreneurship, labour leasing	narcissistic individualism	digital media: virtual style(s) of one's own	[1980?-?] post-industrial society

Fig. 3: Subject figurations (overview)

It is important to counteract the impression of a set of simple periods in the table. It does not depict a simple periodization. These models can overlap and possibly even form *hybrid variants*, which may indeed be more interesting than those presented. In addition we know that even within the 'core time' of the figurations presented different developments arise (cf also Reckwitz 2007: 113ff). There was, for example, *romanticism*, with its distinctive features, during the bourgeois figuration; then there were the different *avant-garde movements* at the beginning of the 20th century, which again provided contrasting features, during the post-bourgeois

variant; and during the postmodern figuration, world-wide 'counter cultures', which are anti-individualistic, anti-consumeristic, and highly critical of a capitalist marketisation of life. However, taking this complex view
of Modernity is inspiring and provides rich material for further research
and investigation. In the context of the book, we gain more understanding of the complex interplay and connectedness of culture, subjectivities,
language and technologies, in both creating subjective figurations, but
also in reflexively engaging with and challenging them.

Notes

1 An amusing study done by Carlo Ginsburg is showing this – the story of the
Friulian miller *Menocchio* (Ginzburg 1979, 1986) with the subtle title ,*Il for-
maggio e i vermi*', a metaphor which Menocchio uses to talk about the angles
in heaven that – by the end – seals his sentence of death –, as well as the more
prudish works of the French École d'Annales – for example Lucien Fèbvre's
Rabelais (Fèbvre 1947) –, the literary criticism analyses of Garraty (1957),
Neumann (1970), Niggl (1977) or Scheuer (1979), as well as the intelligent
socio-historical considerations particularly on the shrift by Alois Hahn (Hahn
1982; Hahn/Knapp (eds.) 1987) – they all agree that the ability to reflect on
the self and the individual development is based on very new experiences of
the beginning Modernity and finds its expression in literature not before the
18th century.

2 Even *Montaigne* mentions this case in his essay "Von dem Hinkenden", where
he ex post – he was observing the law process – remembers the unusual ,de-
fraud' (cf Ginzburg 1989: 185).

3 Bräker 1997 (an autobiography with the meaningful title *Lebensgeschichte und
natürliche Ebenteuer des Armen Mannes im Tockenburg*).

4 Eberhard 1802 (title of her autobiography: *Fünfundvierzig Jahre aus meinem
Leben: eine biographische Skizze für Mütter und Töchter*).

5 In the autobiographical key passage, namely just before Wilhelmine's confir-
mation, the duality between body and spirit – in her case the competetion
between "beastlike pictures" and the immaculateness of the mind – has been
taken as a fixed constant: "Am letzten Tage vor dem großen wichtigen Schritt
zerfloß meine Angst in mildere Thränen, ruhiges Gebet und Stille. Ich fühlte mich ermattet, aber dennoch wie neu geboren; fühlte mich entlastet von
diesen Gespenstern der Einbildungskraft, und lernte hier früh, wie wichtig es

sey, seine Einbildungskraft zu zügeln. – Ich ward von jetzt an *Jungfrau* an Seel' und Leib, voll Unschuld und Würde, und blieb befreit *auf immer* von jenen Bildern!" (ibid: 114)

6   "Und da ich mich, wie schon oft gesagt, in keiner Seele glaubte entdecken zu dürfen, nahm ich in diesen mutlosen Stunden meine Zuflucht zum Lesen und Schreiben, lehnte und durchstänkerte jedes Buch, das ich kriegen konnte, in der Hoffnung, etwas zu finden, das auf meinen Zustand passte, fing halbe Nächte durch weiße und schwarze Grillen und fand allemal Erleichterung, wenn ich meine gedrängte Brust aufs Papier ausschütten konnte." (Bräker 1997: 173)

7   Bräker writes: "Da ich hiernächst um die nämliche Zeit anfing, mich auf Lesen zu legen, und ich zuerst auf lauter mystisches Zeug – dann auf die Geschichte – dann auf die Philosophie – und endlich gar auf die verwünschten Romanen fiel, schickte sich zwar alle dies vortrefflich in meine idealische Welt, machte mir aber den Kopf nur noch verwirrter. Jeden Helden und Ebenteurer alter und neuer Zeit macht' ich mir eigen, lebte vollkommen in ihrer Lage und bildete Umstände dazu und davon, wie es mir beliebte. Die Romanen hin-wieder machten mich ganz unzufrieden mit meinem eigenen Schicksal und den Geschäften meines Berufes und weckten mich aus meinen Träumen, aber eben nur zu größerm Verdruß auf. Bisweilen, wenn ich denn so mürrisch war, sucht' ich mich durch irgendeine lustige Lektur wieder zu ermuntern. Alsdann je lustiger, je lieber, so daß ich darüber bald zum Freigeist geworden und derg-estalt immer von einem Extrem ins andere fiel." (ibid: 205)

Wilhelmine Eberhard is more pretentious: "Ich las wenig, aber ich hatte zu wählen gelernt und wählte nun sehr gewissenhaft. *Milton, Rowe, Dusch, Ra-bener, Gellert, Kleist, Richardson* u.a. waren meine Unterhaltung für einige Jahre. Ich verehrte diese Männer, wie ich meine Lehrer verehrte, mit warmem Enthusiasmus. Es fiel mir nicht ein, zum Zeitvertreib zu lesen, denn ich wußte nicht was Langeweile war, und betrachtete meine Muße zum Lesen als eben so viel nothwendige Lehrstunden; so hatte mir ja mein Lehrer das Lesen vorges-tellt." (Eberhard 1802: 143f)

8   Popp 1991 (title of the autobiography: *Jugend einer Arbeiterin*).

9   Nolde 1931 (title of his first autobiography: *Das eigene Leben*).

10   "Mir war durch die Versammlungen eine neue Welt erschlossen worden und alles in mir drängte nach eigener Betätigung. Ich wollte mithelfen und mit-kämpfen und wußte doch nicht, wie ich das anfangen sollte. Unter all diesen Einflüssen war ich aber eine ganz andere geworden." (Popp 1991: 14)

11   Vgl. bes. Nolde 1931: 145ff. The most important thing for him is the way how to *see* the world: "Der Wissenschaft der Völkerkunde aber sind wir heute noch wie lästige Eindringlinge, weil wir sinnliches Sehen mehr lieben als nur das Wissen. Auch Bode war noch großer Gegner künstlerischer Geltung des

Urprimitiven. Unter einem Berg von üblicher Tüchtigkeit und Gelehrsamkeit war sein Sinn des Sehens vergraben." (Ebd.: 158)

12 Cf. ibid, pp. 85ff, 137ff, 221ff, 263ff, 282ff.

13 Katja Kessler, the wife of the chief editor of the red top BILD, Kai Dieckmann, an intimate friend of Bohlen's.

References

Alheit, P.(2005). Autobiographie und Literalität. Zum Wandel autobiographischer Formate in der Moderne. In: J. Ecarius und B. Friebertshäuser (Eds.). *Literalität und Biographie. Perspektiven erziehungswissenschaftlicher Biographieforschung.* Opladen: Barbara Budrich, 66-81.

Alheit, P., Bast-Haider, K. & Drauschke, P.(2004). Die zögernde Ankunft im Westen. *Biographien und Mentalitäten in Ostdeutschland.* Frankfurt am Main, New York: Campus.

Alheit, P. & Brandt, M. (2006). Autobiographie und ästhetische Erfahrung. *Entdeckung und Wandel des Selbst in der Moderne.* Frankfurt am Main, New York: Campus.

Alheit, P. & Dausien, B. (1990). Biographie. In H. J. Sandkühler (Hrsg.). *Europäische Enzyklopädie zu P und Wissenschaften.* Hamburg: Meiner, Bd.1, 405-418.

Alheit, P. & Schömer, F. (2009). Der Aufsteiger. *Autobiographische Zeugnisse zu einem Prototypen der Moderne von 1800 bis heute.* Frankfurt am Main, New York: Campus.

Bohlen, D. & Kessler, K. (2003). *Nichts als die Wahrheit.* München: Blanvalet [Erstauflage 2001].

Bräker, U. (1997). *Lebensgeschichte und natürliche Ebenteuer des Armen Mannes im Tockenburg.* Mit einem Nachwort hrsg. von Werner Günther (Reclam-Ausgabe), Ditzingen [zuerst Zürich 1789].

Cole, T.R. (1992). *The Journey of Life. A Cultural History of Aging in America.* New York: Cambridge University Press.

Eberhard, W. (1802). *Fünf und vierig Jahre aus meinem Leben. Eine biographische Skizze für Mütter und Töchter.* Leipzig: Kummer.

Eisenstadt, S. N. (2000). *Die Vielfalt der Moderne*. Weilerswist: Velbrück Wissenschaft.

Elias, N. (1989). *Studien über die Deutschen. Machtkämpfe und Habitusentwicklung im 19. und 20.* Jahrhundert, Frankfurt am Main: Suhrkamp.

Fèbvre, L. (1947. *Le problème de l'incroyance au XVI siècle*. La réligion de Rabelais, Paris: Albin Miche.

Garraty, J. A. (1957). *The Nature of Biography*, New York: Knopf.

Ginzburg, C. (1986). *Der Käse und die Würmer. Die Welt eines Müllers um 1600*. Frankfurt am Main: Syndikat.

Ginzburg, C. (1989). *Nachwort zu Natalie Zemon Davis: Die wahrhaftige Geschichte von der Wiederkehr des Martin Guerre*. Berlin: Wagenbach [ital. Originalausgabe 1979]

Goethe, J.W. (1998). Aus meinem Leben. Dichtung und Wahrheit. In: Werke, hrsg. von E. T. *Hamburger Ausgabe in 14 Bänden*. Bd. 9 (HA 9). München: C.H. Beck.

Hahn, A. (1982). Zur Soziologie der Beichte und anderer Formen institutioneller Bekenntnisse. Selbstthematisierung und Zivilisierungsprozess. In: *KZfSS*, Jg. 34, 407-434.

Hahn, A. &Knapp, V. (Eds.) (1987). *Selbstthematisierung und Selbstzeugnis*. Frankfurt am Main: Suhrkamp.

Morgan, G. (1986). *Images of Organization*. London: Sage.

Moritz, K. P. (2001). *Anton Reiser. Ein psychologischer Roman*. Stuttgart: Metzler.

Neumann, B. (1970). *Identität und Rollenzwang- Zur Theorie der Autobiographie*. Frankfurt am Main: Athenäum.

Niggl, G. (1977): Geschichte der Autobiographie im 18. *Jahrhundert. Theoretische Grundlegung und literarische Entfaltung*. Stuttgart: Klett.

Popp, A. (1922). *Die Jugendgeschichte einer Arbeiterin, von ihr selbst erzählt*. München: Ernst Reinhardt [zuerst 1909].

Ortheil, H. J. (2001). *Das Element des Elephanten. Wie mein Schreiben begann*. München: Piper [Erstauflage 1994].

Scheuer, H. (1979). *Biographie. Studien zu Funktion und Wandel einer literarischen Gattung vom 18.* Jahrhundert bis zur Gegenwart, Stuttgart: Metzler.

Schulze, G. (1992). *Die Erlebnisgesellschaft. Kultursoziologie der Gegenwart.* Frankfurt am Main, New York: Campus.

Reckwitz, A. (2006). *Das hybride Subjekt. Eine Theorie der Subjektkulturen von der bürgerlichen Moderne zur Postmoderne.* Weilerswist: Velbrück Wissenschaft.

Reckwitz, A. (2007): Die Moderne und das Spiel der Subjekte: Kulturelle Differenzen und Subjektordnungen in der Kultur der Moderne. In: T. Bonacker & A. Reckwitz, Andreas (Eds.). *Kulturen der Moderne. Soziologische Perspektiven der Gegenwart.* Frankfurt am Main, New York, 97-118.

Schuller, T. (1997). *Modelling the Lifecourse.* Bremen: Universität Bremen.

Zemon Davis, N. (1984). *Die wahrhaftige Geschichte von der Wiederkehr des Martin Guerr.* München: Piper.

Chapter 6

The myth of birth: autobiography and family memory

◊ LAURA FORMENTI, ASSOCIATE PROFESSOR,
UNIVERSITÀ DEGLI STUDI MILANO BICOCCA, ITALY

[...]
Born.
So he was born, too.
Born like everyone else.
Like me, who will die.

The son of an actual woman,
a new arrival from the body's depths.
A voyager to Omega.

Subject to
his own absence,
on every front, at any moment.

He hits his head
against a wall
that won't give way forever.

His movements
dodge and parry
the universal verdict.

I realized
that his journey was already halfway over.

But he didn't tell me that,
no.

"This is my mother",
was all he said.
(Wisława Szymborska, "Born")

There is a ubiquitous dimension in all autobiographical work: when someone decides to tell or to write the story of his/her own life, birth is immediately evoked. "I was born the... at...". If we are here, living in this world, that means, of course, that we were born. Somewhere, sometime and somehow. We were born from other humans, and this gives to our existence a very concrete framework. Besides, the story that is told about it adds to this framework, sometimes working as a "self-fulfilling prophecy." (Merton, 1949; Watzlawick, 1984). Philosophically speaking, the core of the autobiographical experience is the very fact of having a story; it is a statement about (our) birth and death, about us as limited entities, as Szymborska says so wonderfully.

This paper aims at building a compositional theory (Formenti, 2008, 2009) and a framework for understanding personal narration – specifically, the story of one's birth – within a systemic, interdisciplinary, and constructivist framework. The story of birth, as a fragment of the wider story – or better, a system of stories – that is our autobiography, has the power to question the nature of autobiography itself. In fact, while someone may naively believe that autobiographical memories are subjective, i.e. they *belong* to the subject, I would like to show that in this very case – as in all the other cases – it is evident how much the story contains more than personal meaning, and connects the individual to his/her system of relationships, his/her family, environment and culture.

Several levels of information and relationships are involved in storytelling. Storytelling itself is *about relationships*:

> It is probably an error to think of dream, myth, and art as being about any one matter other than relationship. [...] it is only about relationship and not about any identifiable relata. (Bateson, 1967: pp. 150-151)

Stories of birth can be read on many levels. First of all, we can see how they are "internally patterned", i.e. words are used in relation to one another, and this *codified information* becomes "meaningful" for the reader or the listener. This is the level of meaning in which most biographers are interested. Most research in autobiography is focused on content. But, as Gregory Bateson argued, any communication contains at least two levels of meaning: "content" and "relation". Applied to stories, this means that they can be read as "digital codification", but they also are iconic and metaphoric communication. A story is a metaphor that stands for different things for the storyteller, for the ongoing conversation (its here-and-now context), and for the wider "culture".

On another level, we can question where and how the teller learned about the circumstances of his/her birth, about the "facts". They cannot be "remembered" in a proper sense but must have been told – somehow, sometime, by someone. In fact, often other people are evoked within the story as witnesses, or "first hand" tellers. The story that is told here-and-now is a composition of other stories, fragments of stories, usually told by members of the "family" (not necessarily the biological or legal family: you become a member of a "family" when you know this kind of story and its meaning). "Facts" themselves, the way they are organized, as well as their meaning, which changes over time, are built and transformed within significant relationships in the proximal system – about the past, present and future in the family. (Boscolo and Bertrando, 1993; Formenti and Lombroso, 1994). The story contains information about these relationships; it is a guide for understanding connections between individuals and their proximal systems, between individual and family memory. I hold that there is a peculiar process of understanding which stems from the composition and comparison of these different levels.

The *micro-system* – i.e. the construction of *this* story as a system of concepts and values linking the teller's perceptions, ideas, emotions around the event of his/her own birth – must be composed with the *meso-system* – i.e the proximal system of relationships and the huge corpus of stories that is systematically produced by it. Those who "know you by heart" are the same people who will tell you (or not) how you came to be here, how you came into this world. And by telling, they also offer some implicit answers about who you are and who you can become.

On yet another level, stories of birth are a precious field for research in education, as they cast light on the wider system of relationships called "culture" (whatever this means), i.e. they contain information about the *macro-system*, in social terms, as well as about the very history of *homo sapiens*. "In its ways for welcoming the newborn, a society displays its deep patterns, its consciousness of life" (Gélis, 1988: 9, *my translation*).

The stories that can be told (or not) about birth change in time and space, alongside social and cultural changes, and are strongly influenced by age, gender, class, education. The very circumstances of giving birth are socially and culturally built. These stories contain information about the customs of birth in different places, as well as its symbolic meaning in a specific society (Maffi, 2010). Silence or disinterest regarding some aspects of birth or – on the other hand – giving emphasis to some specific aspect, reflects dominant discourses, presuppositions, and practices. Stories can chronicle, confirm, and of course criticize, lifestyles, health policies, models of education and care. If we become aware of these complex implications, we can make space for freedom and agency, for transformation and learning in birth processes. We can give more visibility to lived and shared experience.

To develop these concepts, I will draw on some texts (1) containing fragments of stories written by women students in education. I consider these stories of birth as *revealing artifacts* about individual, family and social patterns, offering a view of the ecology of ideas that shape individual (women's, babies') bodies and experiences, inter-generational relationships, and health and care in our society. These stories are not reports, of course. I prefer to consider them as pieces of "art", composed of facts and symbols that take material shape – a "form" – made of words.

Two fragments: the story of my birth

> *I am going to be born soon and I will have a sister and a brother. I know this since I hear them all the time. My mum lets them place their little hands on her belly, and I can hear their sweet whispered words. It is nice to be here, I feel protected. I feel my mother's warmth and my father's love always embracing me. But I am looking forward to coming out, and letting them know me [...] In my life I will strive to fulfill my ambitions, which will also become theirs. Hence, they will be happy. And me too! This I know for sure because they always say to me: "Whoever you are, we will be happy." (Cinzia)*

Cinzia chooses to take the perspective of the fetus, writing a sort of fictional text. Her understanding of the whole situation appears permeated by positive emotions and values. She does not speak of birth itself, rather she focuses on what came before and anticipates the future (first level of interpretation).

To be able to construct this form of narration, she must use what she already knows from her parents, but the form of the story is original. This fragment of her story conveys a strong sense of "us": all family relationships (at least the nuclear family) are represented; both parents and siblings are cited. There are some clues about the family's educational model (child-centered, sustaining, positive), as well as the experience of living with these parents (second level of interpretation).

The story also suggests some hints about this family's social and cultural environment: the practice of "talking with the baby" during pregnancy, as a way of letting the other members of the family (father and siblings) build a relationship with her before birth, are nowadays quite common in urban, middle-class, educated families (third level of interpretation).

> My mother very often told me that I did not want to take milk from one of her breasts, so she "fooled" me by making a very uncomfortable position with her body; this story is always accompanied by another one: "Here's the reason for my pains". I do not know if my mother links these events consciously or unconsciously, but I always experienced her storytelling about my birth with embarrassment, sorrow, and some feeling of guilt. (Daniela)

Daniela tells a "heavy" story of being fooled and charged with guilt; she gives voice to her feelings of sorrow and embarrassment about something she could not be responsible for. It is an occasion for her to become aware of this transactional game between her and her mother (first level of interpretation).

Wider family relationships are not taken into account: it seems that everything happened between mother and child, both of them "trapped" in this sad relationship. Different time frames are involved here (Formenti and Lombroso, 1994), at least three of them are the here-and-now time of Daniela's writing, the cyclical, repetitive storytelling by her mother (on different occasions: "this story is *always* accompanied..."), and the there-and-then original events. They concur in the creation of a pattern (second level of interpretation).

This story is also quite emblematic of dominant discourses and policies around motherhood and baby-care: the dyadic relationship between a mother and "her" baby is offloaded with expectations in our society, while resources to sustain new mothers in the proximal system and in public health services are very poor. Most mothers are left alone, expected to breastfeed the newborn with no knowledge about it, and weighed down by many demanding tasks. Since the sixties, new generations of mothers do not have any previous knowledge about childcare ("natural" ways of learning from experience being totally cut out from young womens' lives), and they do not receive much support when they have problems. We can imagine that Daniela's mother did not only have "a practical problem" with breastfeeding, but also a bad solution for it. We can guess that she was caught in the rhetoric of "the good mother", in addition to her specific psychological and family situation. As a matter of fact, differently from in the past, most women nowadays risk being considered "incompetent mothers" (third level of interpretation).

These examples show the potential of stories for research, when they are used both to celebrate and investigate the connections between the different levels of relationships and the ecology of ideas regarding birth. The same goes for death, health, play, work, learning… Since we are involved in educational research, another question is: how can these stories be useful to bring about change and transformation?

Goods reasons for telling

I used to invite adult learners to write the story of their birth, whenever possible, if I judge this not too risky or invasive for those involved, and if there are good reasons for doing it. When is it useful to explore one's experience and family memory about birth? For instance, I consider it necessary for future obstetricians and midwives to develop an explicit narration of their own birth. When I was teaching General Pedagogy at the Faculty of Medicine, I realized that healthcare professionals needed to understand the deep educational implications of their work, for themselves and their patients. I invited those students to develop awareness about their assumptions by exploring their own experiences.

Another group of learners who can learn a lot from (the story of) their own birth is "parents-to-be". Gaudio (2008) argues that narrative workshops and biographical interviews may help new fathers and mothers be active in the transition into parenthood. The aim of her work is to foster awareness, agency and responsibility in parents, as well as to contrast the trend towards the "infantilization" of parents on the part of experts (see also Formenti and West, 2010). I myself had this experience when I was pregnant with my first daughter 20 years ago, and participated in an autobiographical group. Thanks to the narration of my own birth, I suddenly became aware that I had received/developed a horrible story about it, and all the ideas, emotions, feelings of guilt and powerlessness that went along with that story had never been expressed, let alone transformed. That was my very first experience with autobiographical work. And it worked! I felt that I could become a competent and caring mother. Stories can be rewritten.

A less obvious reason touches other groups of adult learners: students in education, social workers, counsellors… With these groups, I use (the story of) birth as a gateway towards deeper reflection on the meaning of education and life itself, an exploration of metaphors and myths about care and human relationships, as well as to gain an understanding of personal and family myths. The stories cited here were written by students who were attending a course in Family Pedagogy; a part of their learning was aimed at reflecting on birth as a family issue and an example itself of the systemic, relational, and aesthetic nature of family life. I invited them to celebrate the metaphorical and mythical essence of their narrations. "A fantasy or myth may simulate a denotative narrative" (Bateson, 1972: 190), but its meaning goes far beyond facts. It creates a connotative framework, like play. Learning how to play with myths is an essential skill for future educators and social workers, which makes them more respectful and curious regarding the multiple versions of each family story (Formenti, 2012).

What is somehow "shocking" for these students (most of them are women) is to discover that an event so crucial for human life seems to have lost its generative meaning. It is silenced in our culture, except in hospitals, where it is reduced to something technical. The experience of writing, analyzing and discussing one's birth becomes thus a learning experience, producing critical thinking, challenging presuppositions, and fostering new attitudes.

Cultural frameworks

What is an appropriate set of ideas for thinking about birth? The dominant discourse in our world is "evidence-based medicine", a form of "religion" (in Bateson's terms) where facts can explain processes, and meanings are removed from legitimate talk. Positivist epistemology features an idea of knowledge based on control. "Risks" and "problems" are very often the main focus of birth. Doctors are scared by lawyers and tribunals. Talk about birth is saturated by denotative language, so that most people (not only doctors) tend to forget other dimensions – emotional, connotative, relational. The meaning of birth for human life – individually and col-lectively – cannot come from purely inductive research: as Bateson said, "we need some philosophy and some religion too". What I want to stress here, is that we are able – thanks to a compositional view of autobiography (Formenti, 2008, 2009) – to see and deconstruct our cultural frameworks and assumptions, in order to answer questions like: where does the mean-ing of (my) birth come from?

It is not a coincidence that all human cultures have myths about the Ori-gin. In the Judaic-Christian tradition, the Book of Genesis is the original myth. It is a creative and generative story about the making of *difference*. In fact, it is by performing an "act of distinction" that God first divides light and darkness and so on. Differences lead to other differences at later times. This is the essence of perception: to see is to build a world (Bateson, 1972). A "perceiving Entity" thus performs the act of creation, followed by categorization: someone *gives names* to things. Language and creation are strictly interwoven.

The same myth told by the Book of Genesis seems to go on and on for each new generation, for each newborn, as Gaia wonderfully wrote:

> I believe that my birth was a mythical event for my mother, and the name she choose for me proves it – she sees in me qualities and features that I do not see, and I am sure that she saw them right from the start, when she took me in her arms – maybe by choosing this name she was already thinking about what I could be. (Gaia)

Knowing not knowing

Thanks to this exercise, I realized that I do not know anything about my birth (Allegra)

Is Allegra right? What kind of knowledge is implied by the story of our birth? We do not have direct memory of it, yet we *were* there, well adapted and fully related to our world, and no less to the body of our mother. Birth and early care affect the baby, who is able to perceive and react, grasp and search. He/she is active from the very beginning. These first experiences are the basis for feeling (more or less) safe as well as for the following experiences of attachment, organization, regulation, curiosity, and playfulness. Early relational experiences create the capacity for learning and for a certain degree of openness towards the world. "Mutual adaptation, or the opposite, happens very fast and generally implicitly, but it leaves a trace of the emotional impact of the interaction." (Horsdal, 2012: 45) It also leaves more mysterious traces in the body. Many physical therapists argue that ancient memories of trauma, loss and pain, linked to birth and early care, keep affecting the body years later. Luckily, we are resilient and we have adaptation strategies.

While we are not able to recall the details of those events, we can make connections between our here-and-now perception and the details from the stories that were told to us. Being exposed to the story/stories of our birth in a context of meaningful relationships *shapes* us, just as the event itself did. Our habits of thinking and acting are in line with it, and also with the idea of ourselves which developed from it. We continue to gather meaning out of it, all the time.

Bateson's idea of the unconscious as the basic mechanism of the mind/body process, shaped by interactions, puts the processes of perception, cognition and basic learning beyond reach most of the time. But we have stories. One story leads to another, and *this* is all we know. Our sense of identity, mental well-being, trust and creativity depends on them. Until we are able to compose a shape, a meaningful story, out of the fragments we have, we cannot keep on keeping on, at least in any meaningful way.

My point here is that the way stories are codified offers clues about (and to) the teller, about his/her proximal system as well as about the wider culture. There is a complex layering of conscious and unconscious information, and even a little fragment contains overwhelming complexity. Birth, as a *pregnant* human event, is a very good example of the intertwining of the different levels of communication, meaning, and life. The process of writing (which differs from oral storytelling, not considered here) triggers a peculiar experience of communication, codification and learning, involving the individual and his/her here-and-now relationships. The story is also a "family issue": it is built with the active participation of family members and it is a piece of family memory itself (even when memories are hidden or silenced). *Someone* tells about birth – the mother, the father, other relatives, or the parents who adopted a child -, and the teller always brings a perspective to the story. The story is a cultural artifact, produced by social circumstances. However, it is also subjective: the author of the story chooses words and themes, and the relationships between them. In the overall composition, many aspects remain unconscious (Bateson, 1967). It is a very dynamic and tangled process.

But, when the story is written, when it takes shape, then it is possible to come to terms with it. I remember when I finished telling the story of my birth, I heard myself saying "Well, this is the story, quite awful indeed, but I am not compelled to repeat it". It felt good. The learning potential of autobiographical work lies in this shift: what is there is celebrated and recognized as such, and this very fact enables the teller to choose the next action, to become an agent (yet, it must be said, with no possibility of controlling its outcome). Choice is our possibility for freedom.

Family myths and learning

> Everybody told that I was tiny and delicate, with a red – maybe too red –face and body. I cried so much, as if I wanted to go back to sleep in my mother's womb [...] Maybe it was because the people around me disliked me. This feeling was confirmed some years ago, when I secretly read my mother's journal [...] "Her father says she is ugly with that head with few and messy hairs, and her blotted red skin"... but after a few pages, some days after my birth, mum wrote: "She is the most beautiful baby I've ever seen. Her skin has whitened, now her hair gives her a funny look... her little body is tiny and soft, she opens her eyes, and inside those eyes you can see all the gleam that was hidden before: big blue-green eyes, a color so special that we gaze at her for hours". With those eyes I was peering at my new world, which I feared at first, and which then excited me more and more with the passing of time. I was born in a simple and rapid way, but it was not easy to take care of me. Since the moment I opened those blue eyes, I began to show my character, complicated and curious at the same time. (Diana)

Family narrative is a complex system of communication processes through which stories are continuously created and changed, individually *and* collectively, within the family (what we define as such *also* depends on narratives). These stories are repeatedly shared and confirmed, but also modified, enriched, re-signified. They become teachings about the "facts of life." (Laing, 1976) "Facts" from the past are passed down from one generation to the other, but only some bits of information become "news of difference". The information contained in these stories is not merely about contents and facts, but about their organization, revealing hidden presumptions and rules. The sociologist Halbwachs (1925) argues that when we enter into a family, by birth or marriage or whatever, there are rules and habits that do not depend on us, which were there before us. The process of learning to become an individual within a certain community combines strategies that both enforce and recognize these pre-existing rules and habits, and distinguishes them from the individual's perceptions, ideas and emotions. This is a struggle, outcomes can never be taken for granted.

In family narrative, each story acts as a here-and-now model for that kind of learning that makes one "a member of this family". Family members can identify with role models and characters who are (re)presented in the stories that are told. Any narrative offers a range of actions, solutions and scripts, creating a terrain for learning and identity. (Muxel, 1997) What appears to be relevant in the building of family narrative is repetition: the repeated sharing of some stories (not *any* story) guarantees both stability and change.

In this framework, we can consider stories about birth as belonging to the larger category of family myths (2). In the systemic approach, this concept has undergone a significant evolution. First proposed by Ferreira, (1963, 1966) it was defined as a set of organized opinions, shared by all the members of a family, about their reciprocal roles and the nature of their relationships. From this view, relationships are built in a hidden way, following rules that are buried under the daily habits and clichés of family life and discourse. Ferreira's engagement with dysfunctional families (he was a family therapist) brought him to connote the myth as a homeostatic and pathological process, creating a systematic distortion of reality, a sort of family defense mechanism aimed at guaranteeing equilibrium and avoiding change. Thus, total adhesion by the subject to the family myth would prevent his/her growth and transformation, not to mention mental well-being. In the same years, Ronald Laing was developing the concept of "mystification" (1965) and Bateson's Group defined the "double bind"

141

(for an overview of this theory, see Sluzki and Ransom, 1976), as ways to create confusion and bring on identity crises. These studies offered an implicit pathological view of those communication frameworks, seen as ways to paralyze individual freedom.

The homeostatic function of myth is considered a mechanism enforced by an implicit prohibition to meta-communicate, discuss or criticize it by family therapists. Both positive ("we are such a close family!") and negative ("we cannot communicate") myths appear untouchable: "A myth is carried out in communication, but it cannot itself be an object of communication." (Fruggeri, 1997: 77, *my translation*) Many myths have been identified by systemic family therapists: the happy family, the scapegoat, alongside some general family themes like misfortune, unity, transparency, lack of communication, and so on. In this view, family members seem like prisoners of the myth: they behave in a way that confirms the shared myth and avoids falsifying it.

More recently, thanks to the "narrative turn", family myths and legends have been acknowledged a positive, constructive and morphogenetic role. Families are considered as auto-mytho-poietic systems, i.e. systems that are essentially made of stories. A certain degree of mythological narration is healthy and necessary in order to build a sense of identity and belonging (Byng-Hall, 1982, 1988, 1990).

Myth evokes complexity: individual myths are interwoven with couple and family myths. (Bagarozzi and Anderson, 1989). Their continuities and discontinuities, sometimes their conflicts, are relevant for learning. What is interesting in family myths, from an adult learning perspective, is the way subjects cope with them and manage differences, both on individual and family levels. When differences become *news of transformation* (Bateson, 1979), then learning is possible. From the epistemological point of view, the mythical dimension belongs to any representation of the family, its members, their relationships and events, such as birth, illness, death, crisis…. Nonetheless, it is often invisible: insiders are blind to the mythical quality of their knowledge about the system. In this view, myths are not a pathological feature of some kind of family: on the contrary, they are constitutive and cross-sectional of life and learning in all human communities and groups. They are the (necessary) basis for further learning.

Aesthetic and critical learning

When we focus on such an event like birth that is not "remembered" by us but re-constructed from fragments of conversations, hints, and a lot of imagination, the question arises about who and how, and in which circumstances, the story was told, what kind of story it was, and what effects it had on our life. In the framework of learning, we need to question the way this story was brought up, developed and transformed during one's lifetime, shaped by new experiences and new conversations.

The specific experience of aesthetic representation (autobiographical writing, but also drawing, sculpting, metaphorizing, poetic writing, etc.) seems to open new possibilities for understanding (stories of) birth and for bringing about transformational learning. The process of writing, sharing, and discussing with others creates space for reflection and choice. Facts may take on new meanings. In the stories included here, the suggestion to think about one's birth as a myth has opened space for a playful, exploratory, sometimes poetic, attitude. The session where the stories were written had a literary opening: a colleague (3) read myths from the Ancient Greeks, telling stories of the births of the Gods. Then, each student was invited to write her own myth of birth. After that, some of the stories were read aloud, followed by a collective discussion about family myths, self-fulfilling prophecies, destiny and agency. The concept of *daimon* was cited from the philosopher Hannah Arendt (1959) and the psychoanalyst Hillman (1996), to signify the mysterious role of individuality that is with us from birth, shaping as much as it is shaped.

It is more than likely that the 'who', which appears so clearly and unmistakably to others, remains hidden from the person himself, like the daimon in Greek religion which accompanies each man throughout his life, always looking over his shoulder from behind and thus visible only to those he encounters. (Arendt, 1959: 159-160)

This is a narrative participatory educational practice, based on autobiographical writing. It composes aesthetic and critical dimensions, individual learning and collective co-operative inquiry (Heron, 1996; Formenti, 2009). It builds on the (perceived) differences between personal narration – most often taken for granted – and what is *communicated* – i.e. what is composed in the story, shared and discussed with others, taking on different points of view and eventually finding a collective composition of meanings – i.e. a *satisfying theory* (Formenti, 2010). Awareness about the impact of family scripts and paradigms, as well as about external and social forces, can help an individual to claim a more personal and freer narrative space for him/herself.

This is especially interesting, as I stated above, for some groups of adult learners:

- young adults, who are engaged in the process of self-differentiation and individuation;
- pregnant women and their partners, as a way to build awareness of one's positioning in relation to giving birth and becoming a parent;
- professionals, who can reflect on birth and its complexity as a crucial passage in life, and a metaphor for life itself and all its transformations

The learning outcomes of this practice can be different for different learners:

- It can open a personal search for the *daimon*: what kind of person am I, for others and for myself? Who should I be, who do I want to be?
- It can sustain the transition to parenthood: what is the relationship between me and "my" child? What kind of parent do I dream of being? What kind of dream do I have about "my" child?

- It can offer a link between personal and professional knowledge: what kind of knowledge about birth and life do I bring into my work? Which hidden values have I learned from my own stories? Am I able to distinguish my knowledge and values from that of others?

These are open-ended outcomes: it is not my intention to boil down myths to facts, "evidence" or plain reality. Life is too complex to be trivialized by some easy interpretation. So, I will close with Luce's poetic and mythological text, where an archetypical image of birth as the dawn of life is offered:

As the world itself, I was born from Chaos… that abyss, that gulf of love and desire. […] In the dead of night. And as the latter prepares to hand on the baton to daylight […] that night, "my night" handed on to me a special "relay": expectations, love, tenderness, pride… (Luce)

Notes

1   These excerpts are taken from a corpus of 95 texts, written by students attending a course in Family Pedagogy (Faculty of Education). The question was: "What is the story of your birth? Write what you know, or imagine, about it". The brief commentaries I add to each story are not meant as a full understanding of their rich and complex meanings, but only (maybe oversimplified) examples of the three levels of information that I want to illustrate. I am aware that my understanding of these stories is strongly influenced by my own experience, as a child, mother, researcher in family pedagogy, as well as my paradigmatic and theoretical choices.

2   To gain a better understanding of myth in human life, we must take on an interdisciplinary perspective. Psychoanalysis, history, sociology, anthropology and literature, as well as religion and philosophy, offer many interesting and profound studies where personal and collective myths are analyzed and interpreted. See Bernhard, 1969; Valastro 2009, 2012. It must be said, however, that myth is almost completely absent from mainstream research in most disciplines.

3   Thanks to Andrea Di Martino for his sensitive and thoughtful choice of texts.

References

Arendt, H. (1959). *The Human Condition.* Garden City, NY: Doubleday.

Bagarozzi, D.A. and Anderson, S.A. (1989). *Personal, Marital, and Family Myths: Theoretical Formulations and Clinical Strategies.* London: W.W. Norton.

Bateson, G. (1967). Style, grace and information in primitive art. In Bateson, G. (1972). *Steps to an ecology of mind.* New York: Ballantine Books.

Bateson, G. (1972). *Steps to an ecology of mind.* New York: Ballantine Books.

Bateson, G. (1979). *Mind and Nature, A Necessary Unit.* New York: Bantam Books.

Bernhard, E. (1969). *Mitobiografia.* Milano: Adelphi.

Boscolo, L. and Bertrando, P. (1993). *I tempi del tempo. Una nuova prospettiva per la consulenza e la terapia sistemica.* Torino: Bollati Boringhieri.

Byng-Hall, J. (1982). Family Legends. Their Significance for the Family Therapist. In A. Bentovim, A. Cooklin, & G. Gorell Barnes (Eds.). *Family Therapy: Complementary Frameworks of Theory and Practice, vol 2.* London: Academic Press.

Byng-Hall, J. (1988). Scripts and Legends in Families and Family Therapy. *Family Process, 27,* 2, 167-180.

Byng-Hall, J. (1990). The Power of Family Myths. In R. Samuel & P. Thompson (Eds). *The Myths We Live By.* London: Routledge.

Ferreira, A. (1963). Family Myth and Homeostasis. *Archives of General Psychology, 9,* 457-463.

Ferreira, A. (1966). Family Myths. In P. Watzlawick & J.H. Weakland (Eds.) (1976). *The Interactional View.* Palo Alto: Mental Research Institute.

Formenti, L. (2008). La com-position dans/de l'autobiographie. *Pratiques de formation/Analyse. 55,* 171-191.

Formenti, L. (2009). Com-posizioni. Percorsi di ricerca-formazione alla relazione di cura. In *Attraversare la cura.* Gardolo (TN): Erickson.

Formenti, L. (2010). Metaphors, Stories and the Making of a Satisfying Theory: Transformational Learning for Professionals in Education. In M. Alhadeff-Jones & A. Kokkos (Eds.) *Transformative Learning in Time of Crisis: Individual and Collective Challenges.* Proceedings of the 9th ITLConference 28-29 May 2011, Athens.

Formenti, L. (2012). *Re-inventare la famiglia. Guida teorico-pratica per i professionisti dell'educazione.* Milano: Apogeo.

Formenti, L. and Lombroso, F. (1994). Costruire il passato: l'uso della mitologia familiare con gli adolescenti. In F. Bassoli, M. Mariotti, & L. Onnis (Eds.) *L'adolescente e i suoi sistemi.* Roma: Edizioni Kappa.

Formenti, L. and West, L. (2010), Costruire spazi di immaginazione auto/biografica. Quando i vissuti dei genitori diventano esperienza. *Animazione Sociale, 243,* 34-41.

Fruggeri, L. (1997). *Famiglie. Dinamiche interpersonali e processi psicosociali.* Roma: NIS.

Gaudio, M. (2008). *Bricolage Educativi. Verso una teoria e una pratica pedagogica con la genitorialità.* Milano: Unicopli.

Gélis, J. (1988). *La sage-femme ou le médecin. Une nouvelle conception de la vie.* Paris: Fayard.

Halbwachs, M. (1925). *Les cadres sociaux de la mémoire.* Paris: Alcan.

Heron, J. (1996). *Co-operative Inquiry.* London: Sage.

Hillman, J. (1996). *The Soul's Code. In Search of Character and Calling.* New York: Warner Books.

Horsdal, M. (2012). *Telling Lives. Exploring Dimensions of Narratives.* London, New York: Routledge.

Laing, R.D. (1965). Mystification, confusion and conflict. In I. Boszormenyi-Nagy & J.K. Framo (Eds.) *Intensive Family Therapy: Theoretical and Practical Aspects,* New York: Harper and Row.

Laing, R.D. (1976). *The Facts of Life. An Essay in Feelings, Facts, and Fantasy.* Penguin Books.

Maffi, I. (Ed.) (2010). *Nascita. Annuario di Antropologia, IX, 12.*

Merton, R. (1949). *Social Theory and Social Structure.* New York: Free Press.

Muxel, A. (1997). *Individu et mémoire familiale.* Paris: Nathan.

Reiss, D. (1981). *The Family Construction of Reality.* Cambridge (Mass): Harvard University Press.

Sluzki, C.E. and Ransom, D.C. (1976). *Double Bind. The Foundation of the Communicational Approach to the Family.* New York: Grane and Stratton.

Szymborska, W. (1997). *Nothing Twice. Selected Poems.* Cracow: Wydawnictwo Literackie.

Valastro, O.M. (Ed.) (2009). *Scritture relazionali autopoietiche.* Roma: Aracne.

Valastro, O.M. (2012) *Biographie et mythobiographie de soi: l'imaginaire de la souffrance dans l'écriture autobiographique.* Sarrebruck: Ed. Universitaires Européennes,.

Watzlawick, P. (1984). Self-fulfilling Prophecies. In P. Watzlawick (Ed.). *The Invented Reality. How Do We Know What We Believe We Know? (Contributions to Constructivism).* London, New York: Norton & C.

Chapter 7

Interrelations between narration, identity and place

◊   JUAN CARLOS PITA CASTRO, UNIVERSITÉ DE GENÈVE

The themes addressed by this book echo with some of the issues we have worked on in some recently completed research (Pita, *forthcoming*). It comprises three main elements. First of all, *reconstructing,* on the basis of the narration of the trajectories of young people who have recently completed their studies in the arts, and whose trajectories as artists are in the making or whose life projects have already encountered obstacles; then *analysing* the identity process so as to *understand* the nature of identities and the functions they might serve.

This research contains links between place and identity on two levels. On the *methodological level*, we have attempted to reconstruct trajectories. The narration proceeds by creating a plot, the *mise en intrigue* (Ricœur, 1983), as well as a process of categorisation of experience into a number of categories to which are attributed different values (Dubar, 2006). This process is related to the work of memory, which led us to address the relationship between memory and location. This reflection then led us to develop a particular device for the "co-production" of "biographic materials" that combines two forms of interviews, one of which – the narration of place – is inextricably linked to the actual movement through a given place.

On the *theoretical* level, our research is related to the current transformation of life trajectories, and amongst other matters its relationship to places. In current views of identity, some authors claim it has become entirely unrelated to place. Identity would not only be without history, but also de-territorialised.

We wish to present here our "co-production" device. The aim is to indicate the contribution of the narration of place to the reconstruction of trajectories and the understanding of identities; and importantly also to underline this different way of articulating experience through a narration that is developed in, and through, a given place. We will then proceed to an analysis of the relationship between place and identity.

I. Introduction

Before coming to the heart of the matter, let us present our research. While our contribution is a second-degree discourse, polarised by a particular interrogation, it none the less clearly distances itself from it.

Our research is focussed on the problem of the transformation of identities. In the context of modernity, identity becomes linked to representations of autonomy and authenticity. The research involves the exploration of its nature (Taylor, 1998), a process of appropriation (Dubar, 2007), and it is related to the possibility of planning one's life trajectory. It constitutes a project of accomplishment of the self, oriented towards the future and realised along a trajectory. "Advanced" modernity destabilises this configuration through its characteristic instability and uncertainty.

It is noted that the tension between the aspiration for self-fulfilment and uncertainty is symptomatic of contemporary societies (Rosa, 2010) and our work attempts to observe how this process operates within a given population, young artists, seen as prototypes of phenomena that have much wider application.

The formulation "fulfilling one's self in uncertainty" (Menger, 2010) summarises what this population seeks to study. Artistic professional activities are distinguished by a certain enchantment. They suggest identification with an activity, which both realises and defines the subject. The subjects must elaborate them, they are not already there. They are thus located at the opposite end of the spectrum in relation to hetero-determined professions. The labour market is however extremely competitive and flexible (*ibid.*). Access into these careers is characterised by a high degree of inequality in terms of success as well as insecurity. The organisation of the labour market demands mobility. On the one hand the artist's project is shaped by identification with an activity that is supposed to enable self-fulfilment, and, on the other, these careers are uncertain and unpredictable. This tension is at the centre of our research and the young artists provide an ideal "laboratory" in which to study the implications of this tension in terms of identity.

The construction of these trajectories takes place at the time when these young people attempt to enter artistic professions, and the above tension is thus at its climax. We chose to focus on two artistic vocations, the fine arts and clothing design studied in francophone Switzerland. The biographic materials produced enabled us to assess what is at stake in this entry process, while at the same time giving this process a diachronic depth and a subjective dimension. Identities were revealed. 13 young people were interviewed. We proceeded by separating the narratives in three "archaeological cuts", at the convergence of the narrative characteristics of our materials, the periods and categories proposed by the narrative, and of theoretical and institutional categories: the periods of the artist's vocation, training and insertion. This last period extends over five years.

II. Reconstructing

It is in relation to our research device for the reconstruction of trajectories that the link between memory, place and identity was established for the first time in our work. The reflexion began on a theoretical level.

Memory(ies)

The narration of a trajectory is inextricably linked to a process of recollection. Memories are always inscribed in a lived temporality. Declarative memory is first and foremost a reflexive memory. The tradition of inwardness (Taylor, 1998) gives a central place to this reflexive process. Here, identity, consciousness and memory are considered to be inseparable. This is consistent with experience and day-to-day language in which:

- Remembering something implies the memory of the self. It is always my memories that are formulated. Memory is thus a model of *mienneté (mineness)*.
- There is an original link between conscience and the past (Ricœur, 2000, p. 116), which resides at the very heart of memory. It is thus in personal memory that temporal continuity resides.
- This continuity constitutes the necessary condition for those who wish to inquire into past events from the lived present. Memory is inseparable from the capacity to go back in time.
- Memories are organised in archipelagos, sometimes separated by abysses (*ibid.*). These are the abysses of oblivion, an ever-threatening negativity.

Augustine may be considered as the inventor of interiority, and also as the founder of the tradition of the interior gaze. For him, it is always the interior human being who is remembering and this interiority is the intimate place where memories remain as vast "palaces of memories". If we follow Augustine, when we remember something we always remember our selves. He thus affirms a strong correspondence between memory and subject. "There, I encounter myself as well, I remember myself, what I did and what my impressions were while I was doing it." (Augustine, quoted by Ricœur, 2000, p. 119). But he also affirms a distance between self and one's self. It is this reflexivity which is inseparable from and constitutive of declarative memory.

Locke too is central to the question of the relationship between identity and memory. He contributed to forging the triad "identity-consciousness-self" (Ricœur, 2000). For Locke, consciousness is first and foremost defined by its memory. Identity is then fundamentally reflexive, and belongs to the category of *mêmeté ("sameness")*: despite different locations and times, it is that thing, and not another, that was in these times and locations; it is that thing which is said to be the same. The concept of personal identity contains the possibility of considering one's self as one's self, one and the same thinking being in different times and places (Locke, quoted by Ricœur, *ibid.,* p. 125). Personal identity is a temporal identity: "The identity of such a person extends as far as consciousness can retrospectively reach past actions or thoughts; it is the same self now and then and the self which executed the past action is the same as that which reflects upon it in the present" (Locke, quoted by Ricœur, *ibid.,* p. 126). Identity is thus also located in space.

The link between aggregated memories (the archipelagos), temporal continuity and the remembering subject is however a fragile one. Husserl, from a phenomenological perspective, helps us to understand this fragility. He distinguishes between impressions, which designate the vivid presence of conscience, and retention, which designates that which is the immediate past, with its relative temporal extensiveness. This distinction leads to another: between primary memory, still related to retention, and secondary memory, detached from the latter. Retention is thus always attached to perception and its impression (pathos). A detachment from perception may occur. The object is then no longer present, attached. It has, so to say, passed. An in-between space is introduced between this detached temporal object and consciousness. This is what partly defines the constitution of secondary memory. In this case, it will have to be reconstructed.

Reminders

The relationship between memory, interiority, reflexivity and temporal continuity is now established. We also used another dimension: an inquiry into the social life pole of memory. In the field of life histories this area of investigation with people in training is less evident. It makes the reflexive dimension of memory more relative. This aspect however allows us to enrich our perspective.

Let us start by a deceptively simple statement: "one does not simply remember oneself, seeing, experiencing, learning, but mundane situations in which we saw, experienced, learned" (Ricœur, 2000, p. 44). The situations one remembers always involve one's body, those of others, a certain lived space as well as a shared world. This is obvious as soon as one considers the body, for it is marked by an individual but non-reflexive memory, a memory of habit. Bicycling, or other often repeated gestures, are good examples. Experience is thus embodied, takes its place in a body-self. This memory does not involve reflexivity. The reflexive gap, constitutive of reflexive memory, is not necessary. However, this memory of the body should not be confused with the memory of the body relating to events. The latter is the product of the rupture of the familiar regime that allows us to construct a narration. Corporeal memory is distributed between worldliness and reflexivity.

The memory of places is related to some extent to this worldly pole. Places may be approached as the "storage room" of memory, since memories are often associated with places. "…it is not by mistake that we say that what has occurred has taken place" (Ricœur, 2000: 51.). The place bears the trace of the relation, it is not indifferent to the "thing" that occupies it (*ibid.*). Places of commemoration are typical of this link.

Let us take one more step. Narration and construction have common features; one is time, the other is hard material. The city is the archetype of this form of inscription. It is a kind of narration.

A city confronts within the same space different times, and offers a layered history of tastes and cultural forms. The city allows us both to be seen and read. There, the narrated time and the inhabited space are more tightly associated than in the isolated building. (Ricœur, 2000, p. 187)

We therefore considered places as possible reminders of life episodes (Casey, 1987), and thus as helpful to the subject in the work of memory.

Complementarities

In order to reconstruct the trajectories of the young people we interviewed, two tools were mobilised. The first is the biographic interview. Here the aim was to "co-produce" a narration relating to the entire trajectory within the artistic domain. These interviews explored the entire education-profession axis in their trajectory. They also focussed on socio-cognitive events, rather than on the expression of representations and discourses. I enquired less into what they thought, but into what happened, what they attempted, what they lived. The instructions for the biographic interviews can by summarised in the following way:

> Tell me what happened that was important for you in your trajectory in the artistic domain. It is a bit of an autobiography.

The biographic interview thus mobilised the genre of the autobiography.

The place narration followed the biographic interview. It was anchored in and extended the latter. The instructions relative to the place narration can be summarised in the following way:

> Tell me what happened that was important for you here, why is this place important in your trajectory.

As indicated above, the interviewer also invited the interviewee to concentrate on socio-cognitive events. The place narration involved moving to a number of places (four or five) chosen by the person, where an interview of approximately 30 minutes was held.

This device fully took into consideration the reconstruction of trajectories as a process, as a work, which progressively builds up into a grand narrative, taking into account the totality of interviews "co-produced" with the "subject-author".

III. Wording one's self

Can one identify differences between the narration formulated during the biographic interview and the place narration? Two main distinctions appear. First of all, the notion of telling as opposed to exploring. Second, a formulation of institutional agents which, if it is difficult to see in the biographic interviews, emerges in the place narrations.

Telling versus exploring

The biographic interview invites the "subject-author" to co-produce a mostly autobiographic narration. This kind of text can be defined as a "retrospective narration in prose which a real person provides of his or her own existence. Here the emphasis is on the narrator's individual life and, in particular, on the history of his or her personality" (Lejeune, 1996, p. 14). Here the autobiography was produced with the help of the researcher, and one should not attempt to hide this "co-production". However it is important to recognise that it is the "subject-author" who is producing his autobiography with the help of a researcher, who supports the process and attempts to understand it.

The figure below represents the kinetic economy of the biographic interview with Iléana, a young clothing designer. We will use it here to expand on some of the characteristics of our biographic interviews. The ordinate (the vertical line) indicates the number of years evoked within each page, the abscissa (the horizontal line) the evolving age of the interviewee. When we interviewed Iléana, she was 28. The here and now of the interview is thus on the right hand of the abscissa.

156

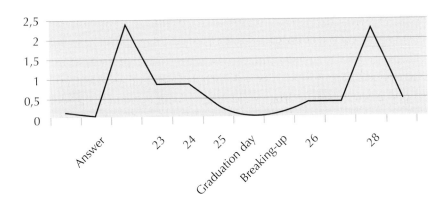

This figure allows us to visualise the unfolding of Iléana's story on the education-profession axis. Iléana's childhood is absent from the figure, since her recollection was so fast. The further the narration advances on the abscissa, the more it develops certain sequences. Three sequences are particularly developed: the sequence "Answer", in which one hour is narrated over half a page; the sequence "Graduation day", in which one day is narrated over one page; the sequence "Breaking-up", in which one month is evoked over one page. The analysis of these three sequences has been fundamental in understanding the development of Iléana's identity. A hypothesis guides the production and use of this figure: the biographic narration develops in priority that which is important from the point of view of the subject. It helps shift the subjectivity of the researcher towards that of the "subject-author". It thus constitutes an important hermeneutic safeguard.

Convergences with the autobiography emerge from our biographic interviews. Here one finds what one is looking for. This genre is distinctive in that it infers a relationship in the identity of the author, the main character and the narrator. The autobiography is however significantly affected by a form of doubling between the present subject who configures different past subjects so as to trace permanence and change in his or her development.

A particular relationship binds the narrator and main character in the autobiographic genre. It may be modulated according to the "pre-eminence given to the present, marked by the supremacy of the position of the narrator, or on the contrary mainly oriented towards the past, with the hegemony of a recollected main character" (Baudouin, 2010, p. 148). But whatever the chosen option may be, this autobiographic doubling is an essential dimension. The autobiography configures a past experience, encapsulated in a narrated time, which does not coincide with the here and now. Essentially the autobiography leads to the present. This is what the figure above enables us to visualise.

From the perspective of narrative logic, the work of autobiography demands a work of periodization (Lejeune, 1996), which leads to a segmentation of the trajectory into temporal units of several years. These provide as many partial and successive closings, which allow for the unfolding of the story. For each period it is possible to determine one identity that progressively stabilises, as well as one or several episodes considered significant with regards to the person one has become. Within each of these episodes, one sequence is particularly developed. The highest points on the graph identify these.

Our place narrations are located in part within this autobiographic logic, particularly when they concern artistic vocation and training. Based on a given place, the "subject-author" seizes the autobiographic genre and responds to its particular resources.

This is the case of the narration formulated by Iléana at the hospital. Her biographic interview outlines a reconstruction of her trajectory during her entire education-professional axis, and privileges the dimensions concerning professional identity. What is striking in her biographic interview is the speed with which she narrated the period during which she attended the School of Design. She only slows down when referring to the end of her training. The narration of this period seems incomplete, unfinished. It is the narration she provided at the hospital, which offers deeper understanding of the period of training.

Excerpt 1

It was a turning point in my life to have been through the hospital! I had an extremely violent anxiety crisis and landed at the psychiatric emergency service. [...] What happened is that this completely changed my vision of clothing design. [...] It made me want to attach myself to essential things, to lose nothing, to not lose the essential in my life. For me clothing design became something completely futile. Producing clothing to produce clothing, that no longer had any meaning for me! (Iléana)

Iléana tells us here of a turning point in her life. This past experience changed her artistic perspective. She goes on to describe what she has attached value to in her artistic work since then. The "essential" is here in opposition to the "futile". While this opposition may be found throughout Iléana's biographic interview, the place narration at the hospital allows it to be analysed, etching it out in the lived experience that was at the origin of this opposition. It was possible to see the emergence of her affirmation of an artistic practice privileging the expression of "*the guts*", in a cathartic process in which the artistic "*work on the cloth*" is paramount, leading to a disregard for "*commercial*" design.

In the narration at the hospital, Iléana gives life to a past Iléana, who, confronted with an event, transforms and establishes her values. This experience takes place away from the time/space of the School of Design. The researcher's instruction to narrate one's trajectory in the artistic domain certainly privileges professional identity. It is interesting to see that the above account of values is absent in the biographic interview. In contrast, the place narration however allows these to be made clearer. For Iléana, explaining how I became who I am requires narrating this experience, because some experiences are necessary to the development of the autobiographic narration (Baudouin & Pita, 2011). They are massive and polarise the creation of the plot (Ricœur, 1983).

Excerpt 2

> [Concerning Iléana's arrival at the hospital] I arrived with my mother and my boyfriend... It was a day when I wished to commit suicide [...] I called my boyfriend for him to come immediately, because sometimes I thought: "I'm going to jump!" So we went to the doctors, at the emergency service. She gave me antidepressants or tranquilisers. After that, I stayed for a month. I did not leave home. During two weeks I did not shower. I did nothing. After, my boyfriend threw me in the shower. That was a turning point... I mean, the shower... I thought... "Ok, I'm alive again!" (Iléana)

Let us note in passing that Iléana "*comes back to life*" following a bodily experience. It is her body that is the trigger of her awakening. In this sequence, Iléana reconfigures her past, tells of what the main character had to confront and how she was transformed by it. The use of deictic is striking. The uses of here, there and it are frequent. They allow us to perceive a work of memory in which place is a support.

Excerpt 3

> I do not want at all to be the person I describe, what I say of myself in this hospital. No, I really don't want that. Here, it is more or less everything I do not want to be. (Iléana)

Here Iléana explains. And she does not desire to be the person whose actions she tells of. Her story thus tends towards the self-portrait, although it is mainly autobiographic, as we shall see below.

Portraying the self

In a similar way to autobiography, the self-portrait carries a subjective dimension (Baudouin, 2010). It is distinguished however from autobiography in particular ways: the self-portrait is not retrospective and narrative; it privileges a "non-chronological thematic perspective" (*ibid.*). It consequently leads to a "convergence or even an identification [...] between the I of the narrator and the I that is in this instance not narrated but evoked (*ibid.*, p. 129). It is a matter of evocation and not narration. The self-portrait proposes an exploration of a set of themes the author uses to portray him or her self. The "I" of the narrator is superimposed on the evoked "I". The tension on the level of identity implied by the autobiographic doubling does not operate here. The author of the self-portrait is not concerned with the narrative reconstruction of divers Is in relation to the present I. He or she does not narrate, but explores different themes in order to say what I am. There is thus a strong nuance here in relation to the subject of the autobiography, who narrates him or herself to say who I am.

A law of proximity thus emerges. As soon as it concerns periods relating to the artist's vocation or training, the narration mobilised the autobiographic genre. However where and when the period of the artist's entry into work is evoked, it is the self-portrait genre that dominates. The place initiates diverse themes and operates as a support to the self-portrait. Our "biographic materials" thus change nature. The unfolding of identity that is foundational to our project is by-passed. The synchronous returns and the diachronic axis are abandoned. But at the same time the key categories of identities are formulated.

Excerpt 4

> Listen, I am bringing you here because we are in a place that is interesting for me [...] I like stations and airports, because one can observe people. There are many different cultures. I like a lot these places. The idea was to bring you into a movement of displacement, because I am fascinated by displacement. I am rather happy when I am neither in a point A nor in a point B but in this kind of no man's land that resides in between. I feel calm and relaxed. (Camille)

Through the narration at the airport, Camille proposes an exploration of dimensions that characterise her, "*I like...*" Here, at the airport, Camille tells us of herself today. The movement through the space constitutes a support for a presentation of herself, through the themes sparked by the airport. Here the past Camilles are no longer present, she does not provide us with an autobiography. The focus is on Camille today. The same occurs with Christophe, a Fine Arts graduate, when he brings us to his workshop.

Excerpt 5

> It is a place to which I love coming, because it is located at the outskirts of the city. It is at the edge of the city, we still hear the cars in the background, but also the forest, the river. [...] This is a liminal space, which is a bit freer. [...] "On the outskirts" is a term that characterises me well, it means being both inside and outside. Yes, it is such a position that artists must have. They need to be a bit outside, to have a certain distance, a capacity to see. [...] But at the same time you need to be inside. (Christophe)

Christophe uses the particular position of his workshop to argue for the positionality of the artist, the category through which he defines himself. Just like Camille, he presents himself here through the place and its geographic characteristics. It is through them that he tells us of who he is: an artist, both inside and outside.

A shared world

A narration is inconceivable without a certain number of agents. They intervene through the narrative grammar (Greimas, 1966), which allows us to interpret the trials proposed by the narration. They mandate, bring resources, oppose and qualify the subject.

The place narration helps to describe institutional agents. It facilitates the description of the collective, whether it be under the auspices of the autobiography or the self-portrait. Here too, the law of proximity operates. The more the places from which the narration emerges concern the period of entry into work, the more it focuses on an institutional agent. The place narration thus articulates a generalised other (Mead, 1933/2006), but also a subject in its quest for belonging and recognition in the sphere of social cooperation (Honneth, 2000). It facilitates the evocation of a common world within which the subject seeks anchoring. It thus completes the biographic interview by addressing that which the latter tends to relegate to a secondary level.

This focus is evident with Christophe. The narration he developed on the occasion of a visit to the Forum, an institution that deals in journalism and organises thematic meetings, shows us a Christophe who, in the present of the narration, evolves in an institutional setting.

Excerpt 6

> This place, I would say now, is a kind of stage. [...] I do have room for creativity. The Forum is 8 roundtables, 30 films, an exhibition [...] I proposed themes for the roundtables, speakers and developed some of the questions. [...] I have a real place! [...] But it is not entirely myself. I mean, there is a frame, I can not do whatever I want. But this is a frame I feel close to, it is close to my interests, even if it is a bit more institutional. (Christophe)

Christophe has started a career as a documentary film director, at the intersection of art and political engagement. His biographic interview tells us how he progressively invested in art and politics and how his positioning of himself as an artist progressively stabilised. When his biographic interview stops, after having described his professional identity, and as he comes close to the present of the narrating Christophe, he evokes an experience in which he became conscious of the *"violence of the system"* and of the impossibility of living for his art. He is at a turning point. He must construct himself without abandoning the identity which has crystallised. The Forum concerns this particular period. He evokes this "*stage*", this "*now*". The Forum gives Christophe a "*place*" in an institutional "*frame*", bigger than him but that, nonetheless, allows him to maintain his creativity. His place narration describes this frame at length.

Excerpt 7

[Referring back to the biographic interview] There was this question of de-territorialisation and re-territorialisation… Well this remains! At some point you can de-territorialise yourself, liberate yourself from the constraints of a field or an institution, and at another moment you need to share. And the moment of sharing can be related to a given field or institution. (Christophe)

The Forum fulfils Christophe's need to find a territory for his work, a frame, so as to share it. He is in a process that aims to fill the solitude of an "autistic" creator. But on this occasion Christophe goes further.

Excerpt 8

It is the question of recognition. It is important for me. […] They congratulated and thanked me for my work, they recognised me! In the first month you enter a new institution, there is something like a work of translation to do. What is this institution? How does it operate? Who does what? Where is it heading? So there is a work of translation of this institutional frame and then there is a moment of negotiation. There is the moment of negotiation. There is the institution, and there is myself. I don't want to do anything for this institution! One needs to find a middle ground. (Christophe)

It is a question of recognition and its corollary, social esteem. But it is also a process of negotiation. It is thus a process of identity reconstruction within a shared world that is indicated by this place narration. Following the difficult experience described above, Christophe found himself on the verge of a "no-man's land of meaning" (Mazade, 2011), or at least finding nothing satisfying to him. His identity for himself was destabilised, and his identity for the other, provided by his older relational anchoring, crumbled. The Forum is a "structure of plausibility" (Dubar, 2007), which will allow him to advance towards a reconstruction capable of maintaining a link with the identity he forged through the period of artistic vocation and training.

IV. Adherences

The trajectories we were able to reconstruct in our research allowed us to unfold identities configured by a desire to affirm and maintain an autonomy and authenticity on the one hand, while on the other were beset by instability, mobility and sometimes a kind of emptiness. Seeking integration they were confronted with an organisation of the work in de-territorialised networks and lost their sense of their own place.

A thesis is therefore being proposed, that of a situative identity, which would develop in contemporary societies in which the characteristics of advanced modernity are spreading. This form of identity is defined in a coherent way in relation to the demands of a society with a great rate and speed of change as well as uncertainty (Rosa, 2010). It has two implications. The first is an abandoning of the pretentions of autonomy and authenticity, as well all trans-situational projects. Identities would thus take shape outside of any desire to fulfil aspirations of an ontological kind, and outside any attempt to attain a definite form. The second is the lack of relationship between identity and place, which will be addressed here. Can one say, in the case of the mobile and networked identities which we have considered, that they are in no way attached to place, that their identities take shape outside of any adherence, that place is no longer significant in the shaping and development of identity in a durable way?

"Our perception of who we are [...] depends directly of our relation to space, to our contemporaries, to objects and our environment" (Rosa,

2010, p. 275). Our relation to self is currently affected by a principle of acceleration. The quantitative increase in this process leads to a qualitative transformation of this relation to self. We would thus see operating a shift from stable identities towards dynamic relations to self, characterised by "permanent biographic revisions" or at least an increased contingency of the old fixed elements of identity. (*ibid.*, p. 277). These revisions, desired or constrained, have become recurrent. And, "when the past, the present and the future must constantly be interpreted and associated in new ways, the notion of who one was, who one is and who one will be is constantly transformed". (*ibid*, p. 291). These subjects would thus find themselves confronted with the impossibility of evaluating a single one of the many main dimensions of their identity. Identity's stability "no longer rests on substantial identifications" (*ibid.*). Identity thus risks being absorbed by flexibility, change and transition. The consequences of these perspectives in terms of place are important. In effect, identity and place would grow further apart. "Nothing of the place (temporal) where its existence unfolds adheres "essentially" to the subject, and, conversely, the subject no longer invests in place" (*ibid*, p. 298).

Our place narratives challenge these perspectives and cannot be forced into this frame of analysis. Rather, the place narratives we collected validate the continuing strong link between identity and place. Identity seems to continue to adhere to place. And their interrelations concern the dimensions considered by the "subject-author" as essential. The empirical fragments we presented here show that the subject appears attached to a place, whether this attachment be marked by a form of nostalgia or by current concerns.

Lost Paradise

When Iléana takes us to the School of Design, which she attended five years before, she expresses with emotion a continuing adherence between this place and her identity.

Excerpt 9

It is this school that allowed me to love creating with my hands, it is here that I feel good, in these moments where I feel the closest to myself… to my roots… […] I completely identify with this school. I feel at home! No, I don't know, it is such an important part of my life! For me, it is still part of myself. […] It is a part of myself, of my life, and I cannot forget it. Sometimes I no longer recognise myself… You know, I no longer have this energy. I was never like this, without energy, without this desire to do things. At the time, I was well. (Iléana)

When we meet Iléana, she is in the midst of a process of reconstruction. Entry into the world of clothing design was not possible. She must change, but without "*losing herself*". To change, without letting go of this part of her self, which she discovered at the School of Design. For her identity, which unfolds during our research, the School of Design constitutes a place, located in time, where "*energy*" circulated, through collective emulation, where the desire "*to create*" was transmitted "*between friends*". For Iléana as she digs into her own archaeology, something of her self is attached to this place, which continues to be "*a home*" at the time when she is reconstructing herself. One must consider this statement and assess its importance. The relation of adherence is affective; it is related to an important period of her life, when she "*discovered*" herself in the company of others in an institution, which offered her social esteem through its recognition.

This place should be situated in the dynamic that the biographic interview allows us to reconstruct. It contrasts with the dereliction experienced by Iléana at the end of her studies, during the sequence "Falling Apart", which the analysis of the kinetic economy of her interview reveals. The School of Design completed, Ileana fell out of a shared world, and was confronted with the solitude, the loss of creative drive relating to the loss of the collective, and also a particular anguish related to the feeling of evolving in a kind of "emptiness". Iléana remains attached to this place. In her trajectory it constitutes a major landmark, despite the numerous reconstruction projects she has engaged with over the 5 years since she completed her studies. For this identity, adherence to place lives on. This place remains "*home*", a lost paradise.

Consistence

Camille too addresses the link between identity and place. It resembles that evoked by Iléana, but is devoid of nostalgia. In a small restaurant of her choice, she speaks of the close connection that binds her to her city.

Exerpt 10

> Where are our roots? I have often asked myself this question, because when I completed my travel in China [...] I realised that everything happens from the place where the people I love are. They were my pillars! And so I needed to be close to them to be more creative. I realised this when I came back from China, because before, I was ready to live elsewhere, to develop my career elsewhere. I came back, I lost my boyfriend, my brother was sulking and my parents no longer spoke to each other.... I had no place, no home. (Camille)

Camille's trajectory is different from that of Iléana. At the end of her studies, she was projected into the international network of fashion design. She led a frenetic life, participating in events on different continents. She left her city and her landmarks for nearly two years to become an international designer. However, when she came back, she felt that her landmarks, her anchoring had vanished. She no longer had a "*home*". She was literally from nowhere and everywhere at the same time, organising business meetings in the different airports in which short stops were possible, living from project to project. She became an incarnation of this identity made up of networks and de-territorialised, without anchoring.

168

But her life fractured when she grew conscious of the diffraction of her identity and particularly a certain affective emptiness. After having been nowhere and everywhere, she came back *"home"*, to her city, where her pillars, her life supports, are. She felt *"the ground crumbling beneath her feet"* as a result of her de-territorialisation. She became conscious of the important of a place that gives her a certain consistence, and admits that she needs her pillars *"to be creative"*. However, this return *"home"*, based in a small Swiss city, required a professional reconstruction. Camille will no longer be a designer. But she could no longer live with the implications of this career.

V. Conclusion

Certain conclusions can be made, based on what we have developed above. In terms of the reconstruction of trajectories, the place narration does seem to provide a strong stimulus. We have however outlined a law of proximity, based on which the narration changes in nature. The more the place and what was lived there is temporally close to the "subject-author", the more it mobilised the genre of the self-portrait. The place offers a set of characteristics, which will be used in order for the subject to say what he or she is. The "subject-author" then undertakes to uncover the characteristics that define it. The farther away the place is in time, the more the "subject-author" tends to mobilise the genre of autobiography, and undertakes a narration of the "development of his or her individual personality" by configuring a distant subject, who suffers and acts and about whom the "subject-author" formulates continuities and changes. This "law" also operates with regards to the possibility of accessing a shared world within which the subject seeks to locate itself. The closer the place is to the current experience of the subject, the more its narration involves a collective dimension, allowing us to study a shared world.

In terms of the links that bind place and identity, three elements have emerged. First, as soon as the identity proceeds with its unfolding, certain processes remain constant as affective anchoring and subjective landmarks in a process of identity transformation. The "subject-authors" attest here to identification with a place. Second, our biographic materials demonstrate the importance of the collective dimension attached to places, and the energy, which emanates from it. Finally, they attest to an impossibility of living free of any bounds, in a heightened mobility. The place is invested with a need for stability and anchoring. It is opposed to emptiness. Here the subject is always in a place, but the latter is evoked negatively. The analysis of our trajectories shows that an identity without history and de-territorialised is a fiction. While not impossible on a logical level, it is unlikely on an existential one.

References

Baudouin, J.-M. (2010). *De l'épreuve autobiographique*. Berne: Peter Lang.

Baudouin, J.-M. & Pita, J.C. (2011). Récit de vie et pluralité interprétative en sciences de l'éducation. Le cas des histoires de vie. In A. Petitat (Ed), *La pluralité interprétative. Aspects théoriques et empiriques*. Paris: L'Harmattan, 263-286.

Casey, E. (1987). *Getting Back into Place. Toward a Renewed Understanding of the Place-World*. Indianapolis: IUP.

Dubar, C. (2007). *La crise des identités. L'interprétation d'une mutation*. Paris: PUF.

Dubar, C. (2006). *Faire de la sociologie. Un parcours d'enquête*. Paris: Belin.

Greimas, A.J. (1966). *Sémantique structurale*. Paris: Seuil.

Honneth, A. (2000). *La Lutte pour la reconnaissance*. Paris: Cerf.

Lejeune, P. (1996). *Le Pacte autobiographique*. Paris: Seuil.

Mazade, O. (2011). "La crise dans les parcours biographiques: un régime temporel spécifique?" In *Temporalités*, 13, 2011, put on-line le 05 juillet 2011, Consulted1 février 2011. URL: http://temporalites.revues.org/index1472.html

Mead. G.H. (1933/2006). *L'esprit, le soi et la société*. Paris: PUF.

Menger, P.-M. (2010). *Le travail créateur: s'accomplir dans l'incertain*. Paris: Seuil.

Pita, J.C. (*forthcoming*). *Incertitude et réalisation de soi. Vocation, formation et insertion de diplômés d'écoles d'art.* Berne: Peter Lang.

Ricœur, P. (2000). *La mémoire, l'histoire, l'oubli.* Paris: Seuil.

Ricœur, P. (1983). *Temps et récit 1. L'intrigue et le récit historique.* Paris: Seuil.

Rosa, H. (2010). *Accélération. Une critique sociale du temps.* Paris: La Découverte.

Taylor, C. (1998). *Les sources du moi.* Paris: Seuil.

Chapter 8

Non-traditional students and imagined social capital: the resources of an embodied mind

◊　ANDREA GALIMBERTI, UNIVERSITÀ DEGLI STUDI MILANO BICOCCA, ITALY

This chapter presents some conceptual reflections about auto/biographical work with non-traditional students in higher education. I developed this methodology as a part of a Ph.D research project centered on the following research question: how does the *imagined social capital* (Quinn, 2005) influence non-traditional students' perception of their learning and identity at the university?

"Stories from Bicocca", a pilot project funded by the EU Grundtvig Lifelong Learning Programme, was the starting point in building a framework for my own research. The aim was to promote the inclusion of adults at risk of social and institutional marginalization. The Bicocca University team chose non-traditional students in higher education as the target group.

The theoretical background is the systemic approach (Bateson, 1972; Varela et al, 1991; von Foerster, 1982), social constructionism (Gergen, 1999) and the theory of complexity (Morin, 1995). According to these perspectives, auto/biographical work follows some general premises:

- "self-construction" is a systemic, conversational, and compositional process;
- there are other levels beyond the individual level of construction (the "agent"): relationships and contexts, where individual actions and meanings can be seen as effects of interactions;
- stories and meanings are not only subjective. They are developed in a context with its own possibilities and constraints. Different contexts create different narrations.

The term auto/biography, with the slash, seems to fit these ideas. It was coined to draw attention to the complex interrelations of the construction of one's own life and that of another person (Merrill and West, 2009). Based on this framework, I will explore two theoretical approaches, in particular the concept of the "embodied mind" by Varela et al (1991) and the "conceptual metaphor" by Lakoff and Johnson (1980). They connect both with my research and with the general topic of this book by highlighting the role of body experience in generating a plurality of representations of the world (including university, learning, and oneself).

Non-traditional learners at the university: a Grundtvig LLP project

The pilot project "Stories from Bicocca" started in 2009-2011 as part of the Grundtvig project "European Biographies. Biographical approaches in Adult Education" whose general aim was "to enrich and improve methods of biographical work with adults, and to make biographical approaches better known in European adult education institutions, as powerful integrative and experience-based pedagogical tools for reaching and integrating socially marginalized persons into society" (as described in the project's presentation brochure). Each partner institution (from Austria, Germany, Italy, Poland, and Turkey) carried out pilot projects introducing new biographical approaches into their work. The results were gathered in a common handbook and computer disc in English.

As a partner in the project, under the direction of Professor Laura Formenti, the Bicocca University team chose to address non traditional students, who are described in the literature as under-represented, and whose participation in higher education (HE) is constrained by structural factors. They include, for example, students whose family had not been to university before, students from low-income families, students from (specific) ethnic minority groups, older students and students with disabilities (see also The RANLHE study at http://www.dsw.edu.pl/fileadmin/www-ranlhe/documents.html). These students are considered at risk in terms of access, retention, active participation, academic success, and social integration. (http://www.dsw.edu.pl/fileadmin/www-ranlhe/files/national_stat.pdf)

During the first phase of the project, however, the category of "non traditional student" was transformed by the team, and given a more experience-related definition, namely "the idea of being a-typical in relation to some university standard". In fact, after autobiographical exploration of the term "non-traditional", the team came to consider it ambiguous, since it could be associated with many different, contradictory, meanings. This first phase of the project was aimed at creating a team of "researcher/ students", who were invited to experiment with auto/biographical methods (Demetrio, 1996; Dominicé, 2000; West et al. 2007; Formenti, 2009) through personal exploration, to reflect on their implications, specifically in terms of ethics, and to design narrative workshops which would be offered to non-traditional students.

The basic idea was to gather learning stories from students who appear not to fit the usual institutional expectations, for example adult students who decided to re-enter higher education after (or during) a work period, or students who had changed faculties. Within the Italian HE system, these students are considered in a negative light as a mere social cost and/ or a difficult category to deal with; (programme) changes are viewed as "errors" and workers are simply "non-attending" students. In line with international literature, there is some evidence that these students have a higher risk of non-completion due to different kinds of difficulties related to their "a-typicality".

The challenge is to integrate identities that appear not only different, but opposites (student vs. worker, or adult, or parent…); the social feedback (generally negative) to their learning choice; and the way they dealt with previous experiences in education and in higher education.

Auto/biographical workshops: from collecting stories to understanding experiences

There were three, three-hour auto/biographical workshops for writing and sharing, in small groups, personal narrations that could:

- give voice to individual learning stories within the university;
- highlight differences and connections between the participants' experiences;
- develop meaning and understanding through dialogue;
- foster reflexive processes, and possibly some sort of action or further project.

Overall 50 students participated in the workshops. Their texts were shared and, with the author's consent, published online in a website specifically created to make them visible to other students and members of the nstitution.(See storie della Bicocca, http://sites.google.com/site/storie-dellabicocca).

The decision to create a website was thoroughly discussed with the team and the participants, and it sought to:

- give space to learning experiences that appear "unorthodox" if compared to a "normal student career";
- enrich some of the linear simple ideas that seem to drive institutional decisions with more nuance and complexity. For example, ideas about: dropping out as a "failure" (while from the point of view of a single student it can be a "discovery", or a "better choice"); the learning career as being automatically linked to a professional

career; or the support that is needed by non-traditional students, commonly seen as "filling a gap" regardless of their experience, knowledge and motivation;

- highlight the resources brought by non-traditional students, recognizing what is expressed in their narrations, in motivational, emotional, and symbolic terms.

"Stories from Bicocca" thus represented the starting point of my research. I started to develop my own PhD research by analysing the narrative materials produced during the workshops, searching for some ideas that could help me formulate my research questions.

Imagined social capital: a concept for re-thinking the interplay between students and institutions

The notions of *social capital* and *habitus* (Bourdieu & Passeron, 1970; Bourdieu, 1988) are frequently used in research about non-traditional students (see Bowl, 2001; Longden 2004, 2006; Thomas, 2002; Thomas and Quinn, 2006), to show how institutional structures and student's assumptions interact in shaping a variety of possibilities. If the student and the institution share similar aims, language, and world-views, there may be no misunderstanding or clash of frameworks, and the student's career will probably meet the institution's expectations (*fish in the water*). On the other hand, when the student *habitus* is "unorthodox", it is more likely that this is an obstacle in the learning career, with a higher risk of drop out (*fish out of water*).

This point highlights structural factors that can open or close possibilities in students' careers. Biographical research uses Bourdieu's ideas extensively, linking them to personal narration: stories show the impact of structural factors on individual lives.

Field (2008) describes how social capital and lifelong learning could be connected. There is, in general, a mutual, beneficial relationship between these two concepts. This relationship should not, however, be interpreted as a simple one, since it depends, in fact, on a range of other elements. For example, when the network producing social capital is based on very close and strong interpersonal links, the space for reflexive learning seems to decrease. Field suggests using the concept of social capital in a heuristic way, posing questions like: "If we have more social capital – stronger and more extensive networks – then are we more likely to learn new things than people with less social capital?" (Field, 2005). Quinn (2005) adds further reflections to the debate. She gives the notion of social capital a new dimension: networks that give benefits are not only "social", but also symbolic and imagined.

> Symbolic networks may be the networks of those we know who are given a symbolic function, imagined networks may be with those we don't know personally, or who may not even exist, but with whom we can imagine desired connections. These networks provide resources of power and resistance and appear to be more useful for survival than formalized support networks are. (Quinn, 2010: 68)

Taking a symbolic and imaginative stance implies transforming language and a new way of considering belonging, student identity, learning, and educational spaces. The focus is on the ability to create symbolic relationships, to "invent" a community to belong to and to be able to tell a "good" learning story (i.e., a story that is useful for persevering). Structural factors remain important, but the question is: how do these factors affect everyday negotiations? What creative solutions are found to cope with them and to include both the symbolic and the material in a coherent identity?

Our aim should be an education system that permits harmony between the symbolic and the material worlds of learners (Quinn, 2010: 77)

The concept of imagined social capital brings a new dimension to the ongoing reflection about social capital in existing literature. Quinn, in fact, suggests considering imagined social capital to be like any other kind of social capital. This implies fundamental acknowledgement of it.

Even if created by people for themselves, imagined social capital has an essentially social and cultural dimension. This raises pedagogical questions like: what conditions are needed in HE institutions to promote spaces where symbolic connections, future dreams and fantasies are shared with others? What would the effects of such a kind of space be on education? What could be an active and effective educational policy to counter drop out, also aimed at fostering and honoring differences and divergent thinking? In my view, this is an occasion to stimulate a sense of belonging and reflexive processes among students, without imposing a proper or right way to live within the institution on them. In other words, the possibility to "offer mutuality without incorporation" (Quinn, 2005: 4).

Metaphors and thought: theories for the embodied mind

My research required the development of a theory of the mind based on language and concepts. I drew on different disciplines with a common constructivist approach and an embodied and enacted view of knowledge. Varela et al. (1991) offer a new perspective on the nervous system: instead of conceiving of it uniquely as a collection of open systems (i.e., that exchange information with the external world), they introduce another level of description which makes it possible to consider them closed systems. On this level, the nervous system is not an input/output machine, but a self-reproducing system, built to maintain its balance. In order to do this, it interacts with the environment, selecting what does not disturb its structure. Varela uses the concept of "structural coupling" to illustrate the relationship between the (structure of the) organism and the (structure of the) world: they interact and influence each other very concretely on one level, while on another the organism works in a way that preserves its structure, compensating for any disturbance.

This approach rejects the traditional idea of representation as a linear correspondence, implied by the input/output machine metaphor, in favour of a theory of representation as a circular process of action and perception. They are connected and inseparable: cognitive structures (and thoughts) emerge from sensory motor patterns. Living organisms, then, "enact" the world as a series of distinctions embodied by the cognitive system as a result of its interactional history with the world itself.

Lakoff and Johnson (1980) bring this "motor theory of cognition" further when they introduce the role of metaphor as a bridge between the body experience and concepts. They state that our conceptual system is empirically rooted: interaction between body and world (even if culturally mediated) generates experiences with a certain degree of "immediacy". Thanks to this, the individual builds concepts like "object", "case", etc. as kinaesthetic models. These embodied and very concrete concepts are the basis for creating more abstract ones because of the process of metaphor.

Metaphors, in fact, offer the bridge for translating the primary body experience in other domains of existence: its main function is to provide a partial understanding of an experience in terms of another kind of experience (Lakoff and Johnson, 1980; Kovececs, 2002). The primary body experience is the starting point for mapping all other kinds of experience, which appear less defined. For example, metaphoric "ideas are objects", translating the first concept (quite abstract ideas) into the terms of the second (more concrete objects). All the actions that apply to objects from then will also apply to an idea: one can grasp it, weigh it, and throw it away. Other examples are "time is money", "skills are tools", and so on.

According to this view, abstract concepts are always the result of a metaphorical process. As the authors showed in their book *Philosophy in the Flesh*, even philosophical perspectives have metaphorical roots (Lakoff and Johnson, 1999). A metaphor acts as a bridge between the two terms it links. It states a similarity, not something factual. The domain of experience created via the metaphor is perceived as the original one, rooted in bodily experience.

When we start to perceive time in terms of money, for example, this affects life experience. This translation is possible because our culture conceives of time as a countable quantity. Complex concepts are usually mapped by a plurality of metaphors, not just one: each of them highlights some aspect while concealing others. Time itself can be perceived through a plurality of metaphors, hence generating a plurality of experiences. The choice of the metaphors and experiences that are allowed, or avoided, or dominate, is a cultural choice: individual embodied experience is connected to culture.

A conceptual system that is structured by and around metaphors has a fundamental characteristic: it cannot be exhaustive. In this view, a fixed "truth" doesn't exist, because a mobile, generative ocean of meanings can map concepts (and experiences) only partially. There is always a possibility, in fact, for experiencing and thinking differently. This possibility is shaped by culture. This idea of partial truth is also a cornerstone in the theory of complexity (Morin, 1995).

Since body experience is the basis for the metaphorical process, it is a goldmine for thinking and knowing. However, there is always the risk of reducing this richness. In fact, a certain degree of coherence between different metaphors is necessary, in order to structure a discourse. When the level of coherence is high, metaphors become "consistent": they overlap because of their similarity. In this case there are few differences in the conceptual dimension: the empirical basis is taken for granted and forgotten. The result is that the relationship between "map" and "territory" (Bateson, 1979) is experienced as real, not metaphorical. This, philosophically speaking, is the objectivist stance.

The attempt to define a situation using a consistent set of metaphors is similar to describing it from an objectivist point of view. Metaphorical and empirical bases are left out, as well as what the metaphors conceal. Every consistent set of metaphors will probably conceal a number of features "of reality"; these features can only be revealed by other metaphors which are incompatible with that set (Lakoff and Johnson, 1980). The result of this process is the affirmation of a unique truth and a unique world, by eliminating both plurality and differences. It becomes impossible to perceive other potential meanings of the same experience.

From the stories: imagined social capital and metaphors

The project "Stories from Bicocca" can be seen as a way of promoting and making visible the students' imagined social capital in the narrative workshops where participants were invited to tell their stories using metaphors and symbolic language. The senses and imagination in fact were extensively used in these narrative workshops to create conditions where learners could imagine (new) symbolic connections, while telling their stories.

The embodied mind is the starting point: thoughts are connected with the body experience via metaphor. But, as we said, there is always the possibility of inhabiting a sphere of meaning in an objectivistic way. In this case, only a narrow range of metaphors were used to structure the dominant narration, and the empirical, embodied roots of concepts were forgotten. As a result, the plurality of (possible) meanings of experience was reduced to a single vision, and divergent thinking stopped. In the university context, there is often a unique vision of the learning experience and a rigid definition of valid/invalid knowledge. Non-traditional students and their stories bring unexpected representations, enriching the repertoire of the community, as long as it is open to the differences and can thrive on them.

"Universities facilitate the production of imagined social capital by opening up the strange and the unfamiliar to be reframed and reused by students in new symbolic networks. Is this 'making strange', then, the distinctive role of the university within lifelong learning?" (Quinn, 2005:15)

Below I present some extracts from three auto/biographical narratives produced in the "Storie della Bicocca" project. All of them were published on the website with the author's permission. The authors are adult students who entered or re-entered HE. I selected them from a variety of texts because of their richness in terms of using explicit or implicit metaphors and making reference to imagined and symbolic networks.

They show how one's learning identity and university experience can be composed of a plurality of meanings through a plurality of metaphors and images.

ANNAMARIA – The university bubble awakened my energy

Annamaria uses metaphors of actions to illustrate her project:

> I loved perfection, certainty, clear and definite things, but I wasn't able to build my future as an adult!

> I found the courage to change, to risk, to walk along a road that I didn't expect to walk on any more: university.

> I don't know what the future holds for me. I can only hope that I will be able to build it, here and now, savouring the present, alone, but also with my beloved ones.

The university, in Annamaria's words, also is a protective place, a shelter. I think that this is very far from the rhetoric of university as an open space, a crossroads for students getting ready to challenge the future and the economic world.

> I don't know when I will finally have the job I dream of, but in the meantime I hope that this "university bubble" will hold up and guarantee me proper training.

The energy and passion arising from learning are considered to generate a source that enables Annamaria to cope with uncertainty.

> This experience (this workshop but also university) generated and will generate new things, rising from the energy that university awakened in me.

The certainty I now feel, adrift in this uncertain navigation, is that…
I don't want to stop sailing!

Today is a new day,
I changed the aspect of my life.
No more high heels,
now it's time to walk,
to go further
where I never could imagined.
I thank life,
because I have the possibility
to make a dream come true.

DANIELA – Light-headedness and the university machine

Daniela uses an original image to illustrate the condition of being an adult student in Higher Education. She put herself into an imagined network of "undesirables".

And for the second time we expire. Like mozzarella, we are no longer desirable.

Daniela expresses her difficulties in relation to the university using metaphors of coldness (calculations, mechanisms) and confusion (a shaggy ball of thread).

When I went back to enroll at the university I used to tell to myself a story made of calculations, reasons, lies. "It will be an investment for my professional career". I found myself on an internal journey, where education is a process with clear and functional objectives.

Besides re-entering education, I was also reconverted. In the past I had enrolled at the Literature Faculty. I was just a shaggy ball of thread at that time and I didn't have enough strength to go through such a new world, so I never attended the lessons. It's a fact that sometimes life offers you experiences you aren't ready for... but sometimes you can to pass by start once again. Eventually, I found myself in a university class at 35.

The girls around me scared me: I spied on them in their ingenuity, their biggest worry seemed to be a grade, they appeared to be so naïve, but actually I was scared by how easily they were able to move inside the huge mechanism of the university. I was so envious of them, maybe because they weren't afraid to knock on a door, to ask, to fail. The steepest paths are those which give you a clear view of yourself at a certain point, for a few clear moments. Today I know that I'm here for some other reasons: I don't know if I'll ever work as a consultant, maybe being a pedagogical consultant is more a state of mind, a way to skim along life. Maybe it is just nice to have a certain type of mind, maybe I'm here just for the pleasure of it.

When pleasure for learning takes the scene, metaphors change:

When you have these burdens to reckon with, you forget those times in your youth when you spent hours and hours on books, without even realizing it was dinnertime. But the pleasure of learning cannot be erased, it makes itself comfortable in the corner and waits. It waits together with all the feelings that made it grow: the satisfaction of solving a problem, the intuition of understanding the world and how it has worked for centuries. The light-headedness of being caressed by an unheard-of verse, the rapture of meeting great unaware teachers along the way.

The pleasure is "enacted" by Daniela by using rich bodily metaphors.

The pleasure, that pleasure. It has no titles, no grades. It has oxygen, energy, emotion. It has no chains that bind, no hunchbacks, no rules or donkey ears. That pleasure is never enough.

The image of me that I come across is one of a curious woman who desires to be passed through by emotions. That's how I started this course, just saying "How beautiful".

Today I'm even more convinced that my experience shapes me as a person in the first place and then as a professional, because it is made of encounters and experiences. I don't know whether I'm learning to do a certain job, I don't even know how I will be living a year from now. What I do know is that I'm dedicating my mind and heart in a very personal way where deadlines are in the background, creating space for new ideas and challenges. I don't know whether I'll manage to graduate or not but I'll take the many things that I have learned here with me.

ANNA – Reverent fear and the foolish ideas

Anna's narration about her motives to be a student starts from a sense of emptiness associated with inadequacy.

I felt empty inside... like something left over... in the meantime the years passed, the children grew up, and this empty space got bigger and bigger; and it produced a sense of inadequacy. I wanted to escape from home and doing something different...

She was inspired by a very special imagined social capital.

I also needed money, so I accepted any occasion to work... saleswoman, clerk, attendant in a hospital: psychiatric department. The contact with craziness pushed me to begin a new vocational process, searching for "the human world". I wanted to know why we move in a certain direction. Do we make our own decisions? I was 45!!! I didn't know, and actually I don't know by now, where the road is leading but I enjoy it. I left my job at the hospital, stopped cleaning bedpans and vomit, but I miss those foolish men and women.

Because I found the courage to start over thanks to them. I took my life in my hands and I gave it a new direction, with new colours and a lot of poetry.

Anna uses her imagined social capital when she is asked to find meaning for her choice of study at the university. The metaphors she uses express the way she embodies this meaning, in a very deep way.

I had a reverent fear of university, like something beautiful but I was unfit for, and then I was infected by craziness!

Foolish idea… my idea.

Building bridges

What do these stories tell to us? How can we interpret them to gain a better understanding of non-traditional students' experiences? All of these stories build bridges: between past and present, between different people, and between different experiences. They all have in common a movement from difficulty to discovery. The main discovery consists in making sense of the university experience and of living in it in a personal and meaningful way.

Using Varela's language, we may see a "structural coupling" between these students and the university: they talk about the "disturbance" brought into their lives and identities by this new environment. All of them are able to create a satisfying and coherent theory about it through auto/biographical narration. Their theories are also "good stories", useful for finding a new personal balance in the university experience. In building their theories, they use all sorts of materials: past experiences, imagined communities, a constellation of metaphors…

Also the body experience is quite relevant, as illustrated in the metaphors they use: the basic dimensions of space ("empty space", "huge mechanism", "university bubble") and time ("time to walk", "we get to our expiry date") appear to structure forms of embodied knowledge. The narration itself becomes, in turn, a series of messages to the body, in line with the emerging personal theory about "how I can live at the university".

Finally there is another level to consider. These stories were composed through imagination, self reflection and dialogues with other participants in the workshops; during these moments the "author" and his/her "product" were the centre of attention. Once the story was published on the website, it entered a "political space" where plurality and unpredictability play the main role (Arendt, 1958). Meaning spreads out in all directions, according to readers' assumptions; these processes allow individuals to create bridges with the experiences of others and use them in new ways. According to Arendt, "political space" is the sphere of freedom and action, where something new and unpredictable can happen.

References

Arendt, H. (1958). *The human condition*. Chicago: Chicago University Press.

Bateson, G. (1972). *Steps to an Ecology of Mind: collected essays in anthropology, psichiatry, evolution and epistemology*. Chicago: University of Chicago Press.

Bateson, G. (1979). *Mind and Nature: a Necessary Unit*. New York: Hampton Press.

Bourdieu, P. (1988). *Homo Academicus*. Cambridge: Polity Press.

Bourdieu, P. and Passeron, J.P. (1970). *La reproduction: éléments pour une théorie du système d'enseignemen. Paris*: Editions de Minuit.

Bowl, M. (2001). Experiencing the barriers: non-traditional students entering higher education *Research Papers In Education* 16, 141-160

Demetrio, D. (1996). *Raccontarsi. L'autobiografia come cura di sé*. Milano: Cortina.

Dominicé, P. (2000). *Learning from our Lives: Using Educational Biographies with Adults*. San Francisco: Jossey-Bass.

Field, J. (2005). *Social Capital and Lifelong Learning*. Bristol: The Policy Press.

Field, J. (2008). *Social Capital*. London: Routledge.

Foerster von, H. (1982). A Constructivist Epistemology. *Cahiers de la Fondation Archives Jean Piaget, 3,* 191-213.

Formenti, L. (a cura di) (2009). *Attraversare la cura. Relazioni, contesti e pratiche della scrittura di sé.* Gardolo (TN): Erickson.

Gergen, K. J. (1999). *An Invitation to Social Construction.* London: Sage.

Kovececs, Z. (2002). *Metaphor. A pratical introduction.* New York: Oxford University Press.

Lakoff, G. and Johnson, M. (1980). *Metaphors we live by.* Chicago: University of Chicago Press.

Lakoff, G. and Johnson, M. (1999). *Philosophy in the flesh.* New York: Basic Books.

Longden B. (2004). Interpreting Student Early Departure from Higher Education through the Lens of Cultural Capital. *Tertiary Education and Management,* 10, 121-138.

Longden, B. (2006). An Institutional Response to changing Student Expectations and their Impact on Retention Rates. *Journal of Higher Education Policy and Management,* 173-187.

Merrill, B. and West, L. (2009). *Using biographical methods in social research.* London: Sage.

Morin, E. (1995). *Introduction à la pensèe complexe.* Paris: Seuil.

Quinn, J. (2005). Belonging in a learning community: the re-imagined university and imagined social capital. *Studies in the Education of Adults,* 37 (1), 4-17.

Quinn, J. (2010). *Learning communities and imagined social capital: learning to belong.* London: Continuum International Publishing Group.

Thomas, L. (2002). Student retention in higher education: the role of institutional habitus. *Journal of Educational Policy 17,* 423-442.

Thomas, L. and Quinn, J. (2006) *First Generation Entrants into Higher Education: an international study.* Maidenhead, England: Society for Research into Higher Education and Open University Press.

Varela, F., Thompson, E. & Rosch, E. (1991) *The embodied mind. Cognitive Science and human experience.* Cambridge (USA): MIT Press.

West, L., Alheit P., Andersen, S. A. and Merrill B. (2007). *Using Biographical and Life History Approaches in the Study of Adult and Lifelong learning: European Perspectives.* Frankfurt-am-Main: Peter Lang.

Sites:

RANLHE Access and Retention: Experiences of Non-traditional Learners in Higher Education. Retrieved August 2, 2012, from http://www.dsw.edu.pl/fileadmin/www-ranlhe/documents.html

European Lifelong Learning Project 2009-2010 Access and Retention: Experiences of Non-traditional Learners in Higher Education. An overview of national statistics on retention and withdrawal. Retrieved August 2, 2012, from http://www.dsw.edu.pl/fileadmin/www-ranlhe/files/national_stat.pdf)

Storie della Bicocca, http://sites.google.com/site/storiedellabicocca

Literacy and the social environment: when the context sets the agenda for learning

◊   CHRISTOPHER PARSON AND SAMRA TABBAL AMELLA

Introduction

Our contribution proposes a reflection on the question of the supports and resources available to adult migrants seeking to improve their basic literacy skills. Our empirical material is taken from a biographical interview undertaken in the course of an on-going research project (Tabbal Amella), which aims to understand how adult migrants who have never attended formal schooling "enter into the world of written language"[1] for the first time as they engage in "French as a foreign language (FLE)" provision in Francophone Switzerland. The ultimate aim of this research is to identify the experiences that have helped people to find a "breakthrough" in terms of literacies learning as adults. Our approach is informed by the tradition of life histories in adult education, in an attempt to better understand the relationship between adults and the "world of the written language". These adults have not come into contact with reading or writing during their formative years and, as a consequence, find themselves "outside the world of written language" during their childhood:

An individual's practices can also be situated within his own story…
In these circumstances, it will be necessary to use an approach
based on life histories. Several aspects appear: on the one hand,
literacy is a resource that individuals mobilise in order to change
the course of their lives; on the other hand, literacy changes individuals, who find themselves in a contemporary world in which
literacy practices are changing. The literacy practices in which an
individual engages vary throughout the course of his or her life,
because they are the result of demands and of changing resources
as well as of the possibilities that he or she perceives in them and
the interest lent to them. (Barton & Hamilton, 2010: 52)

There has been little research into the question of how adults, who have
never received any formal schooling, engage with literacy, learn how to
read and write. This research project uses a methodological approach
proper to the field of adult education and learning in general and more
specifically to the field of life histories in adult learning.

After a brief presentation of the key issues addressed by the research
project from which our case study is taken, we will analyse the interview
with Thierno, an adult learner from (Equatorial) Guinea currently resident
in Switzerland. We will attempt to identify the supports on which he has
been able to rely and the resources he was able to mobilise in order to
develop his literacies learning. We will focus on the particular characteristics of the environment, of the social and cultural contexts in the various
countries through which he travelled. We will be trying to understand
the living conditions, the structural, economic and socio-cultural contexts in which Thierno has evolved. We will also identify the interactions
that have contributed to the development of his learning in the field of
literacy (reading and writing), even though he was never able to rely on
the support of any formal schooling, as defined in the West. Finally, we
will be asking ourselves how adults that have been characterised in terms
of their weak levels of human agency (*agir faible*) (Soulet, 2010) manage
to improve their ability to act when it comes to engaging with learning.

Brief overview of the research project

In our research we have been looking at the question of literacy/illiteracy[2] amongst adults particularly in reference to the field of "language training in the context of economic integration" (Bretegnier, 2007, 2011; Etienne, 2008; Adami, 2009; Leclercq, 2011; Adami & Leclercq, 2012), which is expanding rapidly in the context of European Francophone academic interest, and within which the use of *biographical research* is an observed trend (Molinié, 2006; Bretenier, 2009). A life history narrative, in as much as it represents a "place of reflexivity and a tool for introspection" (Gohard-Radekovic and Rachédi, 2009), is likely to *help us understand the relationship that a learner maintains with his literacies learning. We formulate the hypothesis that knowledge of the learner's life history allows us to interpret certain mechanisms of resistance to learning, proper to some learners, or on the contrary, the facility to learn that certain others display.* According to Adami (2008),

> immigrants evolve in a social, professional and relational context that we should be familiar with if we hope to understand the types of interactions in which they are most often involved. It is thus important to know where they live, where they work, what contacts they have with the indigenous population in order to ascertain in a more subtle way the socio-linguistic modalities of acquisition of a target language by means of verbal interactions. (p. 12)

Our research is rooted in the field of life histories in adult education (Dominicé, 1990; Pineau and Le Grand, 1996; Bertaux, 1997, 2005) as well as in contemporary (auto)biographical approaches (Baudouin, 2010; Demazière et Dubar, 2004). In spite of a certain number of observable convergences in technical strategies in the ways in which children and adults learn to read and write, our aim is to study the specificity of adult learning by exploring the question from a *biographical perspective* and by reconstructing *life trajectories*. We would like to highlight the *biographical* nature of this moment of entry into the world of written language by placing the focus on *what people say* about the way in which this process has unfolded *in the long term* ("in the course of a life"). We are seeking to understand what occurs in terms of the daily practices of the subjects we have interviewed, outside the purely "school" environment or any face-to-face learning situation. Our interest is therefore firmly directed towards the *marginal spaces* outside any formal institutionalised literacies learning/training context.

As far as methodology is concerned, we have opted for biographical interviews. These have been held with adults who are following post-alphabetisation courses and with whom we have made contact through the auspices of various voluntary sector providers (associations) in Geneva and Lausanne. By analysing these interviews, we seek to discover the social practices through which learners have been able to develop literacy skills outside formal learning/training institutions. The narratives produced by these adults allow us to focus attention on the life histories of these individuals, to learn something about their life conditions and their real, contextualised social practices.

In this chapter, we will be highlighting the social practices and interactions likely to aid Thierno, a 48 year-old man from Guinea, in his attempts to appropriate written language. His mother tongue is Fula and as a child, neither he nor any of his brothers and sisters received any formal education. At the age of 13, although he could neither read nor write, he started going to the local Koranic "school", which was run by a "wise old man" in his village. He learned to recognise, memorise and orally reproduce certain *surahs* of the Koran in classical Arabic. At the age of 15, he left Guinea for Senegal where he worked for his uncle, a businessman, for several years. He then moved to Ivory Coast in 1998 where he got a job with a friend who ran a tailor's shop. He learned how to sew and also to read a little in French. In the year 2000 he decided to migrate to Europe in search of work and a better life. After a first failed attempt in France, he settled in Portugal and then in Spain, where he worked as a bricklayer until 2009, then forced by the financial crisis to move to Switzerland. He again found work on building sites for several months, with intermittent periods of inactivity. He is now unemployed, and attending adult literacy courses at an adult learning centre in Switzerland. He now reads well in French, writes "phonetically" and with some difficulty.

A few theoretical elements

Literacy

The notion of *entering the written language* as defined by Fijalkow (1997) is the departure point for our analysis: "from an anthropological point of view, entering the written language, involves [...] the accomplishment by the subject of an *acculturation* process with regard to its linguistic and social practices, which differ considerably from those of oral language."(cited by Le Ferrec, 2008, p.103). Our intention here is to show the evolution of this process of acculturation, of the relationship developed by Thierno with written language, throughout his various successive migratory journeys. This acculturation, as well as representing a simple "object of learning", is always a reflection of a more pragmatic "intention": he learns to read and write "with a view to...". This process of acculturation is also linked to an injunction, usually dictated by the context itself. We shall see that these reasons for action are indeed directly dependent on the social and cultural norms in place in the environment through which he is moving. Thus, as Adami explains (2008),

> we should no doubt consider the question of adults' relationship to literacy in a less technical and more anthropological way, in other words by looking at aspects of decoding or access to meaning through verbal communication. For readers from a working-class background, the praxeological dimension of language is a determining factor and it is through this prism that they tend to view written language. (p.9)

In his work on literacy, Goody (1979) uses an autonomous model in which literacy is apprehended as "a collection of self-contained skills, that model the mind" (Fraenkel and Mbodj, 2010: 10). He considers literacy as a variable that can be studied through its technical aspects, independently of the social context. However, the distinction drawn by the school of *New Literacy Studies*, notably by Street (1984, 1995), Barton (1994) and Gee (1991), between the autonomous model of literacy and the ideological one seems pertinent here. The emergence of *New Literacy Studies* in the 1990's saw the development of a series of research projects using an ethnographical approach, based on the recognition and analysis of social practices in very diverse social and cultural contexts. This approach is in some ways a critical response to the *autonomous* model of literacy, and puts forward an *ideological* model, which envisages literacy as a set of "social practices" (Street, 1995; Barton and Hamilton, 2010). It allows us to apprehend the importance of structural changes in his environment, not only in terms of resources and supports, but also in terms of sense, of meanings – often contested – with which Thierno was confronted throughout his successive migrations.

Migration, bifurcations and learning

The question of entering the written language as it emerges from Thierno's life history narrative is characterised by the specific nature of his status as an immigrant seeking to integrate himself in a host country. Indeed, for Veillette and Gohard-Radenkovic (2012), "we cannot comprehend the situation of foreigners and the diversity of their paths "of integration through language" without re-contextualising them in a country [such as Switzerland] that represents a good deal of complexity" (p. 89). At the same time, for Gohard-Radenkovic and Murphy-Lejeune (2008), it is equally important to apprehend the paths of mobility from the country of origin to which they belong. The authors propose a re-reading of the experience of geographical mobility in terms of "starting capitals" and "mobilised resources", in which the analysis of migratory paths reveals the development of strategies and intercultural competences as well as new linguistic capitals, which denote a transformation of the "mobility capital" (Murphy-Lejeune, 2003) of migrants. Migration can then be presented as an opportunity for developing an individual's *agency*. The rupture caused by Thierno's geographical displacement to a new social, cultural or linguistic context, plunges him into an environment where, according to Soulet (2010), "the normal conditions for action are absent" (p. 277), where the individual finds himself in a state of "latency" that he qualifies as "weak agency" (*op. cit.*), that is, in a context where he is obliged to "act in a *structural situation of* vulnerability" (*op. cit.*) and of "uncertainty". But how does a weak form of agency then acquire the "capacity to transform the situation" (*op. cit.*, p. 281), and become "*poietic agency*" (*op. cit.*, p. 282)?

The recourse to a narrative, resulting from a biographical interview, allows us to refer to Thierno's life course and thus to analyse his long-term *trajectory*. Through the reconstruction of the course of his life, together with his geographical movements, it is possible to apprehend the evolution of his literacy-learning path. We will see by following his path as a migrant that Thierno's lack of formal schooling has varying consequences depending on the expectations and demands of different societies towards this immigrant.

Thierno's journey: geographical mobility and the construction of language skills

For Thierno, the development of his literacy-learning evolves systematically throughout his successive migrations. As he moves from one country to another, he integrates social spaces in which he creates interactions with the native population. In order to become integrated in these new spaces, he develops a particular kind of aptitude, a specific linguistic skill (oral and written comprehension, oral and/or written expression), which he needs to progress in that environment. Throughout his life course, learning oral and written French is deconstructed into various component skills that he must master if he wants to succeed in his social and employment integration, in the contexts in which he finds himself. The type of skill developed is not directly dependent on an intentional choice made by Thierno, rather his learning progresses as a consequence of "pressures" exercised by the host society and by the status that he occupies, and subsequently from the needs that are generated by this context. In other words, the successive stages of Thierno's migratory journey confront him with different environments and ever-changing conditions of access to adult education in general and to literacy-learning in particular. It is thus possible to identify in his narrative an evolution in his rapport with written language in relation to his geographical mobility. His mobility systematically results in him being in contact with a network of people, thanks to whom opportunities for learning to read and/or write present themselves.

In order to illustrate our proposal, let us take a look at the interview with Thierno and follow the course of his geographical mobility, focussing on the following aspects: structural contexts; employment; forms of education; relationship to language(s) and to literacy; linguistic aptitudes developed; figures of "educators" playing a significant role in his learning oral and written language. We will identify the supports on which he could rely in order to engage with literacies at each stage of his migration, and also the resources that he was able to mobilise in order to facilitate learning. Let us now travel with Thierno from Guinea all the way to Switzerland.

(I) Guinea

During his childhood, just like many children in rural areas of Guinea, Thierno did not attend school. In the social and economic context in which he grew up, working in the fields was more important. Not going to school, during this period of his life course, represented the "norm":

> I never went to school when I was young. [...] Because at the time, my parents said to me, right, you have to go and work in the fields, go and cultivate the manioc, that sort of thing, you know. [...] So I didn't go to school, but you know, me, my country was colonised

by France. So me, in my country, they speak French there. Only I didn't go to school. And I didn't used to go visiting the town either. Me, I'm a villager, you know, I lived in the country, and that's the only place I stayed. (Thierno)

With regard to the population that interests us here, the definitions of literacy that we have referred to above do not reflect the totality of situations in which adult learners may find themselves. The criterion of schooled/not-schooled is difficult to define: in some cases. People may have attended school sporadically, have learned to read and write informally (with family members), or have attended Koranic school (Adami, 2009). This was Thierno's case, for at the age of 13 he went to the village Koranic school, run by a local "wise old man":

I'm a Muslim, we have to learn to read the Koran, that's an obligation. So we did it, our parents made us do it. I did that. [...] We used to live in this village, because we are village people, and over there, there wasn't much, we didn't have much in the way of means. So, we just learned there. Well, it wasn't much but we had this wise old man who lived in the village there, and he was our teacher. (Thierno)

The Koranic school, such as it was instituted in West Africa and Sub-Saharan Africa, whilst bearing some of characteristics of traditional "banking education" as described by Paulo Freire (1970), provides access to a form of schooling for all children, even though the region is extremely poor. Akkari (2004) defines the Koranic school by identifying six core characteristics: *openness* (access for all Muslims without discrimination with regard to age, intellectual standards or physical integrity); *ritualisation* (use of rote learning and mobilisation of the body through the rhythm of the voice); *permanence* (in time and in different geographical zones throughout the world); *malleability* (optimal combination of oral and written language, in resonance with the cultures of oral and written traditions); *resistance* (in spite of the dominance of the colonial model of education); *diversity* of the curriculum, of goals, of space and of temporality (organisational modes). Thus, for Akkari, "the opening up of the Koranic school to all social groups and to all cultures makes this an institution of "basic teaching" available to all and by definition egalitarian" (*op. cit.*, p. 184). The Koranic school is often the only access available to a form – albeit somewhat limited – of literacy. Although the pedagogical methods used rely on memorisation and repetition, in terms of linguistic skills, Thierno was able to develop some degree of comprehension and oral expression in classical Arabic, the language of the Koran.

(II) Senegal

Thierno left Guinea at the age of 15 or 16 in order to stay with an uncle who "did a bit of business". He explained to us that he was "obliged to stick by him, in order to do at least a little bit of business, to be able to make a living". He speaks of a "difficult" period. In Senegal, mastering spoken French was not high on his list of priorities. He found himself in a context where there was no pressure on him to learn how to speak French or to read and write:

> At that time, well, I didn't know how to read or write. I still don't know how to. [...] At that particular moment, that's why, if I'd said to myself that I should speak French or learn to read and write in French as well, I could have done it. But at that time, I didn't have this idea. [...] Me, personally, I never went and studied in Senegal because, you know, first of all, it just didn't occur to me to do it. No one else told me to either. And so, I didn't go, I didn't have any opportunity to do it. (Thierno)

On the other hand, he completely immersed himself in "Wolof culture", to such an extent that native speakers were unable to detect his Guinean accent. The manner in which Thierno blends into the Senegalese population, thanks to his mastering of the Wolof language, has been theorised in the work of Véronique (1984), looking at the way in which second languages are acquired by migrants, contrasting the acquisition in a *natural milieu* as opposed to acquisition in a *guided milieu*. Véronique has shown that the process of linguistic acculturation amongst immigrant groups takes place in the majority of cases in the *natural milieu*, in everyday contact with native speakers, in a context in which the languages spoken by the immigrants are put under pressure by the *dominant* languages (Adami, 2009: 34). As explained by Adami (2008), the more frequent the contacts with native speakers, the faster and more easily they progress. From this point, interactions in the natural milieu become the privileged form of acquisition of the target language by immigrants. Thus, in this situation of immersion, "learning and communication blend into each other" (*op. cit.*, p. 13):

I learned the language. If you'd heard me speaking the language, you'd have taken me for a Senegalese. But I'm not Senegalese. I just speak their language very well. And that's why, when a Senegalese sees me, when we say hello, he'll say to me "But my brother, where are you from?" When I tell him that I'm from Guinea, he'll say "no, that's not possible, me, I know lots of Guineans, but when they speak Wolof, when they talk, if you listen to their accent, you can tell they are from... Guinea..." And so we didn't speak any other languages. Let's say we just spoke Wolof. (Thierno)

The passage above confirms that "migrants learn *by* communicating whereas learners [enrolled in language courses in a formal, institutionalised setting, in other words, in guided learning situations] learn *to* communicate" (Véronique, 1984, quoted by Adami, 2009: 37). In this case we can understand that for Thierno, as for many migrants, "the acquisition of the target language is not an end in itself, but a means to integration." (Adami, 2009: 38).

In terms of supports, Thierno tells us two things regarding learning to read and write in Senegal: "It just didn't occur to me to do it" and "No one else told me to either". To understand how adults characterised by weak forms of agency mobilize their potential for action, let us refer to the characteristics of "*poietic* agency." Soulet defines this as "an individuated capacity to act, *i.e.* marked by forms of action undertaken by an individual, whose sense is given by the individual himself and whose object is both himself and the framework in which he takes action" (2010: 283-284). In this sense, it is "an intertwining of the biographical and the structural" (p. 284), that is, a combination of "individual resources" generated by his experiential capital and of "structural constraints" in terms of "social structure" and/or contexts of interaction (*op. cit.*, p. 285). The reasons invoked by Thierno for not having learned French do indeed find their source in both a personal dimension ("It just didn't occur to *me* to do it") and in a social or contextual dimension in so far as he did not feel pressured or constrained to start learning, either by a third party or by his environment ("*No one else* told me to either"). For Thierno, at that particular moment in time, the conditions for "individuated agency", in other words, "*a social fabrication in the situation,* which requires the presence and the support of differentiated social environments" (*op. cit.*) were not in place.

(III) Ivory Coast

On arrival in the Ivory Coast, Thierno's perception of norms in schooling and adult literacy change: high levels of literacy seem to be generalised throughout the country[3]. In this new context, the fact that he hasn't been to school is experienced as a failure, a shortcoming. Thierno suddenly sees himself as different, feeling marginalised in comparison with the indigenous population:

> In 1986, my adventures led me to Ivory Coast. And at that time, I didn't know how to read, nor write, in French. [...] The Ivorians don't speak any other language than French. And if you can't speak French, too bad for you, it's up to you to find a solution. [...] In Ivory Coast, you can go to a village, even one that's right out in the bush, but even out there, you're going to find colleges. [...] I mean

there isn't a single Ivorian that speaks French badly. All the people in Ivory Coast speak good French and they've been to school. They go to school when they are three, until… And it's you that decides if you are going to drop out. There isn't a single Ivorian who hasn't reached tenth grade or final year. Before dropping out. Every single Ivorian. That's what I saw. (Thierno)

On arrival in Ivory Coast, Thierno experiences a *bifurcation,* as defined by Soulet: "a context in which the rules of the game are no longer clear and the social norms no longer coherent" (2010: 281). He finds himself in an unfamiliar, distal space, in which he is unable to call upon the habitual modes of functioning developed in Senegal, where poor literacy skills were not a significant handicap. Baudouin (2010) has characterised the nature of this kind of rupture as *exotopic*: leaving an environment in which he was familiar with social and cultural norms creates a new, problematic situation for Thierno. On the one hand, the rupture "produces unpredictability and uncertainty [and] on the other hand, the resources available up till that point are no longer pertinent in the present situation; they become inadequate in relation to the new context" (Soulet, *op. cit.*). The fact that he had never attended formal schooling, which had not in itself been a problem in Guinea or in Senegal, becomes a handicap in Ivory Coast. The advantages of schooling now take on new meaning and pertinence given the (perceived) facility of access to primary education in the Ivorian context: poor French language and literacy skills now form a barrier to communication and an obstacle to integration in *this* society that needs to be removed. In this respect, Barton and Hamilton (2010) remind us that literacy practices must adapt to changing circumstances and that subjects must demonstrate a capacity for adaptation in order to face up to such changes:

There can be no doubt that literacy practices are not static, and the fact of constantly having to adapt to changes introduces a good deal of complexity. All particular change is linked to broader social practices and this leads to a certain number of contradictory tendencies, making certain activities more difficult, whereas others may be simplified. In some ways, these changes erode the literacy practices that bind communities together and render previous practices obsolete. Seen from another angle, these changes offer an occasion to reshape and reinforce the power of literacy in the life of the community. New demands constantly modify the role that these literacy practices play in the organisation and control of their lives by individuals. As a result, changes are brought about in the complex balance of relationships and resources, of expertise and the need for support. (p. 61)

Thierno's narrative also highlights an aspect of language amongst migrants that Adami (2009) considers to be typical. Their primary concerns are not related to education or language learning. They appear to give relatively little importance to language in terms of form or structure. Lahire (1998) has shown that indeed for most working class families, language is not an object that exists by itself, for itself, rather language is for them a means to action and is apprehended essentially in terms of its *praxeological* dimension. For Thierno, it is quite clear that becoming a more competent reader is a priority for him if he wants to be able to interact with the native population and have any chance of achieving social and economic integration in Ivory Coast:

> The most important thing at the time for me was that I wanted to learn to read first. At least like that, I could communicate with people in the cities. Because in Ivory Coast, there's no other language spoken in the towns, only French. So if you haven't mastered French, it would be very difficult to live in that country. At the very least, even if you can't write it but only speak the language, and if you can recognise your name when you see it written down, at least, even if you aren't very quick, but you know how to get by, recognising your name… yes, yes, that's my name written there. Or maybe it's "Henri" that's written here, and so, you know that. And so I managed to muddle through. (Thierno)

In Ivory Coast, the friend who taught him to read in French – and at the same time to *speak* French – comprised the support that he needed in order to at last realise his potential for action as an adult learner.

(IV) Portugal and Spain

Thierno manages to systematically establish a network of peers in order to "find a job", *leitmotiv* of his numerous geographical relocations. A "job" constitutes a resource that allows him to find his feet as he moves from one country to another:

> Well, you know, I came to Europe in the year 2000. But it was also work that brought me here… that got me on the move again. [I was working] as a bricklayer, on building sites. Well, in Paris I never worked there, because … the months that I spent there, well, I didn't manage to find any work. And so I left, I went to Portugal, that's where I found little jobs and that's where I settled down. [...] Some firms took me on in Portugal and then they sent me to Spain. So I did that a few times as well. Anyway, when the financial crisis hit in 2008, I left Portugal. Towards the end of 2008, I came to Spain, and I stayed there for a while. But I could see that it was the same situation, almost exactly the same crisis in Spain as in Lisbon. That was no good. And I've got a family, so I had to keep going forwards, because anyway, we're in Europe. And so that's what pushed me into coming here to Switzerland, in 2008. (Thierno)

The various encounters that occurred during Thierno's journey can be seen as a series of supports that allowed him systematically to come to terms with the structural context. When this did not happen, he would move on and migrate to another geographical location hoping to meet a new friend, or establish another special relationship, which would help him to rebuild his life in this new context.

(V) Switzerland

On his arrival in Switzerland, Thierno is rapidly able to count on different institutional and interactional supports:

> And so I arrived here. OK. When I got here, I was lucky. I arrived around the month of July, I'm not sure if it was the 26th or 27th July. When I first arrived, it was difficult. I had nowhere to sleep. There were lots of things I needed when I arrived; I came with very little money. I slept at the Salvation Army hostel. When I got here, on the 29th, just after, I saw a friend. He was here. He hasn't got a job either. He was looking for a job. Then an agency called. He said to me "Right, listen, you've just arrived, first of all you don't know [the town], today is your first day here, so I'll go with you". They'd called me to offer me a contract. (Thierno)

His wife, who had been through school and passed her baccalaureate, also plays a support role:

> Sometimes she came herself [to help me do] my homework and the exercises I get here [at the adult literacy centre], when I go home, she helps me with them [...] Well, if I get homework and I have problems, I mean even like how to use a computer, she guides me. [...] These are things I never had time to learn. Not even how to use a computer. [...] Thanks to her, I'm learning a bit now. (Thierno)

Thierno's trajectory also allows us to see how, as his narrative progresses, the kind of learning with which he engages has evolved. For Barton and Hamilton (2010), "it clearly emerges that literacy takes on distinctly different forms according to the context" (p. 48). This is just what we have identified in Thierno's account. His arrival in Switzerland and his enrolment in literacy training at an adult literacy centre represent his first engagement with any kind of "formal" education, in the sense of institutionalised education, structured according to a chronological order and with a specific curriculum in which the rôle of the trainer/educator is clearly defined.

> The postulate of the constructed nature of literacy implies that any theory of literacy goes hand in hand with theories of learning. Literacy practices change, and new practices are frequently acquired by means of informal learning processes and the fabrication of meaning, as well as through classic forms of education and training. This learning takes place in specific social contexts and part of this learning involves the incorporation of social processes. (Barton and Hamilton, 2010: 52-53)

Enrolling in courses to learn how to read and write in French in Switzerland also involves learning about how the system functions on the social, institutional and judicial levels:

> I'm looking for a job now. [...] Even if I find work, I'll have to, that's what the unemployment office told me, if I find a job, I'll have to stop [the courses] and go to work. (Thierno)

Accessing literacy training, as Thierno discovers in the context of Geneva, places him in a position in which he feels trapped between a desire to emancipate himself and integrate (by learning to read and write in French), and a sense of constraint and alienation (accepting whatever job the cantonal employment office (OCE), which is responsible for paying unemployment benefit, decides to allocate him). Thus, engaging in language training as an adult means being caught between political, institutional and economic requirements, and issues or stakes linked to the development of his "biographical power". Again, we see that conditions of access to education and training are dictated by the context. If the OCE plays a significant role in terms of financial resources and access to training (it is the institutional structure that finances his adult literacy courses), the other side of the coin reveals that such antagonistic pressure can bring a swift halt to Thierno's engagement in literacy training. Indeed, he finds himself confronted by a triple discourse with regard to his presence in the literacy courses: the discourse of encouragement produced by his teacher in her role of educator accompanying him on his learning journey (learning stakes); the double discourse of the OCE linked on the one hand to its function as controlling and sanctioning organ (economic stakes) and, on the other hand, to its role of (re)integration, which, whilst it exercises strong pressure on Thierno to make sure he attends his courses, is likely to force him to abandon them as soon as a job that fits his profile becomes available (economic and social stakes).

Synthesis and conclusion

Our analysis of the interview with Thierno has made it possible to identify a certain number of "supports" and "resources", which we can synthesize here by posing the following questions in the manner of Martuccelli (2006: 327): How does Thierno manage to cope in his life? What are the supports he can count on and what resources can he call upon in order to develop his agency? How does a person characterised by various forms of "weak agency" (Soulet, 2010) manage to mobilise his power of action to serve his learning needs or, in other terms, how can he "(re)construct the conditions for potential action in the world" (*op. cit.*, p. 284)? Here, then, is what we have been able to conclude from this interview:

(I)   Thierno is dependent on the context in which he finds himself at any given time; as the context changes, the availability of supports and resources varies; unequal degrees of access to these supports affect possibilities for developing his human agency;

(II)   Thierno was able to build special relationships with third parties, and thanks to these he was able to progress in learning to read and write;

(III)   As demonstrated by work in the field of *New Literacy Studies*, social practices linked to literacy change through time and space; they allow the development of a type of specific linguistic competences or aptitudes in relation to the supports made available by the context, and in relation to the needs and expectations of the local environment;

(IV)   The mobilisation of his capacity for action is linked to the availability of various supports (a friend, for example…), that allow him to mobilise other resources (…which put him in touch with his social/employment network thanks to which he manages to find work…) and which ultimately integrate the person in a new context conducive to learning (…and which create opportunities for multiplying interactions with native speakers and developing his linguistic capacities);

(V)   Support found in the structural elements of the environment combine with individual resources generated by experiential capital, which are themselves forged by constraints inherent to the structure of the environment.

Following Thierno's progress throughout his narrative has allowed us to identify the evolution of his relationship to literacy. "The interweaving of the biographical and the structural" that Soulet refers to as *poietic* agency also contributes to the construction of what Murphy-Lejeune calls "mobility capital". At the end of his narrative, we find ourselves in the Swiss (Geneva) context in which engaging in learning becomes a new field of tension that leads us to pose a series of ethical questions concerning the posture of the learner: What is he learning for? For whom is he learning? Who is directing his learning process/journey? What values can he attribute to his learning/training in such circumstances? However, these questions open a new area of debate that we have pursued elsewhere, notably in a paper about a series of ethical questions posed by basic adult education and training (Parson and Tabbal Amella, 2012).

Notes

1   The term in French here is *"entrer dans l'écrit"* which evokes the image of a person who has never engaged with literacy in any formal way crossing the "border" into the world of reading and writing, traversing frontiers of understanding/incomprehension, access to knowledge etc. All translations from the French are by the author (Chris Parson).

2   In French: «*en situation d'analphabétisme*». In English we tend to refer to *literacy* as an ensemble of skills, events and practices relating to written language (Street, Barton), whereas in francophone countries *illiteracy* has been apprehended as a state in which adults find themselves and which must be combated, eradicated etc by educational and political action.

3   According to UNICEF, total adult literacy rate in Ivory Coast for the period 2005-2010 was 55%. Secondary school participation (net attendance ratio) for the same period was 32% for males, 22% for females.

References

Adami, H. (2008). Tests de sécurité pour salariés en insécurité à l'écrit: stratégies de lecture en contexte professionnel. In *Transformations, 1*, 107-120.

Adami, H. (2009). *La formation linguistique des migrants*. Paris: CLE International.

Adami, H. (2011). Parcours migratoires et intégration langagière. In J.M. Mangiante (Ed), *L'intégration et la formation linguistique des migrants: état des lieux et perspectives* (pp. 37-54). Arras: Artois Presses Université.

Adami, H. & Leclercq, V. (Ed.) (2012). *Les migrants face aux langues des pays d'accueil. Acquisition en milieu naturel et formation*. Villeneuve d'Ascq: Editions du Septentrion.

Akkari, A. (2004). Vers une anthropologie de l'école coranique. In A. Akkari and P. R. Dasen (Ed.), *Pédagogues et pédagogies du sud* (pp. 183-205). Paris: L'Harmattan.

Barton, D. (1994) *Literacy: an introduction to the ecology of written language*. Blackwell: Oxford

Barton, D. & Hamilton, M. (2010). La littératie: une pratique sociale. *Langage et société, 133(3), 45-62.*

Baudouin, J.-M. (2010). *De l'épreuve autobiographique*. Berne: Peter Lang.

Bertaux, D. (1997). *Les récits de vie*. Paris: Nathan.

Bertaux, D. (2005). *L'enquête et ses méthodes: Le récit de vie*. Paris: Armand Colin.

Bretegnier, A. (2007). Langues et insertions. Recherches, interventions, réflexivité. Paris: L'Harmattan.

Bretenier, A. (2009). Histoires de langues en formation. Construire une démarche de recherche-intervention alter-réflexive». In M. Molinié & E. Huver (coord.), *Praticiens-chercheurs à l'écoute du sujet plurilingue. Réflexivité et interaction biographique en sociolinguistique et en didactique*. CAS n°4, LESCLaP, Université Picardie Jules Verne.

Bretegnier, A. (dir.) (2011). *Formation linguistique en contextes d'insertion. Compétences, posture, professionnalité: concevoir un cadre de référence*. Berne: Peter Lang.

Demazière, D. and Dubar, C. (2004). *Analyser les entretiens biographiques. L'exemple des récits d'insertion*. Québec: Les presses de l'Université Laval.

Dominicé, P. (1990). *L'histoire de vie comme processus de formation*. Paris: L'Harmattan.

Etienne, S. (2008). Compétence linguistique et alphabétisation des migrants, quelles approches? *Cahier de l'Observatoire des pratiques linguistiques, 2*. Migrations et plurilinguisme en France (pp. 25-31). Paris: Editions DIDIER.

Fijalkow, J. (1997). Entrer dans l'écrit: oui, mais par quelle porte? *Repères, 15*, 113-129.

Fraenkel, B. and Mbodj, A. (2010). Introduction. Les *New Literacy studies*, jalons historiques et perspectives actuelles. *Langage & Société, 133*, 7-24.

Freire, P. (1970). *Pedagogy of the Oppressed*. New York: Continuum.

Gee, J. P. (1991). *Social Linguistics: Ideology in Discourses*. Falmer Press: London.

Gohard-Radenkovic, A. et Murphy-Lejeune (2008). Mobilités et parcours. In G. Zarate, D. Lévy et C. Kramsch (dir.). *Précis de plurilinguisme et du pluriculturalisme* (pp. 127-134). Paris: Editions des archives contemporaines.

Gohard-Radenkovic, A. and Rachedi, L. (2009). *Récits de vie, récits de langue et mobilité*. Paris: L'Harmattan.

Goody, J. (1994). *Entre l'oralité et l'écriture*. Paris: PUF.

Lahire, B. (1998). *Tableaux de famille. Heurs et malheurs scolaires en milieux populaires.* Paris: Gallimard.

Leclercq, V. (2011). La formation linguistique des migrants: lignes de force en didactique. In J.M. Mangiante (Ed), *L'intégration et la formation linguistique des migrants: état des lieux et perspectives* (pp. 19-35). Arras: Artois Presses Université.

Le Ferrec, L. (2008). Littératie, relation à la culture scolaire et didactique de la lecture-écriture en français langue seconde. In J.-L. Chiss (Dir.), *Immigration, Ecole et didactique du français* (pp. 101-144). Paris: Didier.

Martuccelli, D. (2006). *Forgé par l'épreuve. L'individu dans la France contemporaine.* Paris: A. Colin.

Molinié, M. (Eds) (2006). Biographie langagière et apprentissage plurilingue. *Le Français dans le monde/Recherches et applications, 39.*

Murphy-Lejeune (2003). L'étudiant européen voyageur, un nouvel étranger. Paris: Didier.

Parson, C. and Tabbal Amella, S. (2012). *Éthique et formation de base: entre réciprocité et contradictions… exigences et découragements…* Communication, Colloque «Formes d'éducation et processus d'émancipation», Université de Rennes 2, 22-24 mai 2012.

Pineau, G. and Le Grand, J.-L. (1993). *Les histoires de vie.* Que Sais-je? Paris: PUF

Soulet, M.-H. (2010). Changer de vie, devenir autre: essai de formalisation des processus engagés. In M. Bessin, M. Bidart and M. Grossetti, M. (2010). (Ed.). *Bifurcations, Les sciences sociales face aux ruptures et à l'événement* (pp. 273-288). Paris: La Découverte.

Street, B. (1984). *Literacy in Theory and Practice.* Cambridge: CUP.

Street, B. (1995). *Social Literacies.* Longman: London.

Veillette, J. and Gohard-Radenkovic, A. (2012). Parcours d'intégration d'étrangers en milieux plurilingues: le cas du Canton de Fribourg (Suisse). In H. Adami & V. Leclercq (Eds), *Les migrants face aux langues des pays d'accueil. Acquisition en milieu naturel et formation* (pp. 89-133). Villeneuve d'Ascq: Editions du Septentrion.

Véronique, D. (1984). Apprentissage naturel et apprentissage guidé. *Le Français dans le monde, 185,* 45-52.

Chapter 10

Narrative learning for non-traditional students: a model for intervention in higher education[1]

◊   MARIA FRANCESCA FREDA, GIOVANNA ESPOSITO, MARIA LUISA MARTINO,
JOSÉ GONZÁLEZ-MONTEAGUDO

Introduction

This chapter will discuss the use of a narrative device, based on four narrative codes, in supporting and improving learning for non-traditional students at university. We will discuss a European research project, IN-STALL, which is researching an innovative methodology, the Narrative Mediation Path (NMP), based on the use of narration. The project has a two-fold purpose: on the one hand it fosters the acquisition of a Key Competence, 'Learning to Learn', which is central to the improvement of students' academic performance; on the other, the project seeks to evaluate the narrative methodology designed specifically to develop that competence. We will focus here on the theoretical bases of the methodology used, and will illuminate this with reference to a pilot project undertaken with a group of non-traditional students at Federico II University, Naples.

Narrative and Biographical Methods in Teaching and Learning

The use of auto/biographical narratives clearly has a place in both research and training. As a research instrument, written narratives offer first-hand biographical material covering the individual's recent history as well as social, cultural, family and educational experiences. This subjective perspective fosters an experiential approach to historical and socio-cultural issues. It could be argued that the creation of life stories is important in the development of motivational learning contexts; focusing on the lives of students and oriented towards the achievement of a level of education that integrates cognitive, emotional and social aspects.

Experiential learning, and sharing with others, provides a basis for learning and change. Through learning the learner symbolically travels from dependence to autonomy, from passivity to activity, from selfishness to altruism, from self-rejection to self-acceptance, from imitation to originality, from narrow to broader interests (Fraser, 1995). From here it is suggested that the sharing of autobiographical writing and personal accounts in small groups can promote personal understanding as participants reflect on their lives in an informal atmosphere of free exchange. In contrast, education has often been seen, traditionally, as mere instruction and the transmission of a set body of knowledge. While more recent times have seen important changes in the social context, educational policies and the development of pedagogical methods which have challenged this approach, it is still the case that education is generally viewed, as noted throughout this book, as primarily a rationalistic and cognitive process neglecting the affective, emotional and interpersonal dimensions. Naranjo (2004) maintains that this stance is congruent with the patriarchal system, based on authority, hierarchy and rationalism.

However, this is not the end of the story: new ideas have developed to challenge the traditional and conventional models of educational practice. Concepts such as interpersonal and intrapersonal intelligence, emotional intelligence, emotional education and emotional literacy, conceived in the eighties and made popular in the nineties, have at least raised some opposition and critical interrogation. According to Steiner (2003, p. 34), "emotional education consists of three skills: the skill to understand emotions, the skill to express them in a fruitful way, and the skill to listen to everybody and to feel empathy in relation to their emotions". Furthermore, self-understanding implies, among other things, "an activity of reminiscence, which involves a contact, through remembering, with the past experience; this retrospective clarification is stimulated by the written and oral expression" (Naranjo, 2004: 185).

Autobiographical learning, we would argue, can be a most effective instrument for emotional and interpersonal education because it can be helpful for working with the past, by processing conflicts and crisis. Narrative methods can help us to work in depth around the personal and family worlds of the students, integrating and creating skills in the cognitive, operative, and affective dimensions. Working with spoken and written personal narratives improves self-knowledge, allowing a more mature approach to be taken to problems, difficulties, crises and interpersonal relationships. The exploration of personal, educational and social journeys is an important way to work on issues around personal identity.

In this chapter we will focus on narrative learning (Biesta et al., 2011; Dominicé, 2000), examining a model of intervention designed for Non Traditional Students (NTS) in higher education. This model of narrative learning will be thoroughly tested and validated in the European funded project INSTALL (Innovative Solutions to Acquire Learning to Learn), to be developed in a partnership between Italy (the lead partner), Romania, Denmark, Ireland, and Spain. The aim of INSTALL is to foster the acquisition of the key competence described as Learning to Learn, by developing and implementing a group training process that utilizes an innovative methodology, the Narrative Mediation Path (NMP), developed for Non Traditional university students.

Disadvantaged Students and Non Traditional Learners: The Challenges of Inclusion in European Higher Education

The definition of disadvantaged students often includes those belonging to a disadvantaged part of society; migrants, students from migrant households, women, working students and disabled students. It is common to include this category of students in the wider typology of those who are defined as "non traditional learners" (Council Conclusions on Social Dimension of Education and Training, 2010/C 135/02). These students, besides their disadvantage, may wrestle with several other issues such as, for instance, starting their studies later than the norm, or being first-generation students enrolled on a full-time basis (Eileen, 1997; Miller and Lu, 2003). Despite the differences, the two separate conditions of 'disadvantage' and 'non – traditional' students, share some similarities (Merrill and González-Monteagudo, 2010). Moreover, in both categories, students are exposed to the risk of achieving their goals at a later stage in their university career, facing, as a consequence, the risk of dropping out (Metzner and Bean, 1987; Choy, 2002). Bearing in mind how the two categories overlap, our work is concerned with the wider typology of Non Traditional Students.

In general, we take the view that Non Traditional Students are more at risk of dropping out of their studies and/or of poor academic performance because of their disadvantaged socio-cultural backgrounds, which have made their academic development and integration into university life more problematic (see also West and Galimberti, this volume). The need to deal with their disadvantage leads them to take longer in the achievement of their university goals and, sometimes, as a consequence, to abandon their studies. INSTALL aims to reduce the risk of such drop-out by designing narrative training paths with the purpose of promoting the Key Competence of Learning to Learn (L2L), to help them to improve their University performances. INSTALL targets the Non Traditional Student group during their crucial transition from the first to the second year of the university course of study, the time when they are most vulnerable to

216

dropping out: in Italy for example, 17 to 20% of drop out occurs in the transition from the first to the second year of university.

The research carried out by partners, in the INSTALL project, shows that these students experience low academic achievement in the first academic year, which affects their entire academic experience, and ultimately can put them at risk of drop-out. This is extremely important as, reportedly, 20 to 45% of European students are non-traditional learners (Eurostudent III 2005-08, Social & Economic Conditions of Student Life in EU, Higher Education Information System). This is confirmed by the results of the research carried out by partners: approximately 25 to 35% of their respective academic populations comprise underachievers exposed, potentially, in various degrees, to long term patterns of social and educational exclusion.

We move now to the theoretical bases and narrative methodology developed in the project; we will outline the modality through which the narrative device has been applied, by describing a pilot-study carried out with a group of students who were struggling to meet deadlines and gain appropriate academic achievement.

The Theoretical Framework of the INSTALL Project: The Key Role of Narration and Mentalization

As stated above, the INSTALL project is concerned with fostering the acquisition of the key competence of Learning to Learn; in a university context this includes being able to study, as well as knowing how to study. Importantly, it involves becoming aware of one's learning process and needs, which then helps with the identification of both the available resources, and of any obstacles which need to be overcome, in order to learn effectively. L2L key competence is, therefore, regarded as a reflective meta-competence, or rather a higher-order competence, which consists of becoming aware of what, how and why one knows. We want also to examine the concept of reflexive competence, in order to explain the modalities through which INSTALL seeks to develop this with non-traditional students struggling with their studies.

The terms 'reflexivity' and 'reflection' share the same Latin root that refers to the verb "re-flectere" (double bending), indicating the activity and the mental process which enables a thinking subject to attain self-knowledge. Reflection is commonly referred to as an important step on the journey to reflexivity, because through reflection the subject can recognize himself/herself as a subjective source of meaning making (Freda, De Luca Picione, Esposito, 2012, in press). Then, through reflexivity, the subject may become more aware of the relational and inter-subjective processes s/he is involved in and how this may shape experiences of self.

The INSTALL project is based on the assumption that, in order to develop the required competence for study, it is necessary to facilitate what can be described as a mentalization process, through a self-formative and development path. Mentalization, also known as reflexive competence, or reflexive function (Allen: Fonagy, 2008; Fonagy, 2002; Fonagy et al., 2009; Fonagy & Target, 1997; Meehan et al., 2009) is an imaginative ability that allows people to imagine and interpret their mental states (desires, thoughts, emotions, etc.) of themselves and others. From this standpoint mentalization is a significant process concerning one's own and others' behaviour, experienced by the subject within several inter-subjective contexts (Bateman and Fonagy, 2012). Essentially it is a social as well as a mental skill, necessary for the subject's effective adaptation to different contexts. University can be seen as one of those contexts in which the individual deals with stressful events and development tasks requiring functional and adaptive behaviours.

With regard to the two processes mentioned above, reflection and re-flexivity, we argue that, within the university context, mentalization is a process that aids the understanding of the reasons for one's own and others' behaviour (reflection); and to an understanding of how these determine the relationships in which the student is involved, and experiences of self (reflexivity). In effect, mentalization, is a method of approaching and understanding relationships. It is the ability to see the significance of the processes involved in relationships, and, in particular in this project, the role that s/he plays in determining the direction of relationships in the university context, which is important if the student is to re-position herself in more productive ways. (Freda: De Luca Picione, 2012). We believe that the student can engage in a reflexive way when, within the INSTALL framework, the group-facilitator uses a process-oriented approach, taking relationships with the overall educational setting as the focus of reflection. The intervention designed to develop mentalization involves working on the here-and–now of the group inter-subjective processes and relationships. It encourages the group to understand mental states and relational processes by making comparisons between the relationships experienced within the INSTALL group and the wider university (Karterud, 2011; Karterud and Bateman, 2012). Students then need to focus on the types of action/reaction evident in this comparison, in order to understand what was going on in relationships at different times, and to recognize the impact of the role s/he plays in determining the outcome/tenor of relationships in each context. The relationships and interactions in the training group are therefore used as resources for developing mentalization abilities.

The link is clearly made between here and now events/feelings and those experienced within the wider university. External/university events will always trigger feelings and reactions in the here and now of the group, and the group facilitator must be sensitive to this and move between these two contexts in a way that ensures a flow is retained in the group. Work in the group is based on the relationships between the group members and the wider inter-subjective relations within the university; and this is made possible by transference phenomena. According to the mentalizing approach, transference is not viewed in a classical psychodynamic sense (where transference phenomena can be interpreted in light of the past and conceptualised as associations with past episodes or people); the group facilitator uses a device called "mentalization of transference". Participants are encouraged to think about the interactions they are involved in, and they are also asked to focus on the other's 'mind' and to describe their own perception of themselves, and of the way they think they are perceived by the other members or by the group facilitator (Karterud and Bateman, 2012; Stokkebæk, 2011). Through this application of the transference, the student can be aware of the states of mind/attitudes/feelings at the heart of his/her own actions; and then, in light of the other members' points of view, can formulate a mindful account of how their relationships within the group reflect their relationships within the university.

We believe that paying attention to their own and to others' mental states facilitates the movement from reflection, understanding the reasons of their actions/feelings, towards enhanced reflexivity, leading to an understanding of the way the student relates to others, including the university. Essentially the main objectives are to promote a sense of an agentic self (Bateman and Fonagy, 2012) and to encourage a new configuration of the student's interactions within the University context, one more oriented to purposeful development and more effective in achieving academic goals.

Reflexive activity, although it is associated with, and included in, a meta-cognitive approach, often ascribes a fundamental role to emotion and to the need to name emotions in order to recognize and orient them, in an attempt to change dysfunctional behaviours. Therefore, the group facilitator using a mentalizing approach needs to focus on the affective dimension of educational relationships, in order to foster reflexive processes within the here-and-now of the educational intervention. Bateman and Fonagy (2012) coined the phrase "mentalized affectivity" to highlight the attention to such interconnected dimensions: it assumes that the action, functional and adaptive in any environment, depends on the ability to reflect on different mental states (cognitive and emotional) between which a close interrelation is assumed, for better but also, sometimes, worse.

In the project, narration – the invitation to build a formative life-story – is the medium chosen to foster mentalization processes. A number of theorists support the key role that narration plays in developing men-talization. It has a bi-directional and circular relationship with narration. Mentalization presents itself as a narration – whether spoken or writ-ten – insofar as the individual is constantly engaged in creating stories concerning his or her own and others' mental states. The process is also defined as "a psychological self-narrative" (Bateman and Fonagy, 2012); it is carried out through narration and narration can be generated in the interpersonal relationship through mentalization. People narrate their experiences in various styles depending on their ability to mentalize. For example, individuals using more fragmented and less coherent narrations, following a chronological time flow, have less ability to mentalize. Con-versely, those who produce coherent narratives, and use internal instead of chronological time, have better mentalizing competences. Narration, therefore, can be used as a promoter and at the same time an indicator of the efficacy of this kind of intervention (Allen and Fonagy, 2006). Narra-tion acts both as an activator and a promoter of mentalization when it is used in a continuous alternation between narrative and meta-narrative processes. This alternation promotes a transition from narrative sequences – describing the events – to reflective narrative sequences in which the subject uses narration to reflect about her own being, in the experience. This happens through the "narrative group" which activates and improves the potentialities of reflection inherent in the narration, such as the ability to address complex problems and to build knowledge through experience (Freda, 2008a; 2008b; 2011). A narrative group strengthens a student's ability to mentalize by harnessing the impact of the representation of an individual's mind, as seen by a number of people.

The group is therefore a crucial resource for fostering the narrative pro-cesses which enables the students to highlight the behaviors acted out within the here-and-now of the group, thus shedding light on the ones acted out within the wider university context. The narrative input, along with the resulting interrogation of both narrative and meta-narrative dy-namics, fosters processes of reflection and reflexivity. Narration becomes the object of reflection, enabling the subject to recognize herself in the group, to become aware of the self in action, to recognize and to process the representation she has of her-self.

The narrative methodology designed for the project makes use of different discursive codes, at different stages of the training path, pertaining to affective and emotional dimensions, and thus contributes to the students making better sense of the university experience. We will now describe how the individual codes alternate, at different levels and degrees, between what we term the analogical and the digital plan, as well as between affective and cognitive dimensions.

The INSTALL Methodology: The Narrative Mediation Path (NMP)

INSTALL uses an innovative methodology based on Narration, that is, the Narrative Mediation Path (NMP), with the aim of promoting the Learning to Learn Key Competence, by developing, as stated, mentalization competence. Specifically, NMP comprises a group intervention training process targeted at groups of nontraditional students, who have fallen behind with their examinations. They are enrolled in the second year of University and have made an explicit request to participate in the light of their difficulties.

NMP is implemented through a cycle of six meetings conducted by Narrative Group Trainers (NGTs) who have been trained in the theoretical and methodological bases of the mentalizing approach.

NMP combines four discursive narrative codes into one methodology: the Metaphoric, Iconographic, Writing and Bodily codes. Through the four codes the students have the opportunity to mentalize their own personal way of participating in university education, and they are encouraged to develop the learning to learn competence strategically and adaptively in this context. There is a module for each code, each of which make makes use of specific narrative inputs: in the metaphoric one there is a reference to proverbs and mottos related to university experience; in the iconographic code we use vignettes portraying students involved in a typical university situation; in the writing code three narrative tasks are given;

lastly, in the bodily code, the students are asked to "sculpt" the future of the participants in the training, representing it through their own bodies, by means of body performances. These codes have all been used individually in earlier research activities seeking to foster reflexive processes within educational and psychotherapeutic settings. However, the methodology applied here combines all four codes in an innovative way.

Mentalization is a multifaceted capacity, characterized by multiple functional polarities: it is a dynamic process involving analogical and digital levels, implicit and explicit engagement with self and others. So, to respond to this complexity, we use a set of different codes, employing metaphors, images and inputs mediated by writings and sculptures. These activate group meta-narrative discourses and give the opportunity of working, at the same time, at different levels and degrees, on the several polarities. This provides students with the opportunity of looking at problems from a range of different angles.

Each code is distinctive in the way it evokes a different "version of the mind" with which to reflect, and, citing Bateson (see Chapter 1, this volume) to build a specific 'map' representing the student's way of reading his/her relationships within the 'territory' of the university. The use of multiple codes within a single narrative device, which draws on different versions of the mind, is able to produce multiple maps through which the territory can be read and better understood, facilitating the detection of analogies and differences. It also promotes research into, and selection of, the most suitable maps in terms of functional representations, geared towards the subject's purposes. The codes are activated progressively through the training setting; giving students the opportunity of seeing themselves and their situation from different angles; it gradually fosters a changing representation of the self, one more delineated, contextualized and action-oriented.

The Metaphoric input invites the students to choose proverbs and mottoes that represent their own university experience but are embedded in particular cultural contexts. This input directs them to an episte-mology of common sense and recognition of themselves in it; which enables them to see that they are being "narrated" by the specific chosen proverb or motto. Specifically, the metaphoric code allows participants to acquire a knowledge of their own representations of the Self in training/education; the group members are not asked to 'reveal themselves' by giving an account of their educational experi-ence, but rather they are asked to recognize such an experience in a metaphorical representation, suggested by other people. Using this approach, moreover, the sense of the sharing experiences is brought to the fore. This code has the aim of gaining a representation of the university experience from the account of each participant, and also to foster knowledge and awareness of representations of educational university experience in each participant.

The set of metaphorical tools includes, as noted, a list of proverbs and mottos typical of the local culture. The proverbs represent a generaliza-tion of the educational experience, while mottos work as specific slogans suitable to describe one's own formative experience. In the proverbs students identify possible reasons for their problems with exams, such as incompetence and an inability to manage university routine (e.g. "as you make your bed, so you must lie in it"), listlessness (e.g. "slow and steady wins the race"), preference for extra-curricular activities, difficul-ties with peers or the tendency to envy them (e.g. "the grass is always greener on the other side of the fence"). Mottos on the other hand are more aligned with the field of "doing" and to possible strategies which could be adopted to overcome the condition of the underachiever: put-ting confidence in one's own resources (e.g. "yes, we can!"), committing oneself to fate or trusting oneself to luck, playing it clever in order to get a change (e.g. "fortune favours the brave"); or becoming aware of difficulties related to the university context which the student chose (e.g.: "easier said than done"), and or waiting for a change dependent on some external cause.

The Iconographic inputs provide the opportunity of showing oneself beginning to delineate the features of his/her self as a student in action; this happens while s/he is still in the shoes of the hypothetical student who they can tentatively identify with, but which does not yet "clearly" and completely correspond to the self. The Iconographic code makes use of vignettes, which are seen as a projective tool that allows trainees to analyze the deeper meaning and the symbolic value associated with the objects or characters drawn (McCloud, 2001; 1996; Wilks, 2004). Despite the condensed and synchronic dimension proposed by metaphoric inputs, compared with the previous code, the vignette functions at a more diachronic level, suggesting the subjects imagine a typical situation of their university life. The objectives of this code consist of analyzing the educational experience at a diachronic level; and promoting reflection about one's own being-in-action within situations representing the university career.

The writing narrative input asks students to give an account of themselves in past actions, and encourages a clearer view of the construction of experience. Students are asked to produce three narratives: the narration of a low point, a high point and a decision turning point (e.g. see McAdams, 2008; McAdams 2006; McAdams, 2006; McAdams et al., 1997). In this phase of the training path the participants are deemed ready to work on how to use the theoretical and procedural knowledge acquired through the other codes, in order to operate in a strategic way which is effective in successful university achievement. Writing, in response to the request to tell a story about university experience, encourages greater involvement of the students in the construction of the subjective meaning of those educational experiences. Participants are invited to reflect on their own competences and in-competences, in order to analyze them and identify a possible turning point, starting from which it is more possible to focus on any strategic objectives necessary to achieve one's own developmental goals. The narrative writing, therefore, fosters the passage from reflection on the participants' weak and dysfunctional points, to the detection of stronger points in their own experience. This can lead to a representation of the Self in training/education as potentially able to make use of what has been learnt, to be successful in the achievement of goals in university, and later in working life.

Finally, the bodily input invites students to become protagonists in future actions, to represent themselves acting as students in the university context. This code uses the technique of sculpture, a creative, dynamic and non-verbal form of representation. Students are asked "to sculpt the university future of the whole group, by shaping how they imagine it will be by the end of the educational path…" The role of the sculptor is played by the whole group of participants who are asked to create a representation of the most significant relationships that bound them together, and of relationships within the educational context. In this final phase, the sculpture also offers a synchronic and condensed level of analysis of personal experience in the training. The sculpture enables the students to achieve the following objectives: to convey non-verbal and symbolic representation concerning the future of the whole group and to encourage a synchronic, condensed, and shared representation of the ultimate phase of the process, of the achieved objectives and of the goals to be worked towards in the future, after the training is completed.

In summary, the training is designed as a circular reflexive process looking at participants' individual university experience that, starting from a synchronic and summarized representation of it (proposed by proverbs and mottos), gradually leads to a diachronic analysis focused on specific moments and situations (proposed by the iconographic and the writing codes), to finally move back, in the bodily code, to a synchronic level in which the same experience is re-investigated in the light of the reflexive and meta-reflexive processes previously activated.

The training is designed as a path designed to foster the following processes:

a) the progressive cognitive and emotional involvement of the student;

b) the gradual transition from an exploration of the entire university experience to focusing on a specific and individual experience;

c) the gradual transition from a reconstructive function of the formative experience to a planning function allowing the students to act in a more effective way within the university context.

During each training meeting (irrespective of the specific code) the same methodological sequence is used, as follows.

Tab. 1. Methodological sequence

1.	Presentation of a narrative input
2.	Narrative construction of the experience through different discourse codes
3.	Group narrative meta-discourse on the proposed narration
4.	Transformation of the narrative experience

Narrative Codes in the Narrative Mediation Paths: A Pilot Project with Italian Students

We now look at an example of the Narrative Mediation Paths (NMP) methodology used in a pilot project with a group of 18 students at the University of Naples Federico II, Italy. This will enable us to illuminate how the four codes, and the related narrative inputs, have been applied with these Italian students, giving examples of how the narrative methodology has been applied within each code. The students were recruited to the project by means of posters and leaflets distributed throughout the university, email shots and reading about the project through the website of SINAPSI centre at the Federico II University. We will now look at the training process, referring to the methodological sequence described above (Tab 1), and highlighting some significant moments. We will then go on to look at examples from students.

The meetings took place once a week, in extra-curricular time. The Narrative Group Trainer (NGT) was a psychologist and an expert in promoting mentalization competence through narration.

1. Metaphorical Code (1st meeting; two hours):

As explained before, the proverbs are used to address various typologies from amongst which the students can choose the one they feel corresponds best with their situation and university experience. Where the student feels that none of the suggested proverbs are appropriate s/he is asked to write a suitable one. Then in the Narrative Construction of the Experience phase, the NGT asks each participant to tell the group the proverb and motto he/she has chosen and the reasons for that choice. The students' most common choices focused on specific proverbs and mottos such as "More haste, less speed", "Fortuna audaces iuvat", "Mission impossible", "Only the brave". Based on these choices and on the motivations given by the students, NGT activated a Narrative Group Meta-Discourse analyzing proverbs and mottos at two different levels: firstly classifying the typology and the quality of students' representations and use of a specific proverb or motto, then observing their process of attributing the meaning to such a proverb/motto.

Interestingly, two students chose the same motto "mission impossible" but with very different motivations. The first one chose this saying that it was impossible for him to change his university performance; the second one selected this motto as a way of expressing his willingness to change his condition (that of a student being very behind in his studies) apparently perceived as impossible. In one case feelings of incompetence, defeat, and a sense of inferiority predominate, whilst in the other case it shows a powerful trust in the student's own capabilities, a proactive attitude and some ability to change.

Then, from this level of analysis, the NGT, building on the group meta-narrative discourse activated within the training experience, moved to the next phase, namely the Transformation of the Narrative Experience, feeding back to the students the influences such representations and feelings can have on university performance. This, as stressed throughout, was to help the participants to begin to recognize their active role in making sense of their university experience.

2. Iconographic Code (2rd-3rd meetings; two hours per meeting):

Here the participants are situated in a context, through the vignettes, which depict significant events in the participants' university experience, and are encouraged to ask themselves questions about the "doing", that is, about the actions carried out by the protagonist in each of the proposed situations. The vignettes depict typical and significant situations in university experience, such as enrolment (Fig. 1), attendance at university courses, personal study at home, written and spoken university examinations, and periods of waiting with colleagues.

Fig. 1. One of the six vignettes: enrolment in University courses

During the phase of the Narrative Input, each participant was provided with a set of six vignettes. The students were asked to choose one of the protagonists in each vignette, to draw a blank bubble, to put themselves in the protagonist's shoes, and finally to write in the bubble what the protagonist is thinking or saying in that situation. The NGT asked each participant to read out loud what he/she had written in the series of six vignettes, with the aim of creating a story, helping the students to identify different states of mind associated with each vignette; and to use the vignettes to find some continuity between the six narrations, giving a coherent meaning to what they wrote (Narrative Construction of the Experience).

Then, the NGT developed a group discussion (Narrative Meta-Group Discourse) in order to use group inter-subjectivity to activate a process of reattribution of meaning, which was followed by the NGT's feedback on the prevalent dynamics emerging from the stories narrated (Transformation of Narrative Experience). For example, one student narrated, through the different vignettes, how she felt bad about receiving insufficient marks for examinations; of anxiety or boredom during university lessons; and a sense of continuing repetition of content in the lectures. Such cues could be interconnected across the whole narration indicating the student's representation of university life and experience, as a setting, perhaps, which produced anxiety and or where it was not possible to learn, and to have collaborative exchanges (with peers/colleagues, with professors, etc.). The NGT could work on this representation to show how it might influence poor university performance because it was characterized by dysfunctional states of mind, such as anxiety, fear of evaluation, etc.

3. Writing Code (4th-5th meetings; two hours per meeting):

Group members were asked to write three narratives on the following: a low point, a negative event which happened in the individual's university experience; a high point, a positive event in the individual's university experience; and a decision that proved a turning point in the individual's university experience. One student, for example, produced the following narratives:

Low point

A critical moment happened after 4 months after the course of study started. I studied with my colleagues for the first exam in Analysis subject. The written part of the examination went well, but I was rejected at the spoken part. It was a critical event, because since that time I have been afraid to attend other exams.

High point

I decided to try for the written part of the examination, but I had strong doubts about the possible outcome. However, I did it and so, I passed the examination; in that moment I felt the desire to get back in the game. I changed my mind about myself.

Decisional turning point

I had a turning point thanks to this training group. I began to doubt. Before this training I thought it was University to adapt to me, but now I think I have to adapt to the University requests.

In the past, University appeared to me as a challenge against professors, but now it feels like a place dedicated to education and growth.

During the Reconstruction of Narrative Experience, the NGT asked the student to explain the reasons why she narrated the stories reported above, and the significance they had in her personal life. From this it became possible to explore with her the states of mind associated with each episode alongside their influences on her university performance.

During the Narrative Group Meta-discourse, the NGT asked each participant to talk about the thoughts and feelings evoked by the stories they heard. He then underlined the link between the low point and the high point, in order to analyze the different states of mind as well as the differences between internal/external cause attribution for the same event/ examination and the different behaviours of the student. The NGT went on to define an area of competences associated with each narrative, which included an analysis of the way the student made use of the awareness of his/her competences, to begin focusing rather more on strategic goals.

The subsequent stage consisted of feedback, given by the NGT, about the decisional turning point, which the student linked with taking part in this group. This enabled her to examine the suitability of the course of study she had enrolled on, particularly in relation to her real interest in the disciplines included in it (Transformation of the Narrative Experience).

4. Bodily Code (6th meeting; two hours):

The whole group decided what to represent and how to sculpt it, using the participants' bodies to give shape to what they imagined their futures at the university might be (narrative construction of the experience).The NGT asked each participant to describe his/her emotions in relation to the representation; the role s/he played in the sculpture; the significance it had at a personal level and in terms of his/her ideas about future university experience. This allowed the participants to identify themselves as belonging to a shared group representation depicting, at the same time, significant aspects of their personal university experience. During the Group Meta-discourse the NGT gave the group some reflections on the correspondence between the original idea of the group sculpture and what the group actually made, in order to analyze the level of coherence between the expectations for the future and the actual behavior of the group within the university context. As an example we include a photograph of the sculpture made by a number of students (Fig. 2). The students said they wanted to represent a university future made up of different stages, describing different feelings and emotions at each stage. The first step represented reflexivity, the second one the pleasure of studying, while the third one represented grit and tenacity; the last step, finally, (performed by the student appearing at the right corner of the figure, raising a hand) represented the goal of graduation. The student appearing on the left side of the picture, with his body leaning towards the student depicting graduation, represents the effort of going through all the stages to reach the final goal. During the Transformation of the Narrative Experience, the NGT worked on giving the students feedback on the discrepancy between the group's initial plans for the sculpture, and what they actually performed: it looked more like a way of bypassing intermediate steps in order to reach the goal of graduation directly.

Fig.2. An example of sculpture about University Future

Conclusion

This chapter illuminates how narrative, and a particular way of framing key dimensions of it, used in a training setting, can be a powerful tool for building greater self-reflexivity, and agentic understanding. In the process, university, like the self, can be perceived as rather more than a simple given, but can be thought about, represented in diverse ways, and acted upon to encourage more positive relationships and outcomes. The potential role of narrative, and the provision of space to understand the stories we tell, is an important theme across the book. What is distinct in this chapter is the use of various techniques – including sculpture and metaphor – to feel and think about what stories are being told and how these might change for the better, when working with others, in a supportive group.

Note:

1   This chapter is related to the European funded project Innovative Solutions to Acquire Learning to Learn/INSTALL (Erasmus Multilateral Projects, n° 517750-LLP-1-IT-ERASMUS-ESIN). The team leaders are Dr. Paolo Valerio and Dr. Maria Francesca Freda, University of Naples, Italy. The other partners are as follows: National School of Political and Administrative Studies (NSPAS), in Bucharest, Romania, Dr. Dan Florin Stanescu; University of Aarhus, Denmark, Dr. Willy Aastrup; National University of Ireland in Maynooth (NUIM), Ireland, Dr. Úna Crowley; and University of Seville, Spain, Dr. José González-Monteagudo. The project will undertake research and intervention between October 2011 and March 2014 (30 months) in relation to non traditional university students, in order to promote social inclusion and to avoid early drop-out, by means of narrative tools. The information and views set out in this chapter are those of the authors and do not reflect the official opinion of the European Union. Neither the European Union institutions and bodies nor any person acting on their behalf may be held responsible for the use which may be made of the information contained herein.

References

Allen, J. A., and Fonagy, P. (2008). *Mentalization-Based Treatment*. Chichester: John Wiley & Sons.

Bateman, A.W., Fonagy, P. (2012). *Handobook of Mentalizing in Mental Health Practice*. Washington, DC: American Psychiatric Publishing, Inc.

Biesta, G.J.J., Field, J., Hodkinson, P., Macleod, F.J. & Goodson, I.F. (2011). *Improving learning through the lifecourse: Learning lives*. London/New York: Routledge.

Choy, S. (2002). *Nontraditional Undergraduates: Findings from The Condition of Education, 2002.* Retrieved January 12, 2012, from http://nces.ed.gov/pubs2002/2002012.pdf.

Davidsen, A. (2008). Experiences of Carrying out Talking Therapy in General Practice: A Qualitative Interview Study. *Patient Education and Counseling, 72,* 268-275.

Dominicé, P. (2000). *Learning from our Lives. Using Educational Biographies with Adults.* San Francisco: Jossey-Bass.

Eileen, E. E. (1997). The Non-Traditional Student. Paper presented at the American Association of Community Colleges Annual Conference (77th, Anaheim, CA, April 12-15).

Fonagy, (2002). *Psicoanalisi e Teoria dell'attaccamento [Attachment Theory and Psychoanalysis].* Milano: Raffeallo Cortina Editore.

Fonagy, P., & Target, M. (1997). Attachment and Reflective function: Their Role in Self-organization. *Development and Psychopathology, 9,* 679-700.

Fonagy, P., Twemlow, S. W., Vernberg, E. M., Nelson, J. M., Dill, E. J., Little, T. D., & Sargent J. A. (2009). A Cluster Randomized Controlled Trial of Child-focused Psychiatric Consultation and a School Systems-focused Intervention to Reduce Aggression. *The Journal of Child Psychology and Psychiatry, 50,* 607-616.

Fraser, W. (1995). *Learning from Experience. Empowerment or incorporation?.* Leicester: National Institute of Adult Continuing Education.

Freda, M. F. (2008a). *Narrazione e intervento in psicologia clinica. Costruire, pensare, e trasformare narrazioni tra logos e pathos [Narration and intervention in clinical psychology. Build, think, and transform narratives between logos and pathos].* Napoli: Liguori.

Freda, M. F. (2008b). Understanding Narrative Role in Depicting Meaning and Clinical Intervention. *Yearbook of Ideographic Science, 1,* 81-93.

Freda, M. F. (2011). Understanding Continuity to Recognize Discontinuity. Integrative *Psychological and Behavioural Science, 45,* 335-346.

Freda, M. F., & De Luca Picione R. (2012), Relational And Organizational Value Of Self-Positions. *International Journal for Dialogical Science, 6,* 51-60.

Freda, M. F., De Luca Picione R., and Esposito G. (2012, in press). *Reflexivity: applying a reflexive process to an educational context.* Yearbook of Ideographic Science (YIS).

Hermans, H. J. M. (2001). The Dialogical Self: toward a Theory of Personal and Cultural Positioning. *Culture & Psychology, 7,* 243-281.

Karterud, S. (2011). Environ-mentalizing the Matrix: Commentary on Sigmund Karterud's 35th Foulkes Annual Lecture. *Group Analysis, 44,* 374-384.

Karterud, S., and Bateman A.W. (2012). Group Therapy Techniques, in A.W. Bateman & P. Fonagy (2012). *Handobook of Mentalizing in Mental Health Practice.* Washington, DC: American Psychiatric Publishing, Inc.

McAdams, D. P, Bauer, J., Sakaeda, A., Anyidoho, N.A., Machado, M.A., Magrino-Failla, K., White, K., & Pals, J. (2006). Continuity and Change in the Life Story: a Longitudinal Study of Autobiographical Memories in Emerging Adulthood. *Journal of Personality, 74,* 5-36.

McAdams, D. P. (2006). *The Redemptive Self: Stories Americans Live by.* New York: Oxford University Press.

McAdams, D. P. (2008). *The Life Story Interview.* Retrieved January 12, 2012, from http://www.sesp.northwestern.edu/docs/LifeStoryInterview.pdf.

McAdams, D. P., Diamond, A., De St. Aubin, E., & Mansfield, E. (1997). Stories of Commitment: The Psychosocial Construction of Generative Lives. *Journal of Personality and Social Psychology, 72,* 678-694.

McCloud, S. (2001). *Reinventare il fumetto [Reinventing the comic].* Torino: Vittorio Pavesio Productions.

McCloud, S., (1996). *Capire il fumetto, l'arte invisibile [Understanding Comics, the Invisible Art].* Torino: Vittorio Pavesi Production.

Meehan, K. B., Levy, K. N., Reynoso, J. S., Hill, L.L., & Clarkin, J. F. (2009). Measuring Reflective Function with a Multidimensional Rating Scale: Comparison with Scoring Reflective Function on the AAI. *Journal of American Psychoanalitic Association, 57,* 208-213.

Merrill, B, and González-Monteagudo, J. (2010). Experiencing Undergraduate Learning as a Non-Traditional Adult Student: A Biographical Approach, in L. Gómez, D. Martí; I. Candel (Eds.): International Conference on Education, Research and Innovation 2010. Proceedings CD. Valencia: IATED, 5046-5054.

Metzner, B. S., and Bean, J. P. (1987). The estimation of a conceptual model of nontraditional undergraduate student attrition. *Research in Higher Education, 27,* 15-38.

Miller, M., and Lu, M.Y. (2003). Serving Non-Traditional Students in E-Learning Environments: Building Successful Communities in the Virtual Campus. *Educational Media International,40,*163-169.

Naranjo, C. (2004). *Cambiar la educación para cambiar el mundo.* Vitoria: La Llave.

Steiner, C. (2003). *La educación emocional.* Madrid: Punto de lectura.

Wilks, T. (2004). The Use of Vignettes in Qualitative Research into Social Work Values. *Qualitative Social Work, 3,* 78-87.

Chapter 11

The relationship between students originating from sub Saharan Africa and patients, during vocational training courses in nursing in Switzerland

◊   MYRIAM GRABER

Introduction

This contribution aims at understanding how students from sub Saharan Africa, studying for the bachelor degree in Nursing in Switzerland, live and deal with various intercultural issues raised in their daily lives. For this purpose I will highlight a number of issues of significance to these students (Martuccelli, 2006), that are both indicative of their own individual experience, history and personal journey as well as the collective experience of student nurses. Certain issues, whether they are chosen or imposed, usually only become problematic once the students have arrived in the host country and started their training.

These students are of particular interest because they come to train in Switzerland after attending compulsory education in their own country. These different experiences create tension in terms of their identity because of their values and the perceptions of training, health and disease

(Charmillot, 1997), which they bring with them, and the reality they dis-cover, particularly during the practical training course. The culture shock experienced by these students could then impact on the process of their integration into the society of the host country. If we consider nursing to be a profession where communication is paramount we must not forget the significant impact it can have on the body. The latter is encountered by students during their internships. Training prepares them at a theo-retical level, with videos and photos, and, at a practical level, through the use of models to simulate certain types of care, such as bathing (Gineste & Marescotti, 1996). However, encounters with the naked and diseased body of another, particularly of the opposite sex, requiring to be washed, massaged, and dressed, can be difficult. This is even more so when the primary cultural values do not allow looking at a naked person, let alone touching one (Drouard, 2002; Graber, & Mégard Mutezintare & Gakuba, 2010). Fear or anxiety are common responses for any student who has to wash a person for the first time, but for these African students it is even harder. In a similar way, representations of disease and death (Graber, PhD in progress) are highly problematic. The tensions they experience during their training in relation to professional values lead to personal crises. The question is then about how they can articulate their own values and those of the host country, which they must do in order to act in a professional way.

In this chapter I will try to highlight and understand how these students manage their own values and those that they encounter in the host country. How are they able to extend the familiar context to one where the "rules" are unknown, opaque and discovered only through action? We will see that this is only possible for them through a range of activities: firstly, reflexive work (with themselves); secondly, discursive work (with another); and lastly, symbolic work (the social world), that is to say, through a process of re-contextualisation dependent on certain recognition factors (Castel, 1999). We will try to address these questions through the analysis of interviews with these students, taken as life stories, undertaken during the degree in nursing (Graber, PhD in progress).

Conceptual framework

Events

The concept of race is, for Boltanske and Tgevenot, particularly associated with the formation of a justification model, because for them this is the test that measures the "discrepancy between the strength of the individuals and the things they are committed to, translated in terms of failure" (1991, p. 169). There is "a demonstration of a deficiency and therefore an injustice or a lack of fairness in an arrangement" (1991, p.169). However, this definition does not include the dimensions of existence and inequality. Subsequently Dubet and Martuccelli (1998) draw on another model, that of Perilleux (2001, p. 75) to define the notion of proof as "the scale of the test set against the proving to oneself". Baudouin (2010) gives particular importance to the autobiographical text and proposes to develop the concept of ordeals. For him the use of narrative is paramount. He looks at the "meditations articulating experience and putting them into words" (Baudouin, 2010, p. 179). Martuccelli (2006), from a sociological perspective, developed a system of standardised tests (with reference to current processes of individuation), identifying the challenges against which individuals are measured, the obstacles they confront and the resources they bring to bear (p12). He attaches great importance to their experiences and the subjective dimension of these. He notes that people confront the issues of daily life in different ways and that their experiences vary accordingly. Those things encountered by students from sub Saharan Africa, who for the most part completed their schooling in their home country, and then coming to train as nurses in Western Switzerland, are not necessarily the same as those faced by students from other African countries; or for those who grew up and went to school in Switzerland. Training is therefore affected by the concept of race, as stated in Baudouin (2003). The transition from one culture to another, one training system to another, deprives students of their usual framework. This passage represents "a difficult test for their identity, based on resistance, ambivalence and the effort to build new benchmarks" (Merhan & Baudouin, 2007).

These events involve their identities by comparing their performance with the culture of their host country whether in their private lives, in training, or in everyday social life.

Exotopy

Bakhtin (1984) says that in the cultural field "the most powerful engine for understanding a given culture is revealed by an in-depth look at a different culture" (p 347). His concept of "exotopy", i.e. the experience and recognition of otherness, can be used to understand what happens in population movements, a reality, almost a condition of the modern individual. Travel places individuals in countries and situations with which they are unfamiliar. Moreover, when they decide to pursue a vocational training such as the Bachelor of Science in Nursing, they find themselves, overnight, both in a new a learning situation, and an "exotopic system". When they begin their training, they face exotopy because the representations of health, disease and education (that are embedded in the course) conflict with their previous learning and deeply ingrained sense of identity. They feel pressured. The intercultural experience mirrors each to him/herself, and to the other, and vice versa. Otherness is a mirror for identity. While some exotopic experience is always present in migration, it is amplified by training. For these students, the course itself presents a challenge, creating tensions and internal conflict, even if it is taking place in an environment that is conducive to self-integration.

The whole experience is not always constructive for sub Saharan African students, and may result in the de-stabilisation of identity (Graber, Mégard Mutezintare & Gakuba, 2010). Migration takes these students far away from their usual points of reference, to a "distal" space (Merhan & Baudouin, 2007). In this exotopy these students find themselves in a position of uncertainty with regard to standards, values and training systems, and are increasingly faced with new forms of thought; their apprehension of the world that they live in is in a process of self transformation (Bautier & Rochex, 2001). Therefore to develop, while situated in and confronting an "exotopic position" (p140), a new point of view allowing them to articulate, in a meaningful way, a plurality of references, is difficult and requires support.

Social representations

Many authors from different scientific perspectives have considered the definition of social representations, and formulated a variety of theories. In 1989 Jodelet defined social representations as "forms of knowledge developed and shared socially, with a practical aim and contributing to the construction of a common reality for a social group" (p. 36). Later, in 1991, she emphasized the social dimension of representation. For her, these are "interpretive systems governing the world and our relationship to others that orient and organise and conduct social communications" (p. 36). It is therefore a form of knowledge; common knowledge, cognitive phenomena, that involves social classes of individuals by the internalization of practices and experiences, patterns of behaviour and thought (Jodelet, 1989). Social representations concern and define the philosophy of this or that society, acting as a point of articulation between the body and the imagination. Different societies construct different interpretations of illness or health, with the consequence that disease does not translate cross culturally in the same way at the symbolic level. This interpretation is "a symbolic cultural orientation of a given community" (Boula, 2010), considering cultural anthropology "as symbolic behaviour" (Boula, 2010), as a language mediated by the body. So the ways in which this behaviour is interpreted in a society is used to analyse how the body suffers, how a person becomes a patient or is cured. Professionals are faced with different explanatory accounts of health, disease, and, therefore, the language of the body.

Students who migrate do so with their own cultural background and find, during training that the representations acquired before migrating are different from those they now encounter. They are then confronted with the explanatory register of the nurses with whom they are working on the wards in the early days of their internships. This explanatory register forces them to acknowledge their own systems of explanation. It should be noted that the position is reciprocal for the carers. In terms of the students, the mental structures they have in place are no longer sufficient to explain what is happening, their way of thinking is threatened, the vision of care that they had in their own country is inadequate for understanding this new context, resulting in culture shock. Often, the carers do not immediately spot what is happening and do not always have the means to deal with these situations. However, understanding what is going on in the mind of the other can allow carers to take into account these differences and help them to support the students as they adjust to new ways of understanding and interpreting. This also leads to a better understanding of the other's way of thinking. The anthropologist Godelier (2007) speaks in similar terms when he says that the imaginary realities give a clear social existence and the status of "truths" and of "evidence" (p. 37). He thinks it is very important to differentiate the realms of the imaginary and the symbolic. The imaginary "is the thought", that is to say, "ideational reality" (p. 38). For him, imagination is a world of ideas, images and representations that have their foundation in thought. Though these representations are a product of an interpretation of what they depict, the realm of the imagination is very real. These ideational realities remain hidden and cannot be shared by other individuals and whilst they remain internal they cannot influence action. The symbolic field represents all the means and processes by which these realities will be interpreted into material realities and practices and give them a concrete, visible and social existence (Godelier, 2007). The imagination becomes real by being embodied in practices and in social relationships and it can also create new or modify existing ones. Having outlined the theoretical framework we will now look at the methodology.

Methodology and population for the research

We conducted fifteen biographical interviews and fourteen other interviews with internship students from several nursing universities in Switzerland. One student only participated in one biographical interview. We

244

have used Baudouin's (2010) method of analysis of biographical accounts to identify events based on the analysis of "variations" in the speed of the story that demonstrates the differential treatment of biographical periods. From the speed of the narrative it is possible to identify meaningful experiences. Then by using the approach of Dubar & Demazière (2004) three levels of narrative were analysed: first the sequence: what happened; secondly, the characters acting, speaking and playing a role in the story, and lastly the arguments that are made in the narrative to defend a point of view, to make an inventory and convince the interlocutor. In this way we could assign temporary and specific patterns to each student and ascertain, where possible, common patterns among students. For this purpose we used four semi structured work placements with nursing students: Camille, Juju, Jahia and Djafalo. The plurality in this methodology gives access to all dimensions of the subject as well as those invisible ones, which are so important. Too often "we see the immigrant only through his immigration status in the host society, dispossessed from the situation in his homeland" (Lahlou 2008). Biographical interviews give access to the history of the person, that is to say, his narrative. Four students are presented here, based on both biographical and comprehensive interviews.

Camille came to Switzerland in 2004, accompanied by her twin brother and little sister. The three joined their mother who wanted the family to be re-united. Her mother has lived in western Switzerland for some years. Camille had difficulties with the training course; she failed several modules and had to re-do them. In Cameroon she went to primary and secondary school, and in the grammar school studied science, receiving a scientific baccalaureate in Cameroon and then a few months later, the literary equivalent in Chad. She thus passed two baccalaureates in one year. She enrolled at university to read law. Her mother then decided that it was time for her children to come and join her in Switzerland. Camille then had to leave the university where she had just begun. She decided to become a nurse and started to train, but found it difficult. She is in a state of crisis, with her mother wanting her to retain her culture, not understanding that Camille has become an adult. She gave up the training early in the second year.

Juju was born in Madagascar. He went to the primary and secondary school and obtained his school leaving certificate (BEPC) at the Lycée Moderne. He completed a degree in secondary education. After his studies he had to earn a living and become part of the family because his father had left home. He then trained as a programmer. He is single. At home, there are 7 children. His father was a civil servant; his mother is a housewife and has not studied much. After his siblings had left home, "he can finally do something more than they did and that is why he came to study in Switzerland". He arrived in Switzerland in 2005 as a student with an annual permit for foreign students. He has a guarantor who has supported him financially during his training. He found the studies difficult and had to redo a large number of modules. Initially he was successful, but then he failed twice and had to leave the course.

Jahia was born in Cameroon. She has 2 brothers and 5 sisters all "dispersed" among the extended family (living with uncles, aunts and grandparents). She attended primary school, living with her grandparents and then went to high school and lived with her uncle. These changes were disturbing and she had to redo the school year. She got a diploma in mathematics but her parents divorced when she was in the third year at the high school. Following the divorce, she had to repeat her school year because she needed more time to work. She was the one who looked after her little sisters and kept house. Her mother was working in another city. Jahia and her sisters joined their mother the following year and life became quieter. She then studied for the baccalaureat in natural sciences. Her father, a prison guard, died. Her mother, an accountant in public administration, died while Jahia was training in Switzerland. The whole family lives in Africa. Jahia is 29 years old and single; she came to Switzerland to join her friend who was studying there.

Djafalo attended primary and secondary school, and then he studied science in the grammar school, gaining a scientific baccalaureate. He studied at the university, obtaining a two year undergraduate diploma at the Faculty of Economics and Management (FASEG). He joined the

RTP (a political movement of the Togolese people) and campaigned to stop young people from falling into the hands of the opposition party. He is committed to his country. He has an accounting background. He noticed that his childhood friends were suffering because they did not think the same as the political establishment and gradually he changed his mind and party. During the elections he became a member of an opposition group, which protected the ballot boxes containing the votes, he was then arrested and taken to a camp. He escaped with a few other inmates first taking refuge in another African country before he left for Switzerland. He had no desire to leave his country; he is very attached to its educational values. Djfalo arrived in Switzerland as an asylum seeker. He started training once he was settled. Currently he has a residence permit (type B) which also acts as a work permit. He is 31 years old, married and has a child of 7 years. His wife and children joined him in Switzerland.

Analysis of interviews

We have focused on care situations experienced as events during internship that placed some sub Saharan students in an exotopic situation. Firstly we have presented the students faced with washing and bathing, and secondly we have presented students having to deal with representations of disease and death. This helped us to understand how students cope with these situations. Such 'ordeals' are met by most of these students: for the first time quite soon after their arrival in Switzerland, and then repeatedly.

Camille has to wash a person during her internship in a care home. For her, nudity is difficult. She said that, "when a person is undressed back in Africa, you should not talk to them as they say it is cursed. That is why it is dangerous to look at a naked person". However, she notes that, "it is not the same situation for them" by which she means native (as in Swiss) students. She continues by saying that, "she would not wash her grandparents, it would not happen". Camille is in tension: "I have to wash and I dare not look at the naked person, nor do the washing, I'll be damned." Finally, Camille said "I wash the elderly and it doesn't bother me either".

It does not go further. Camille lives with a tension that she still cannot solve. She does these things but without taking a reflexive position so that her own values are suppressed. She will wash because she must.

Juju is in a similar situation whilst he is on probation and must wash a patient. He said, "It does not happen here, at home, your sister would not even sit on your bed. Prior to the internship I knew it existed, so I was expecting the worst and I removed it from my head: I said this is the training, this is my job, if I cannot do it I am stuck, nothing will happen. I must manage to do what I have to. Acknowledging the fact that I am an apprentice, I did the washing because I have to do this to succeed. It helped me a lot, I didn't need outside help but that's me, I looked in my heart to succeed. What helps me is my ambition: I want that degree." Juju justifies the action of washing by making it his job, his training. He finds resources within himself to succeed even whilst his symbolic world is under attack. However we can sense how much his identity is in tension as he reconstructs another imaginary world, one which fits with his new environment.

Jahia found herself in the same situation when the nurse showed her how to wash an elderly patient. She says that at home with the elderly, there is a barrier. She continued: "at first I didn't watch when the nurse was doing the lower part of the patient, rather I looked up, I did not look at this part of the washing, I was trying to talk to the lady but it was strange anyway. I thought she must be my grandmother's age. I put it down to the training I chose to do and anyway I thought, I'll have to do this all the time. I reasoned like that, it's part of my job! It was still difficult care but I wanted to be a nurse so I take care of naked people". Jahia is un-comfortable during this procedure, and we can sense how strange it is for her, but she also says that she will do this regularly, it's part of the job, she reallocates the decision to do the washing and personal care to the professional role. The fact of this reallocation of these forbidden activities gives three students permission to go beyond the values acquired during their primary socialisation process, and allows them to succeed at that task. However Camille remains in conflict while Juju and Jahia reorganise their symbolic world.

We now move on to the representation of disease.

Djafalo faces a case of infanticide, this is what he said: "for me this is difficult, what shocks me is that in a case of infanticide here, we will say the person has a psychological problem, it's hard for me to accept things like that. To me the person is responsible; they chose to do what they did. For us the person is responsible. We will say that the person is possessed and should be dispossessed. He says, "I do not accept the story of being possessed. I will be in the middle." In his primary socialisation, Djafalo would tend to explain infanticide by the idea of being possessed. This is his symbolic world embodied in its African context, its explanatory register. But, currently, Djafalo is less certain about attributing infanticide to the fact of being possessed. However, the explanation here in Switzerland, as a psychological problem, he finds problematic too. The individual must take responsibility for what he has done and he adds "I am in the middle." 'That is to say, that he is in between the two explanatory registers, both symbolic worlds are plausible for him. His representations of infanticide are not rigid. There is a break between the old and new explanation, he is in the process of integrating the new elements into his thinking. This is cultural development at work, but not in an obvious way. He rejects part of his identity and manages at the same time to keep a degree of coherence between both levels. Being in the middle is a strategy, which allows him to decrease the tension, caused by the various explanatory registers, while remaining anchored in his former frame of reference (Camilleri, 1998). It is Djafalo that speaks of death. He said, "When people die even at 80 years, there is always something behind it. There is no natural death. He says, "I do not accept that" he explains, "death is always attached to something, I did something wrong and must suffer the consequences, or it is someone who kills, who is bewitched. This is how it is at home and what I find incomprehensible is readily accepted, yes I am the cause.... he then gives the example of the death of his sister "when my sister died from sinusitis: it was my grandfather who had bewitched her and put her under stones and because of this she died. I don't really believe this, but there are people who willingly accept, that yes, I am the cause of her death, disease, it's a bit blurry and this is why I cannot believe it." The concept of death for Djafalo does not match that of Judeo Christian death as seen here in Switzerland. Its symbolic translation "not a natural death, I did something and I have to suffer the consequences, it is someone who is bewitched" is in tension with the reality of death here. However, it is unclear to him, so he claims not to believe in these explanations. You can spot the tension between the old values and those of his new environment. His cultural identity is being tested, but in moderation, since he himself calls into question the register explaining that death is due to witchcraft or an external cause. It is no longer the same; he thinks and tries to work with the new style of thought from his host country without however completely refuting his former conceptions. His symbolic world adapts to his new situation as he compares and thinks and tries to strike a balance that enables tension to be reduced.

Conclusion

The three events experienced by these African students during their training period are highlighted in a space characterised by exotopy, caused by the internship. This is the test of the significance of nudity, psychological representations of illness and of the significance of death. These issues are repeatedly experienced by most of these students and this in a timeframe very close to their arrival in Switzerland. The consequence is that their sense of identity is strongly shaken, tested and made unstable. They must deconstruct and then reconstruct their thinking, their ideational realities and symbolic systems. They are repeatedly in crisis during this biographical journeying and often alone, not asking for help. However, regardless of representations of health, disease, the body, or of death etc, migrant students continue to participate in their own interpretations of the act of care. Similarly, it is not a question of the carers stigmatising these students by putting them into a mould, but a question of respecting difference.

For that purpose carers need to be open to their own cultural space, by thinking about their own explanatory registers and by not staying at one level but adopting an intercultural stance.

In addition to the issues discussed in the above cases, it is important to look again at two other levels of exotopy: to arrive, first, in a strange country, without knowing the social codes and rules and second, to arrive in a different training system with a new style of learning in comparison with what they have been used to. In the past they learned by heart, did not have easy access to books, or the Internet. Here in Switzerland they find themselves in a system based on reflexivity, and where access to information is often difficult to sort out for them. They are in identity conflict, which they must resolve in order to rebuild and to continue to give meaning to the new situations they encounter. It is in these circumstances that what can be called the distal, exotopy, penetrates the proximal, the habitual. Everything seems unusual, the explanations of illness do not really convince: they have to perform bed baths and yet this is something that "one does not do". These are factors that seem to break with routine, with what is familiar to the student. Illness, or even death, with which he/she is familiar, suddenly become part of a distal universe.. They are no longer the same, have become strange. If the explanations given in the West were the same as those heard in Africa, the ordeal would not take place. There is a form of solidarity between the distal and the ordeal. It is in exotopic situations, where unusual distal elements meet, that the sub-Saharan African students face various tests of their bodily relationship. It is here that the proximal subject, the "identity" turns out to be insufficient, where its shortcomings are revealed. But it is also the place where confronting the trials and resolving the issues can reunite the distal with the proximal and where there can then be self-reconstruction and adaptation.

In other words, they can explain and understand illness and death by articulating scientific and traditional thinking, by introducing scientific elements into their way of understanding illness; or again, perform the bed bath by negotiating it as a professional act so that it becomes possible to carry it out.

References

Bakhtine, M. (1984) *Esthétique de la création verbale*, Paris: Gallimard.

Baudouin, J.-M. (2003) *De l'épreuve autobiographique*, Thèse de doctorat, Université de Genève, Faculté de psychologie et des sciences de l'éducation, section sciences de l'éducation, Genève, Suisse.

Baudouin, J.-M. (2007) Savoir et activité: approche autobiographique et catégorie du distal, in: Astolfi, J.-P. and Houssaye, J. (Eds.) *Savoirs et histoires. Penser l'éducation* (pp. 211-216), No Hors série, Presses Universitaires de Rouen et du Havre: Rouen.

Baudouin, J.-M. (2010) *De l'épreuve autobiographique*, Berne: Peter Lang.

Bautier, E. and Rochex, J-Y. (2001) Rapport aux savoirs et travail d'écriture en philosophie et sciences économiques et socials, in B. Charlot (Eds), *Les jeunes et le savoir. Perspectives internationales* (pp. 133-153), Paris: Economica. Anthropos.

Boltanski, L. and Thévenot, L. (1991) *De la justification. Les économies de la grandeur,* Paris: Gallimard.

Boula, J-G. (2012, site consulté) *Nécessité du détour anthropologique dans les soins médicaux.* http://www. gfmer.ch/Presentations_Fr/Detour_nécessite.

Castel, R., (1999) *Les sorties de la toxicomanie,* Fribourg: Presses Universitaires de Fribourg Eds.

Charmillot, M. (1997) *Les savoirs de la maladie. De l'éducation à la santé en contexte africain,* Cahiers de la section des Sciences de l'Education No 81, Genève: Université de Genève.

Demazière, D. and Dubar, C. (1997) *Analyser des entretiens biographiques. L'exemple des récits d'insertio,.* Laval: PUL.

Delory-Monberger, C. (2004) *Les histoires de vie. De l'invention de soi au projet de formation,* Paris: Economica, Anthropos, 2ème Ed.

Drouard, J-P. (2002) *Texte sur la toilette de l'enfant en Afrique et en Inde,* Module Sciences humaines.

Gineste, Y. and Marescotti, R. (1996) *La toilette du malade en institution,* Aide soignante n° 9, octobre.

Godelier, M. (2007) *Au fondement des sociétés humaines. Ce que nous apprend l'anthropologie,* Paris: Albin Michel.

Graber, M., Gakuba, T., and Mégard Mutezintare, C-L. (2010) *Les étudiants d'Afrique subsaharienne. Représentations et discours des acteurs des Hautes écoles de la santé et du social sur les processus et les conditions d'apprentissage,* Genève: Ies editions, Collection du centre de recherche sociale.

Jodelet, D. (1989, 1991) *Les représentations sociales,* Paris: PUF.

Lahlou, M. (2008) L'identité et la mémoire de l'étranger à l'épreuve des methodologies, in Perregaux, C.; Dasen, P.; Leanza, Y. and Gorga, A. *L'interculturation des Savoirs: entre pratiques et théories* (pp. 29-50), Paris: l'Harmattan.

Martucelli, D. (2006) *Forgé par l'épreuve. L'individu dans la France contemporaine,* Paris: A. Collin.

Merhan, F. and Baudouin, J.-M. (2007) Alternance, exotopie et dynamyques identitaires. Enjeux et significations du rapport de stage, en *Alternance et professionnalisation des enseignants et des formateurs* (pp. 203-223), in S. Vanhule, F. Merhan & C. Ronveaux (Ed.), Raisons Educatives, Bruxelles: De boeck Université.

Périlleux, T. (2001) *Les tensions de la flexibilité,* Paris: Declée De Brouwer.

Chapter 12

Biographical learning: a process for recovering the soul in nursing

◊ LIOBA HOWATSON-JONES AND CLAIRE THURGATE

Introduction

This chapter explores the use of biographical approaches in the learning of nurses. It also considers more widely how this sits within health studies and ideas about professionalism. Rising concerns about how the body is perceived within healthcare structures, which have become more impersonal and less compassionate, and ecologies of learning that can be technocratic, have led to an imperative to frame nurses' learning in other, more holistic ways. The aim of the chapter is to stimulate thinking about how to embed change and learning in meaningful ways that invigorate what we term the soul in nursing. The soul is a provocative concept which we view as encapsulating the essence of caring through a deliberate recognition of and response to the whole humanity of others, and ourselves, in the way we think, in what we say and what we do. We draw on the experiences and reflections of students and teaching staff – the Programme Director and Course Leader (also researcher) – on a recently developed nursing degree programme which uses a biographical narrative approach to explore more holistic ways of learning. The key argument developed in the chapter is that such a biographical narrative approach offers a space for people to make better sense of their lives and to integrate such learning in their personal and professional life, thus – and this is crucial – becoming more attentive and open to the narratives of others.

Background

The context of care in the United Kingdom (UK) has changed dramatically in recent years. Increasingly, the qualified nurse has been removed from the patient's side to be replaced by assistant staff, with assistant numbers more than doubling since 1997 (Buchan & Seecombe, 2006). Healthcare technology is an integral part of this process through "automaticising" many aspects of caring (Barnard & Sandelowski, 2001). The modernisation of nursing careers has also brought new leadership responsibilities as nurses develop their roles into new arenas of practice (GB: Department of Health, 2006). However, recent reports have also identified a decline in the experience of patients, who feel uncared for and ignored (Patient Association, 2009; Francis, 2010; Francis, 2013). It seems that the soul of nursing – about caring for others and developing a connected understanding – has become obscured; patients might even say lost. Yet nursing is still about engaging in a therapeutic relationship with diverse human beings in the most difficult and vulnerable of circumstances. Such knowledge can be used in spiritually engaged ways when we are attentive to others and ourselves (Crawford, 2005).

Nurses fulfil multiple identities; of co-ordinator of care, leader, manager, teacher, learner, employee, as well as the more personal mother/father, wife/husband, partner, child, and friend/colleague. Such emotional connections evoke emotional responses which some nurses may carry with them and which need to be processed to free them up to learn and care for others. The nurse demographic profile has shifted to include greater diversity of gender, ethnicity, and life experience providing a rich backdrop for developing the profession, and learning in a professional context.

The UK government's drive to change what they term the 'skill mix' of the workforce means that nurses' learning can be dominated by policy makers' interests. Nurses oscillate between being proficient and a novice again, as their roles constantly develop, thus demanding new knowledge and skills. Questions of what is defined as learning, of ways of learning and how nurses come to know, led in fact, to a doctoral study (Howatson-Jones, 2010). It was important to look at learning from the perspective of nurses themselves, and reflexively, within the wider context of biographies, rather than simply through the frame of nurse education policy makers or nurse managers. Reflexivity, as used here, refers to how nurses can influence their education and practice and how they think those structures might shape them but might be shaped in turn, more agentically. We make a distinction here between learning and education; we use learning to mean the development and internalisation of new understanding in a broad sense, encompassing informal as well as formal experiences in private as well as public spaces. Education refers to specific formal settings and how ideas might be taught in a variety of ways.

The study illuminated how some nurses felt marginalised from their own resources for learning and wise decision-making as they encoun-tered workplace cultures and learning environments which viewed some of them as 'other'. Theorising ideas about learning brings to the fore consideration of the social and cultural networks in which learners are embedded. Jarvis (2007, p.34) suggests that learners use the resources (capital) available from their lifeworld to make sense of their place in the world and that this contributes to learning through the interaction of thought and emotions. However, Gopee (2002 p609) asserts that unless work and learning organisations invest in learners through promoting social cohesion and collegiality, such learning capital may be lost. Our definition of learning capital uses a work based as well as biographical view of the learner drawing upon personal and organisational networks to further their learning. Such 'capital' is a resource which nurses carry with them into different situations and contexts. Cultures, as referred to here, relate to particular ways of behaving, working and learning, as well as viewing individuals which create distinct atmospheres, and represent a view of the organisation in which they are embedded. Below are some excerpts from the nurses involved in the doctoral study. All the names used are pseudonyms.

> Catheris: And it's very hard....because I came from other country. Because still sometimes you feel.... you can't say, "Can you do this?" And they feel like you can't boss around because you are from other country.

For some the past was still active in their present lives influencing their engagement with learning creating a significant amount of anxiety and fear.

> Dornach: I just had so much trouble when I was younger with my education, with fighting and mum fighting for me. Everything was just so hard. It wasn't really that they gave me any help for three years. Not until I started failing my exams. I was going to walk away from nursing altogether, decided to come back last year really to start again and do my degree for some nutty reason. No, didn't like learning, I didn't like what it put me through. Like, you'll look at things in a different way. I think that is the positive thing. I'm never going to be able to retain information the way that others do. And I am never going to be able to function on a certain level as much as certain people do. So I just have to get over that fear really.

Biographical narrative work became a method for repairing lives in the way that it empowered Dornach to revisit earlier events and come away with a different sense of self. Others identified that using biographical narrative to teach could create 'compelling spaces' for learning.

> Larissa: So it took me back to when I was doing my nurse's training and one of the things I got quite involved with which was the national association for the welfare of children in hospital. They were very much campaigning for parents to be able to stay with children when they were in hospital which they didn't in the 70s. But I really believed in children having parents there, having toys

and having access to child friendly things. So what I did for this talk was I started where I started with nursing. I started thinking about (named institution) where I did my training. And when I looked on their website it was the anniversary of them opening that day. And I started there and built this up and lead it through the process that I had seen developing.

When people are not distanced from each other, they are able to learn from and with each other. Such learning reaches to the embodied and authentic person, helping to recover the soul in working and learning. By embodied we mean that learning is fully part of the person and connected to their whole life so that they are able to be themselves as real people rather than adopting a façade. The soul, as referred to earlier, is about caring and connecting. As such it represents the essence of whom we are and what we do. It may be recognised in the 'Thou' that is realised as part of 'I' (Buber, 1958 p. 43). In other words being aware of our own humanity as well as that of others and how this is also a part of learning. Buber (1958) is particularly concerned with how individuals interact in spiritual as well as human ways when making sense of things.

We became concerned with the apparent disconnect between imparting care, and a loss of soul within this. This view contrasts those approaches which are focused on disembodied cognition to gain 'knowledge': a kind of disembodied cognition that is a central preoccupation and concern of the book as a whole. However, the biographical narrative approach represents a major challenge to such still dominant ideas about nurses' learning. The conclusions reached from the doctoral study were that embedding biographical reflexivity into nurse educational programmes could help to harness biographical resources and enable nurses to use this not only in facilitating their own learning, but in teaching others how to care. However, the people who pay for nurses to attend university courses, and university colleagues themselves, have difficulty recognising the value of this way of learning. They may be primarily focused on what additional professional knowledge and advanced skills nurses could get rather than how nurses might develop their learning in deeper, more soul-full ways.

Debate about the purpose and value of biographical narrative method might also, perhaps, challenge the status quo.

Health Studies

I am like a gazer who should mark an inland company standing upfingered, with, 'Hark! hark! The glorious distant sea!' And feel, 'Alas, 'tis but yon dark and wind swept pine to me! (Hardy, 1898: cited Widdowson, 1997 p. 8)

Biographical methods have been used to study the history of nursing's development (Hargreaves, 2008; Cahill, 2009), the lives of prominent nurses and to capture the experience of often marginalised groups such as the elderly, those with learning disability or mental health issues or those in care (Clarke, Hanson & Ross, 2003; Bornat & Walmesley, 2008; Kellett, Moyle, McAllister, King & Gallagher, 2009). Biographical methods can be viewed as empowering through the collaboration of patients and nurses in learning (Perry, 2005). But the use of biographical methods has also revealed a different discourse which some term 'the new nursing discourse' which can conflict with a hard scientistic view focused on the economics of care (Wigens, 1997). From such a perspective, healthcare, it seems, is becoming objectified as 'something' as opposed to 'someone' and, it might be said, learning similarly so. The alternative nursing discourse contrasts this by suggesting that ways of knowing stem from being authentically in relationship with people (Higgs & Titchen, 2001) and bringing an embodied, whole self into play: this includes emotional and spiritual dimensions in building understanding. Spiritually engaged knowing does not work from the dualism of mind and body. From such debates the subjective has come to the fore in considerations of being and learning as a professional in other arenas which have traditionally espoused the methods of what West (2001 p. 32) calls "big science" (Greenhalgh & Hurwitz, 1999). Narrative medicine where patients can tell their illness stories is becoming increasingly recognised as an important vehicle for understanding the patient experience (Greenhalgh, 2006). However, it can be said that the UK's National Health Service (NHS) is often driven by different, harder discourses, based on particular ways of being that assume objective knowing reflected in academic convention and rational thinking, making it harder to redefine learning policies to take account of more marginalised groups (Burke & Jackson, 2007). It is not surprising when considering the findings of the doctoral research – within the frame of policy makers' agendas for nurses' learning – that nurses feel marginalised from their own biographical and learning capital, and capacity for empathic decision-making, and can thus become disillusioned with learning. Field (2006) considers that approaches to learning are based on cultural foundations which lie at the heart of social capital. It might be suggested therefore, that social interaction is a powerful medium for developing ways of learning. By learning capital we mean, to repeat, the diverse learning experiences nurses have had on which they can draw to develop further. It might also be argued that when we feel uncared for it can be difficult to care about others.

Review and planning of learning

It is stories that convey the lived ideas of nursing and learning as a nurse. The story is an essential component of the biographical narrative approach. The construction of biography can be a conscious act, or unconscious defensive act, that stimulates thinking about development, and in the process, facilitates learning. Being able to make subjective sense of a personal trajectory and create a narrative about it is important for understanding how one has got here and where one might go on to. The doctoral research was applied practically through designing and developing a pathway of degree study within the new Continuing Professional Development (CPD) curriculum for health and social care practitioners, to include a biographical module and opportunities for facilitated discussion groups. CPD curricula are reviewed and modified every five years to ensure currency of educational provision to meet the requirements of learners and the organisations which employ them. The new CPD curriculum was introduced to take account of a shift to more work based learning and new nursing roles, which made some of the old educational provision redundant. Nevertheless, such change processes also appear to take greater account of organisational needs than those of learners. The new applied degree within which the biographical module sits is 'bespoke' with flexible content determined by the learner's individual learning and development needs.

This allows learners and their employers to devise coherent programmes of their own choosing. Getting this creative approach to nurses' learning through programme quality checking processes was an arduous and emotionally demanding experience, but one which we wholeheartedly believed in. The final analysis by the review panel, approving the programme, stated that it was innovative, perhaps ahead of its time, and very worth including. A longitudinal study of students enrolling on this pathway enquiring on the value and effectiveness of this change of approach for nurses' learning is now beginning and the first results are offered here. A module at the start of the pathway asks students to explore their biographies and, from here, look forward to plan their future path of study. The scope of the project is to follow the first cohort of students undertaking the programme through to completion and identify the impact on their learning and practice development.

Student engagement

The biographical module asks students to construct their biographies and critically examine these in a collaborative way. This biographical narrative approach develops from the ideas of Dominice (2000). We began by sharing our own biographies. This sharing is important for developing a space that feels safe. Biographical content is interrogated reflexively in terms of perceptions between participants, the teacher-facilitator and considerations of power within relationships and presentation of selves. Using biographical narrative approaches triggers emotions and embodied memory in the feelings aroused. Such moments may lead to new insights into assumptions, as cognition becomes energised as storytelling builds connections between the past, present and future. But this is only possible if the quality of the learning space is right. The learning space is not only the physical space, but also the emotional atmosphere created within it, through the relationships and communication between participants, including psychological dimensions. Positional power, levels of attending and consideration and consultation, may all contribute to a sense of safety or concern. Students on the module demonstrated profound learning progression towards being active learners – not just course consumers – in the way that they were able to exert some agency in their learning by choosing what to disclose, or not, and how to proceed. When constructing their narrative some students recognised in their own nursing behaviour that the soul of nursing could be missing. This gave them a sense of responsibility for their learning. Their stories held similar emotional echoes to those found in the doctoral research, supporting not only the need for reflexive space, but to note how such space can help nurses to take stock of their lived values and how these can be at work in enhancing nursing. The following are some of the students' reflections:

Jessie: This module has given me the opportunity and the space to stand back and consider my learning journey to date. I went to my local primary school and during my final year I became the eldest of four children. My parents decided that I should go to a single sex secondary school, eight miles from where we lived, rather than the local school which is where all my friends were going. I remember feeling anxious and lost as I entered the unknown. My parents chose the subjects which I would take and I feel that I would have been more motivated if I had been able to choose the subjects which I enjoyed. In fact, I cannot remember being motivated while I was at school. Consequently, I received poor results and left school to attend a Youth Training Scheme. This involved attendance at college and I was not keen, I just wanted to earn some money.

I entered the care profession and again any form of learning involved people telling me what I should know. There was an opportunity at work to undertake a Foundation Degree (two years of a degree programme). Along with a colleague I decided to apply and was successful. This was not easy as I had to juggle family, work and study. My husband was very supportive but my daughter less so.

On completion of the Foundation Degree I had this desire to continue with my studies and to gain a degree. By having the creative space, within this module, I have been able to put meaning to my learning journey and I realise that I need to have someone familiar with me when I study, that small groups promote independent learning and that my motivation to study has arisen from the ability to relate my learning to my role in the workplace. This would have benefited me at the start of my education programme.

Jessie's biography enabled her to understand that her prior learning had been predominately decided for her and she was able to acknowledge how this contributed to her poor motivation and lack of formal qualifications. She was able to realise that she was enjoying her learning as she was more in control; identifying her learning needs and putting her learning into action. Constructing her biographical narrative has given Jessie the space to re-evaluate herself and the emotional effects of learning. Some call this coming to a different self-concept (Plummer 2001). What this means is her sense of who she is, but also who she could be. Fischer-Rosenthal (2001, p.100) views such shaping as a process of 'repair'. This is taken further in Carol's account:

Carol: When I was given the space to reflect on my learning pathway I thought that it would be easy to identify the significant experiences which have impacted on my learning. However, as I began to engage with the process I found myself going round and round in circles, questioning life events and trying to decide if they had an impact on my learning journey.

I realised that in order to undertake this task I needed to understand what sort of learner I was. Using Kolb's learning style inventory I realised that I was a visual, social learner who needed to learn in groups. Once I knew my learning style I was able to identify significant life events and situations which have affected my learning journey.

For as long as I could remember I have always needed a support group to guide and assist me. I had put this down to being the eldest of four girls. The most significant impact on my learning journey was the loss of my fiancé to my best friend who was on the same university course as me. This left me feeling isolated, uncertain, lost and scared of failure.

This module gave me the opportunity to explore this event. My fear of failure was creating a significant emotional and social barrier to my learning; I felt nervous and lacked confidence when I undertook new courses.

However, by having the time and space to consider my learning style and to reflect on past events has enabled me to become more aware of my identity. I need to unlearn the style which I have become comfortable with and step into the realms of one of the other learning styles; I need to empower myself and regain control of formal learning environments and emotionally respond to autonomous working more.

Thereby considering the part this space has enabled me to consider my whole approach to learning. Group discussions throughout this module have helped me to stop seeing the emotion barriers as negative but tools to change practice. It is my hope that I will become a better practitioner from this.

Through her biographical narrative enquiry, Carol was able to interpret, understand and give meaning to the impact of life experiences on her approach to learning. At the commencement of the module, Carol identified that a major life experience, which occurred as a student nurse, had influenced and shaped her subsequent approach to learning. However, through the use of protected, creative space and reflection Carol was able to consciously consider her scenario in hermeneutic terms of the interplay of the parts with the whole. Heidegger (1927/1962) believed that to understand the whole it is necessary to refer to and understand the individual parts. This is only achieved though through reference to the whole forming a hermeneutic circle of meaning making. This enabled Carol to understand the situation and so interpret the meaning to her Being-in-the-world (Heidegger 1927/1962). Or as Gadamer (1976) believes, it allowed a fusion of horizons as Carol was able to understand the interplay between past experiences and present behaviours. Diana's account was more tentative:

Diana: Considering my learning journey has contributed to my own personal development. It has enabled me to develop my leadership skills through enhanced self-awareness. Consequently I have a greater ownership of the learning which is taking place. I am aware of the need for self-evaluation and so consider different outcomes, aims and goals. By taking control of my learning, through the use of an action plan I feel that I have created effectiveness within my role.

A health care team which works in partnership with each other, has mutual respect for everyone's contributions and communicates effectively which can create all the difference in client's outcomes. The importance of understanding learning that takes place empowers the individual to understand the change that needs to be undertaken providing better approaches and outcomes. Although emotional, this journey has challenged self-conceptualised learning and opportunities to develop new skills.

As a professional Diana was exercising specialist knowledge in a position of trust (Nelson & McGillion, 2004). She was able to articulate the theory that supported her particular thinking and actions, and to carry out those actions with skill. She was behaving as she felt she should as a nurse, as she had seen others behave. But these actions did not necessarily constitute learning, more a replication of how others were behaving in the professional environment. What has helped to bring new insights and meaning is reflecting on her interaction with others and her biographical journey. The personal seemed more tentative, uncertain until brought into consciousness. Such framing of professional learning is a way of informing expertise according to professional codes (Eraut, 1994). However, unless knowing how is embedded, through processes of internalisation, it is less likely to be manifested in skilled, lived expression.

Significance for nurses' learning

Using biography narrative enquiry as the underpinning methodology for the delivery of the starter module enabled the students to engage consciously with their prior learning experiences, and understand how these contributed to individual learning journeys and practice. How nurses learn is heavily prescribed in their professional community of practice. Emotional residues can influence our whole approach to life and what we do as nurses. These nurses' stories suggest that emotions have been something to hide from or to overcome in everyday working and learning. The learning these nurses have achieved through reflecting on their lifeworld, and life events, has revealed a different view of who they are and what they view as 'knowledge' or nursing. They have moved from narrating their experiential learning to developing ideas about meaning and potential for personal action. We think this is very powerful in terms of developing agency in their learning. Jessie's and Carol's stories suggest this might even have been therapeutic through enabling them to jettison overly negative self concepts. Nevertheless, we would argue that while biographical work may have liberating effects it should not be viewed as a therapeutic endeavour unless undertaken by suitably prepared practitioners for that purpose. We also want to think about some critical questions which surround such work, not least in what can be said when tutors are in positions of power to determine students' futures.

267

Critical questions

If, as Horsdal (2012) has suggested, we tell our lives from the perspective of the context we are in, then how can the power inherent in a classroom situation be negated sufficiently to enable students to tell their stories freely? We as teachers began by sharing our own biographies and some of the difficulties we had encountered in developing this module. As the creation and sharing of our own biographies occurred within a classroom setting, on the first day of the module, we were not prepared for the very personal accounts which followed. This made us realise that the students felt secure in the space we had created together, but this also made us question how we could contain their anxieties and the unpredictability of the process safely. We continued to work with the students individually as they gave meaning to their biographies and understood more of how prior experience impacted on their approach to learning and care giving. This was a powerful experience for us and consequently we wanted to share this innovative approach to nurse learning with others. However, in true collaborative nature we wanted the students to be partners and we were very open about the co-constructive nature of working and writing together. We joined in the sharing of biographical narratives in class, openly sharing the difficulties we had experienced in setting up this course and our sense of this learning being important. After the assignment had been handed in we broached the subject of wanting to write about this experience for a wider audience and invited the students to become co-writers. Relationships that are supportive and secure enough to allow exploration of thoughts and feelings can provide a form of containment (Holmes, 2005).

Another critical question that emerged is how to justify teaching small numbers in a difficult economic climate. Our results would suggest that the richness of the learning is achieved precisely because the low numbers (there were only three students) enable the building of trusting relationships and a particular quality for the learning space. This, we feel, should be the argument used to defend this innovative approach to help nurse practitioners reinvigorate the soul of nursing. The cost of not doing so may be infinitely greater.

Nevertheless, an important suggestion for accommodating larger numbers that came from the conference (upon which this book is based) could be to teach nurses more widely how to build and share narratives so that they can develop some agency in the process as well and share this with others both in the classroom, but more importantly in the workplace. This could be with student health care practitioners, registered practitioners or patients. It could be a way to start to build a critical mass of different thinking and practice. This might also help to maintain momentum for greater sustainability of the project ideas. This bottom up approach can then demonstrate the value of a narrative approach to learning to those who pay for University study and workplace managers, in realistic ways through changes in practice, which are the outcomes they seek. This also offers a person-centred response to the criticisms advanced in the Francis report (2013) by role modelling caring about self and others as being central to learning processes

Reflexivity

This project has generated learning not only for the students but also for us as facilitators. The findings of the doctoral study suggested that this module was important for nurse education. However the translation into practice took this learning into the unknown. At the time the PhD was completed curriculum discussions were beginning regarding the CPD programme, and the need for a work-based learning pathway had been identified. The coming together of two different knowledge bases and areas of expertise – those of the Programme Director and Course leader/researcher – enabled the dovetailing of ideas which led to a fusion of theory and practice.

Teaching staff learning from this project, and from presenting it to an international audience, has allowed some cross-over of knowledge, from diverse sources, in terms of theoretical and practical understanding of narrative methodology and designing work-based learning programmes. Equally the shared experiences in the classroom opened up revealing facets of ourselves, which might not routinely appear in normal teaching and learning approaches. This approach has also challenged our thinking about learners and practitioners. What has become increasingly clear is the pivotal function of the facilitator of activity undertaken in the classroom in this process. The role of this teacher as facilitator is about forming trusting relationships within the group and creating atmospheres which feel safe and secure, often in quite a short space of time. How to manage disconnecting from this space is equally important and we have chosen to do this in constructive ways that empower the students to start writing their experiences for more formal audiences.

We have become aware that a key aspect of demonstrating the value of using a biographical narrative approach is to identify the significance and reach of the impact this project has had on the individual and their practice. This will be achieved through following up this first cohort of students through their programme to completion. The fundamental questions being asked will be 'what changed, for whom and where?'

Conclusions

Regulatory and economic requirements for the formulation of nurses' working and education can easily inhibit other more creative and meaningful ways to learn, which can also be viewed as risky, subjective and less measurable. And yet, experiencing and dealing with emotional residues is important and challenging work for maintaining a healthy mind, body and soul which can work effectively. The time has come for seeing how best to support people in their journey of development through their relationships with themselves, their organisations, to each other and those they care for both in their private and public lives. Biographical narrative approaches can offer the opportunity to integrate learning in personal and professional life in holistic ways enabling practitioners to build their own narrative and share this with others that they learn and work with. In this way organisational cultures can begin to be changed. By developing this skill practitioners can become more attentive and responsive to the narratives of those they care for and those they work with, so recovering the soul in nursing.

References

Barnard, A. & Sandelowski, M. (2001) Technology and humane nursing care: (ir)reconcilable or invented difference? *Journal of Advanced Nursing, 34,* (3) 367-375.

Bornat, J. & Walmesley, J. (2008) Biography as empowerment or appropriation: Research and practice issues. *The Innovation Journal: The Public Sector Innovation Journal, 13,*(1), 6.

Buber, M. (1958) *I and Thou.* 2nd Edition. Edinburgh: T & T Clark Ltd.

Buchan, J. & Seecombe, I. (2006) *From boom to bust? The UK nursing labour market review 2005-2006.* London: RCN

Burke, P.J. & Jackson, S. (2007) *Reconceptualising Lifelong Learning: feminist interventions.* London: Routledge.

Cahill, J. (2009) A combined review of: Collective biography and the legacy of Hildegard Peplau, Annie Altschul & Eileen Skellern; the origins of mental health nursing and its relevance to the current crisis in psychiatry; Mental health content of comprehensive pre-registration nursing curricula in Australia and Childhood abuse and psychosis; a critical review of the literature. *Journal of Research in Nursing, 14,* (6) 549-552.

Clarke, A. Hanson, E. & Ross, H. (2003) Seeing the person behind the patient: enhancing the care of older people using a biographical approach. *Journal of Clinical Nursing, 12,* 697-706.

Crawford, J. (2005) *Spiritually engaged knowledge: the attentive heart.* Aldershot: Ashgate Publishing Company.

Dominice, P. (2000) *Learning from Our Lives: using educational biographies with adults.* San Francisco: Jossey-Bass.

Eraut, M. (1994). *Developing Professional Knowledge and Competence.* London: Falmer Press.

Field, J. (2006). *Lifelong learning and the New Educational Order*. 2nd edition. *Stoke-on-Trent: Trentham Books.*

Fischer-Rosenthal, W. (2000). Biographical work and biographical structuring in present-day stories. In P. Chamberlayne, J. Bornat & T. Wengraf (Eds), *The turn to biographical methods in social science: comparative issues and examples.* London and New York: Routledge.

Francis, R. (2010). *Independent inquiry into care provided by Mid Staffordshire NHS Foundation Trust – January 2005 – March 2009 Vol 1.* London: HMSO.

Francis, R. (2013). *Report of the Mid Staffordshire NHS Foundation Trust Public Inquiry: Executive summary.* London: HMSO [on-line] Available from: http://www.midstaffspublicinquiry.com/report (accessed 07/02/2013).

Gadamer, H. (1976). *Philosophical hermeneutics.* (Linge, D ed) Berkeley.

Gopee, N. (2002). Human and social capital as facilitators of lifelong learning in nursing. *Nurse Education Today 22,* 608-616.

Great Britain. Department of Health – CNO's Directorate (2006). *Modernising nursing careers: setting the direction.* London: HMSO.

Greenhalgh, T. (2006). *What seems to be the trouble? Stories in illness and health-care.* Oxford: Radcliffe Publishing.

Greenhalgh, T. & Hurwitz, B. (1999). Narrative based medicine. *British Medical Journal, 318,* 48-50.

Hargreaves, J. (2008). The under-used resource of historical research. *Nurse Researcher, 15,* (3) 32-44.

Heidegger, M. (1927/1962). *Being and Time.* (J. Macquerrie and E. Robinson, Trans). New York: Harper and Row (Original work published 1927).

Higgs, J. & Titchen, A. (Eds) (2001). *Professional Practice in Health, Education and the Creative Arts.* Oxford: Blackwell Science.

Holmes, J. (2005). Notes on mentalizing – old hat, or new wine? *British Journal of Psychotherapy 22* (2) 179-197.

Horsdal, M. (2012). *Telling Lives: exploring dimensions of narratives.* London: Routledge.

Howatson-Jones, I.L. (2010). *Exploring the learning of nurses.* PhD unpublished thesis. Canterbury Christ Church University/University of Kent.

Jarvis, P. (2007). *Globalisation, lifelong learning and the learning society: sociological perspectives, lifelong learning and the learning society vol 2.* Oxon: Routledge.

Kellett, U. Moyle, W. McAllister, M. King, C. & Gallagher, F. (2009). Life stories and biography: a means for connecting family and staff to people with dementia. *Journal of Clinical Nursing, 19,* 1707- 1715.

Nelson, S. & McGillion, M. (2004). Expertise or performance? Questioning the rhetoric of contemporary narrative use in nursing. *Journal of Advanced Nursing, 47,* (6) 631-638.

Perry, B. (2005). Core nursing values brought to life through stories. *Nursing Standard, 20,* (7), 41-48.

Plummer, K. (2001). *Documents of life 2: an invitation to a critical humanism.* London: Sage Publications.

The Patient Association (2009). *Patients not Numbers, People not Statistics* Available from: http://www.patients-association.com/Portals/0/Public/Files/Research%20Publications/Patients%20not%20numbers,%20people%20not%20 statistics.pdf (accessed 13/01/2012)

West, L. (2001). *Doctors on the edge: General Practitioners health and learning in the inner city.* London: Free Association Books.

Widdowson, P. (ed) (1997). *Thomas Hardy: selected poetry and non-fictional prose.* Basingstoke: Macmillan.

Wigens, L. (1997). The conflict between 'new nursing' and 'scientific management' as perceived by surgical nurses. *Journal of Advanced Nursing, 25,* 1116-1122.

Chapter 13

Interaction between body and environment in *Steveston Recollected*

◊   CATHERINE KAREN ROY, UNIVERSITY OF BRITISH COLUMBIA

Interaction between body and environment in *Steveston Recollected*

In a world of globalisation where cultures and localities interconnect transformative learning occurs increasingly outside of one's place of origin. Since migrations are some of the outcomes of globalisation, my approach compares tendencies of global learning with the context of Japanese immigration to and inside Canada. In this book, on learner narratives, environment, and the body, I relate the concepts of transformative learning to the experience of the Japanese immigrants who established themselves in Steveston, south of Vancouver in Canada, as a place of transit. In their case, "learning is not solely the communication or transference of a body of knowledge from teacher to learner" (King, 2005, p.13) but rather the engagement of a learner with the world and the resulting personal experiences. From a constructivist approach, these processes of engaging and experiencing with the environment are a form of transformative learning. Why do we need to understand transformative learning? "More than 'book learning' and the traditional classroom, transformative learning is that of which life is made" (King, 2005, p.18) and it is produced within cultural contexts.

275

Susanna Egan remarks that "Canada has been a place of transit, of course, since the ancestors of the Amerindian[s] crossed the Bering Strait some 15,000 years ago… Immigrants to Canada identify themselves in transition, as new nationals from abroad, decentring the very concept of nation, and as hybrid among themselves, sharing geographical spaces and influencing each other's cultures even as their own keep changing" (Egan, 2002, p.36). I am interested in how these immigrants enter into relationships with the environment, learn, and change, and how these particular interactions between the body, meaning the group of Japanese immigrants, and nature, influence the autobiographical story-telling in *Steveston Recollected: A Japanese-Canadian History* by Daphne Marlatt and Robert Minden. Steveston was a fishing community south of Vancouver when Japanese migrants established themselves there during the Second World War, as a result of their enforced evacuation from the Canadian prairies. In place of the series of interviews that Maya Koizumi conducted in the early 1970s with some of these local Japanese immigrants, to compose the first edition of *Steveston Recollected*, Marlatt and Minden's reworked edition of the book offers poetry and photography about their current lives and the early years of their immigration to Canada. These Japanese-Canadians experience their living environment, the Canadian West Coast, as a metaphor for their human experience. In the poem "Steveston, B.C.," for instance, "Marlatt writes of place as geography, the physical geography connecting with the migration of the salmon, an emblem for west-coast wealth and aboriginal cultures; of the parallel migrations of people, including their identification, by virtue of immigration or ethnicity" (Egan, 2002, pp.31-32). The images in this poetic prose passage illustrate embodied learning, which means the notion of interaction with one's environment, in the context of the natural world of the Canadian West Coast referring to the salmon industry in Steveston.

In order to understand the processes involved in embodied learning, I first define it in the context of these Japanese immigrants by examining theories from the collection of essays in *Culture and Processes of Adult Learning* as well as Kathleen P. King's *Bringing Transformative Learning to Life.* To focus on the role that the body plays in the environment throughout this learning process I then refer to the poem "Time," which presents metaphors of body and migration to depict the formation of this culture of migration. Next, I address the issues of memory as raised by these autobiographical and biographical poems and narratives, and particularly by the poem "Steveston, B.C." Since Japanese immigrants construct a memory of places that in turn constitutes identity, I approach the geography of their stories from the perspective of Roberto Maria Dainotto's theory of "fear of placelessness." In my conclusion I consider what autobiographical poetry means for adult education.

The notion of embodied learning for these Japanese-Canadian adults of Steveston, B.C. reminds readers that adult learners are not a homogeneous group and that adult learning happens outside of the classroom. Here, embodied learning means the learning of Japanese immigrants when they are physically present in a new natural environment, like the canneries of Steveston. In this case, these learners perceive themselves as a Japanese minority within a broader – not necessarily dominating – culture. These immigrants then form a Japanese community whose embodied learning constitutes adaptive mechanisms to their environment, the work in the canneries; it means how their physical work in the canneries defines and transforms them into a Japanese fishermen community. Their embodied learning is what these immigrants learn about themselves and their immigration environment through their work. The canneries offer these workers both emancipating and oppressive dimensions of learning because of the constraints of the work itself and the sense of enclosure in this Japanese community. That is, fishing and canning salmon allow them to start a new life in Steveston, but as workers they are virtually confined to the cannery, as Marlatt describes in the poem "Steveston as you find it": "the plant packs their lives, chopping / off the hours, contains *them* as it contains first air, toilets, beds, the / vestige of a self-contained life in this small house back of the carpentry / shed" (21). While some Japanese envisioned an ideal life in Canada before emigrating, on arrival all of these immigrants were faced with the harsh conditions of their work environment. Through their work at the cannery, they incorporated their perceptions of these conditions into new frames of reference and meaning for Steveston; instead of representing a dream territory of immigration, Steveston presents itself as a place where Japanese work hard to make a living.

The new frame of reference of Japanese people is based on their actual work as opposed to what they heard about Steveston prior to their immigration. In turn, it is no surprise that their new perceptions of their immediate world changed these immigrants: transformative learning "is not so much *what* we know as *how* we know it" (King 2005, p.6). For these Japanese, the cannery opened their horizons on their lives as both Japanese and Canadians – never being exclusively one or the other, and neither desiring wholeheartedly to stay in Steveston nor wanting to return to Japan. So, these immigrants work in the canneries as a form of survival and support each other as members of one identifiable community. Adult education and transformative learning, in this context, empowers individuals: "it might reinforce or challenge an individual's sense of identity [or community] and the roles [… that person] chooses to play within the community" (Thorpe, 1993, p.1). Here, these autobiographical narratives present personal lived experiences of people in transit and in connection with the two cultures of their homeland and their new land. Instead of returning to Japan, these workers decide to play a decisive role in the development of Steveston as we know it today.

In their narration of their experiences, these immigrants are influenced by their interactions with their environment because they are moving between their memories of experiences in their former environment and those they have acquired in their new locale. Marlatt describes the Japanese in Steveston as flowing with the river, the cradle of human transit always moving:

And the river runs away with them, flood, storm, all manner of lost / belongings gone, anchorless on out to sea … / The edge, the edge. Settled by it. Camped rather. Cluster of / fishing shacks temporary as those Japanese who slept on boats arriving, each / season, for the fish, to stay, stray into settlement, believing still they were / only here this year, sending money home & staying on to the next, & the next, / […]. Always on the edge of, a Gulf where the river runs. (Marlatt & Minden, 2001, pp.29-30)

This passage explains why Egan refers to migrant autobiographers as individuals who "negotiate relationships and belong in several places at once" (Egan, 2002, p.29). Year after year, they delay their intended return to Japan until they never return to Japan.

The very concept of memory of their heart's homeland is internal and related to the body, as the etymology of the word "memory" in fact suggests. The *Etymologisches Wörterbuch der deutschen Sprache* indicates that the Middle High German word "(er)innern" or "imren" is derived from the spatial adjective of the Old High German "innarro," which means *der* "Innere" and "innerer;" it originally meant "machen, daß jemand etwas inne wird" (*Etymologisches Wörterbuch der deutschen Sprache*, 1989). In this sense, memory is that which allows a person to internalize information. In German, "erinnern" means three things: to remind, to remember, and to recollect; but unlike these English words, the German term also implies a process of internalization. Similarly, "Erinnerung" indicates a return to the inside, and describes the action of trying to revive or find connections with pre-existing knowledge. This idea of internalization makes the German words "erinnern" and "Erinnerung" seem to represent more accurately than the French word "mémoire" or the English word "memory," the processes of reminding, remembering, and recollecting as we commonly experience them.

Marlatt depicts in "Steveston, B.C." that at the same time as this West Coast town is becoming the new dwelling place for these Japanese immigrants, their ancestral homeland remains a kind of dream, something that they carry internally in their memories, as the etymology suggests. Meanwhile, Steveston is merely a place of transit where these fishermen have yet put down roots:

displaced & now relocated as fishermen can be, fishing up nets full of shadow / / food for the canneries to pack, blip blip sonar & even these underwater / migrations visible now as routes, roots, the river roots, out from under / brail net / they lift these fishes with. (Marlatt & Minden, 2001, p.57)

This poem refers to the water, salmon, and movement as a way of describing how these Japanese-Canadian fishermen are navigating through life changes. Marlatt plays with the homonyms "roots" and "routes," as in the routes or paths of a river and the "roots" that the immigrants themselves are growing, or hesitating to grow, in Steveston to draw our attention to their process of starting new lives. At the same time, this word play evokes the idea that migration influences the formation of culture and decentres the concept of nation. Away from their homeland and cut off from their roots, these Japanese people are in migration, just like the salmon that they catch for a living. The ocean and the river are images that help to represent how these immigrants move from their original homeland to new homes in her poetic text "Steveston, B.C.":

Steveston: delta, mouth of the Fraser where the river empties, sandbank after sandbank, into a muddy Gulf.

Steveston: onetime cannery boomtown: "salmon capital of the world": fortunes made & lost on the homing instinct of salmon.

Steveston: home to 2,000 Japanese, "slaves of the company": stript of all their belongings, sent to camps in the interior away from the sea, wartime, who gradually drift back in the '40's, [a] few who even buy back their old homes, at inflated prices, now owning modern ranchstyle etc, & their wives, working the cannery, have seniority now, located.

Steveston: hometown still for some, a story: of belonging (or is it continuing? Lost, over & over…

Less than enchanted by their new environment, the Japanese immigrants must make meaning out of their lives in the cannery. The need to learn to read their own lives differently causes them to transform their views on their past and their new surroundings. They integrate their changing perspectives on their land of immigration and in this way, experience transformative learning: "Transformative learning's framework has at its core the dynamic process that learners experience as they gain new discernment and knowledge, wrestle with its meaning, and determine how to reintegrate their learning and insight into their existing, and changing, perspectives" (King, 2005, p.6). For these immigrants, their transformative learning is also global learning. If

autobiography deals with an individual life, or with the family and community in which the individual life is situated, how are we justified in talking about it in terms of globalisation? Perhaps, because the autobiographer makes meaning out of lived experience, that meaning itself becomes a small contribution to the wider historical tradition of autobiography and, as such, becomes a global phenomenon. (Egan, 2002, p.22)

For the Japanese immigrants in Steveston, the resulting global learning is based on the formation of identity within a specific geography. In this multicultural context, what does it mean to be Japanese-Canadian? Is it to be entirely marginal? Japanese-Canadian immigrants in Steveston are divided between both Canadian and Japanese nationalities. And within the Steveston community, the Japanese part of identity is fragmented further since the fishermen come from distinct Japanese prefectures. Therefore, more than unique histories the global autobiographies of these fishermen belong to specific geographies.

Roberto Maria Dainotto's theory of the "fear of placelessness" argues that one must remember that the culture of those people who form a community in a specific place bring also a history independent of that new place (Dainotto, 2000, p.3), as for instance Japanese immigrants of different regions of Japan who establish themselves in a single community in British Columbia and thus form an apparently homogenous group. It is true that it is not place alone that defines the inhabitants of a region, whether their ancestral home or the place they have immigrated to: cultures do not emerge from place alone but rather, primarily from history. However, according to Dainotto regionalism is not defined by history but by individuals in relation with their environment: "[T]he hankering for grounded, rooted, natural, authentic values shared by a true community is the leading motive of regionalism" (Dainotto, 2000, p.17). In defining regionalism, or in this case, Steveston, place matters more than history. "'Regions'... tend to solve class conflicts within their homogeneous organic identity of people and land: They suggest, if not a wholesome nation, at least a contiguity of wholesome communities, each integral in its place" (Dainotto, 2000, p.25). This concept of regionalism appears in the book *Steveston Recollected,* where the different Japanese dialects are translated into homogeneous English, even if the dialogues and interviews come from members from different regions of Japan. The plurality of their voices is lost in translation, just as the diverse Japanese immigrants form the apparently homogeneous Japanese community of Steveston. These dialogues transform into poetic prose and poems are replaced by photos.

The poetic narratives in *Steveston Recollected* insist on the lived experience of these Japanese immigrants as one group instead of exploring their identities as members of distinct Japanese prefectures. In the face of necessity, these immigrants became fishermen, and their life experiences — as transformative learning explains —show that while adults do not necessarily decide to learn, they can always choose their world views. Also, Marlatt's literary representations of the Steveston community show that

education is an activity that explicitly links the individual with the social because of the world views acquired, changed and influenced in the transformative learning of immigrants, for instance. In particular, Mark Tennant argues that adult education is a vehicle for explicitly addressing significant social issues connected to areas such as the environment, race, health, gender, class, aged people, unemployed people, and the dislocation and exploitation of migrants. (Dainotto, 2000, p.6)

In terms of adult education, the experience of these Japanese workers emphasizes how human movement results in the constructing of new or renewed perspectives on the self, the environment, and one's temporary or permanent position in that environment.

The transformative learning of the Steveston community reminds us about the interactions between learners and those they encounter in a new environment. The resulting communication among both groups leads to a sense of how individuals see themselves in the world, how they perceive themselves and their role in society: "Merizow's broad new theory of adult learning attracted much attention because it helped to explain the process through which many kinds of adult learning experiences and approaches result in deep changes in how we understand ourselves and our world" (Fisher-Yoshida, Geller, & Schapiro 5). Beth Fisher-Yoshida, Kathy Dee Geller, and Steven A. Schapiro emphasize the long-lasting effect of transformative learning on one's personal view of the world. Learning, in this sense, is successful when it leads to change: "*Transformation* as an outcome refers to a deep and lasting change, equivalent to what some people term a developmental shift or a change in worldview" (Fisher-Yoshida, Geller, & Schapiro 6). Individuals who experience transformative learning start reflecting together on this experience and question assumptions (Green, 2009, p.119). In this sense, transformative learning is foremost based on critical thinking, dialogues, and the reorganization of concepts: In fact, "the intrapsychic and / or behavioral process[es] of a learner [are] involved in a transformative experience. It is about what the learner does, feels, and experiences, such as feeling disoriented, critically reflecting on assumptions and frames of reference, engaging in dialogue, or integrating images from our subconscious" (Leahy & Gilly, 2009, p.23). Through dialogues, people experience a sense of collectivity and community instead of perceiving themselves as independent individuals.

This communal feeling was distinct in the Steveston community and what emphasized this feeling was the fact that interviews were conducted with a specific group: the elderly. "Elders represent the collective memory of the group and should be respected for their life experience and wisdom. They are responsible for keeping the group together and for monitoring group dynamics" (Green, 2009, 124). This group represents those with the memory of the first Japanese immigrants to British Columbia who then formed the Steveston community. When Marlatt and Minden conducted interviews with the elders of Steveston, these writers seemed to follow an approach elaborated by Ann Davis, who uses a social construction methodology based on an ENRICHED Dialogue Model. Each letter of this acronym stands for specific criteria as the fundamentals of this approach: empathy, network of relationships, real (or reciprocity), integrity, collaborative, holistic, engagement, and discussion (Davis, 2009, p.135). According to this model, a self-other construction occurs in dialogues with one another and as a result, participants will broaden their worldview, be more mindful of their own culture and will learn to be "mindfully present to others" (Davis, 2009, p.135) and be emphatic:

> The ENRICHED Dialogue model adds to these theories rooted in communication and has the potential to transform one's self-view and worldview by looking at who we are and what we are making together. It is positive, possible, and inclusive of all perspectives. It concentrates on making and doing and looks at communication [naming, making and doing] holistically, not through it, to solve problems of everyday life episodes, situations, and events. (Davis, 2009, p.136)

The interviews conducted with members of the Steveston community seemed to adopt the ENRICHED Dialogue Model as Marlatt and Minden sought to understand the point of view of this community. "This transformative learning environment of relationships, difference, critical reflection, and awareness of self and others transforms one's ways of knowing and being in the world, one's self-view and worldview" (Davis,

2009, p.139). Indeed, Marlatt and Minden sought to understand the perspective of these immigrants when they settled in Canada and saw their community thrive with time.

However, the major limitation in their overall approach (the interviews and the subsequent publication of poems inspired by those interviews) was that the resulting edition of the poems did not include the interviews alluded to. The reframing of perspectives and worldviews that happened during the interviews were then translated into poetry written by the interviewer Marlatt and not by the subjects themselves. Thus, the value of the relational dialogues during the interviews was lost. This result raises the question that if transformative learning is to happen through communication, then the intercultural dialogues between interviewers and interviewees should also have been included, in order to preserve the dual perspectives that emerged from these talks between the interviewers and the Japanese-Canadians who are, in fact, global citizens. In this way, it is possible to understand ourselves and others as global citizens, as Davis argues: "To understand ourselves better, the similarities and differences, in a global context and to continue to develop and form a self/other orientation [individualization], we must explore and consider the multiplicity of views within all spheres of influence" (Davis, 2009, p.149). In this way, participants become aware of each other's culture as they engage in transformative relationships and acquire multiple worldviews based on each other's experiences and embodied transformative learning.

References

Dainotto, R. M. (2000). *Place in Literature: Regions, Cultures, Communities.* London: Cornell University Press.

Davis, A. (2009). Socially Constructing a Transformed Self-view and Worldview. In B. Fisher-Yoshida, K. D. Geller, & S. Schapiro (Eds.), *Innovations in Transformative Learning: Space, Culture, & the Arts.* (pp. 133-54). New York: Peter Lang.

Egan, S. (2002). 'True North' in Transit: Some Thoughts on Autobiography and Globalisation. In R. Dalziell (Ed.), *Selves in Crossing Cultures: Autobiography and Globalisation.* (pp.15-27). Melbourne: Australian Scholarly Publishing.

"Erinnern." (1989). *Etymologisches Wörterbuch der deutschen Sprache.* 22nd ed. Berlin: Walter de Gruyter.

Fisher-Yoshida, B., Geller, & K. D. & Schapiro, S. A. (2009). Introduction: New Dimensions in Transformative Learning. In B. Fisher-Yoshida, K. D. Geller, & S. Schapiro (Eds.), *Innovations in Transformative Learning: Space, Culture, & the Arts.* (pp. 1-19). New York: Peter Lang.

Green Fareed, C. (2009). Culture Matters: Developing Culturally Responsive Transformative Learning Experiences in Communities of Color. In B. Fisher-Yoshida, K. D. Geller, & S. Schapiro (Eds.), *Innovations in Transformative Learning: Space, Culture, & the Arts.* (pp. 117-32). New York: Peter Lang.

King, K. P. (2005). *Bringing Transformative Learning to Life.* Malabar: Krieger Publishing Company.

Leahy, M. J. & M. S. Gilly. (2009). Learning in the Space between Us. In B. Fisher-Yoshida, K. D. Geller, & S. Schapiro (Eds.), *Innovations in Transformative Learning: Space, Culture, & the Arts.* (pp. 23-42). New York: Peter Lang.

Marlatt, D. & Minden, R. (2001). *Steveston, Recollected: A Japanese-Canadian History.* Vancouver: Ronsdale Press.

Tennant, M. (1997). *Psychology and Adult Learning.* 2nd ed. London: Routledge.

Thorpe, M., Edwards, R., & A. Hanson (Eds.) (1993). *Culture and Processes of Adult Learning.* London: The Open University.

Chapter 14

Embodied interviewing: searching for illumination

◊   REBECCA CORFIELD

> *… human cognition is fundamentally shaped by embodied experience* (Gibbs, 1996:93).

Introduction

This chapter is concerned with issues around my research at Canterbury Christ Church University in the UK. The research takes the form of an in-depth auto/biographical narrative investigation into the experiences and motivation of a small opportunistic sample of school governors. The research focus is on factors relevant to the recruitment and retention of governors. Many European countries have school boards or advisory boards in schools which are similar to the UK system of school governors.

All state-funded schools and colleges in the UK have a governing body, typically numbering between 15 – 20 people, to which the Head Teacher reports. A typical governing body is made up of staff representatives, community governors and parents of students. The role of the school governor is a voluntary one and unpaid and a normal term of office is four years. Governing bodies in schools and colleges are accountable for the use of public funds, the quality of education provided and the wider contribution of the institution to the community and its relationship with that community. The duties of a school or college governor include setting the strategic direction of the school or college; establishing policies and objectives; approving the budget; reviewing progress against the budget and objectives; challenging and supporting the head teacher and senior staff and playing a part in appointing staff. The gubernatorial duties are conducted via meetings either of the whole governing body or via smaller sub-committees.

I have been a governor in three different schools in Inner London and I selected this research subject through an interest in seeing how my experience of this role compares to that of other governors. I have felt almost a sense of duty to be involved in some voluntary activity throughout my life, but am aware that this is merely my own experience and I am therefore interested to know what makes other governors volunteer to sit in long, evening meetings for a four-year term of office. Realising that others may have a quite different perspective on this role, I wanted to explore how being a school governor fits in to their lives and the stories they tell about it. It is important to understand more about what inspires someone to become and remain a school governor, as seen through their eyes.

Etherington points out that:

> In the field of counselling and psychotherapy many doctoral candidates choose to focus on a topic that has some personal meaning for them, knowing that this connection will develop and grow over time and keep them engaged in what can sometimes be a difficult and lonely process. (Etherington, 2004: 179)

School governors form one of the largest groups of volunteers in the UK with around 300,000 total governor places in schools. At any one time there are around 33,000 vacancies for school governors according to the UK government's statistics (www.sgoss.org.uk) and there are often not enough volunteers from black and minority ethnic backgrounds. I would also suggest – and this is supported by a gap in the literature – individual motivation is not a subject that is often discussed between governors, even when they first join the governing body, as they are normally too busy attending meetings for much personal discussion; nor has it been a focus for research. In the light of the above, my research questions are: What is the experience of a small sample of governors (including myself) with regard to governorship? What was their motivation to decide to become governors? Which factors emerge as important in their decisions to become and remain governors and how can these be theorised?

The research method is to encourage participants to tell their life stories located around this voluntary work, in the context of wider lives; and to chronicle as they see it, their experience of being a school governor. Through the resulting narrative, I aim to illuminate the key motivators that prompt their involvement and activity in this specific role. I am interested in what prompted them to volunteer and what makes them continue in this work. Being a governor is both shaped by how they perceive themselves, and in turn, shapes them beyond their involvement, through the very experience of being a governor. During my research I am interviewing five people more than once, in order to incorporate a longitudinal element to the research. I aim to gauge how their impressions and feelings about their motivation and involvement may change over time.

Embodied cognition is a position in cognitive science emphasising the role that the body plays in shaping the mind (Damasio, 2000). Represented as connecting inner and outer worlds (Merrill and West, 2009), this is relevant to our understanding of the interview interaction – how the mental and emotional outlook of both participants is shaped by their respective and mutual physical and emotional experiences. Throughout the research process there is substantially more involved than just the words exchanged and any examination of them alone is bound to be limited (Richardson, 1997).

This chapter explores the extent to which the hitherto unseen, hidden or ignored aspects of research that involve the embodiment of feelings are important and can help us understand the nature of the interaction and indeed, the fuller story of the life being explored. In considering the physical aspects of a particular research activity, I will relate certain aspects of my interviews and my reflexive work to wider issues related to research relationships, the body and the environment and consider how my material connects with these headings. I also want to think about how we connect specifics with more general issues and to what extent they are interlinked. I will draw on the ideas from dramaturgy to illuminate these aspects. Having more of an awareness of the totality of the interview experience can only enable us to see any emerging issues more fully. We can attempt to garner more of Mills' "encyclopaedic sense" by exploring issues through more than one perspective (Mills, 2000: 142).

My research involves other people, some of whom I know well, some of whom I have met briefly before and some I met for the first time through my studies. For the latter group I physically make initial contact with them. We get the measure of each other at this first meeting. With the people I already know, I am reshaping and redefining our previous relationship to be more purposeful and business-like. When we meet for an interview, I prepare busily: I am a busy body, and also a busybody ready to enquire and, maybe, pry into their lives. The meeting of two people to undertake research through the medium of an interview is formal in the sense that it has been set up – designed, booked and arranged – far away from a casual chance meeting. Such an encounter does not arise naturally and is not necessarily easy to carry out. Many people may find it difficult to express themselves in this setting (Atkinson, 2006).

We face each other like negotiators across the table, bodies close in a safe space, looking into each other's eyes, refreshments available. We are sitting uncomfortably close, I can feel nervous and can heat up with my anxiety that I make a good impression and that she feels at ease in talking about herself and disclosing the personal material to come. My interviewee does not realise it is so personal but I can hear more than just the words she is saying. By talking about her motivation for being a school governor, inevitably she discloses her possible motivation for all sorts of other aspects of her life. The passing comments she makes about her relationship tell me something about how it is going and her references to her family clearly depict their place in her life. She is describing to me indirectly how she feels about herself, through the medium of her direct revelations about her governorship.

Of course, I am telling her all about myself too: in the language I use, the choice of questions I ask and how I direct the interview, how I react to what she is telling me and my behaviour generally. We each change the way we feel at times as the interview proceeds, relaxing as the interview progresses and we forget the recording devices, for instance, or getting tense when a difficult subject emerges, or some confusion is apparent. Given the multiplicity of currents and undercurrents, exploring the many layers and complexity of the situation will enable us to better understand all the different factors being played out; all the inhibitors and the encouragement being experienced as well as what is being discussed at any moment of time.

In some ways this is daunting. Analysing the words being said and taking them at face value is complicated enough. Every interview from the transcription alone could easily contain a book to be written, without layering on this extra dimension of analysing the physical/emotional/relational dimensions that may be relevant. However, if these relational, bodily and environmental aspects are at work and playing out their effects on the two participants in the interview, then it seems important at least to enquire if they are significant. In the main we often focus on what is done, how and to whom and find plenty to discuss and analyse in those aspects alone. I have revisited the whole process of data collection via in-depth interviewing in my research, adding how it is felt and perceived by one or both of the participants. This was to reach a fuller illumination of an encounter, in order to explore these extra dimensions for their significance. Yet the challenge is in how to do this. How can we express the unexpressed or depict the unseen? Beyond this, how can we evaluate its significance to our analysis? These issues have been explored in the literature, to an extent, but the lived experience of engaging with them is still difficult (Merrill and West, 2009).

Bodily engagement

So I will turn to the embodied experience of interviews. Right from the start of choosing a research topic, selecting and sifting participants, initiating contact and the arrangements that have to be made – these elements create an impression, not least in my own body, about how I would like to be, or what seems appropriate. In my case with my research participants, I was aiming to create an impression of being seen as polite and friendly; impressive and competent; someone with authority but who will also work as an equal; courteous (arrangements to be made at their convenience) and with credibility as a local governor myself for many years and therefore 'one of them'. So this can be summed up as essentially: unthreatening, keen, entreating – and essential too – there is no way I wanted anybody to refuse to participate, even though I explicitly gave them scope to do so.

Each interview conducted involves choosing a location and a setting. The most appropriate form of seating, positioning and environment is selected to put the participant at ease and to elicit a free-flowing and unconstrained dialogue. As I considered the setting or staging of my interview and my part in arranging it, together with my prompt cards and my analysis of the performance that resulted, I began to think along the lines of more of a theatrical setting to the interview. Holliday stresses this aspect of qualitative research:

> Another very important task lies in establishing the research set-
> ting – exactly where, when and with whom the research will take
> place. In opposition to the notion of survey in quantitative research,

the aim is to go deep into a definable setting in which phenomena can be placed meaningfully within a specific social environment. (Holliday, 2007: 33)

This, coupled with the fact that my first research participant had previously been a professional actor herself, triggered a consideration of a possible congruence with a full theatre analogy. Theatre can be defined as a collaborative form of art that uses live performers to present the experience of a real or imagined event before a live audience in a specific place. The location for the encounter was my lounge in my house – a familiar location for my participant as she had been a friend of mine for 15 years. I was the interviewer and carefully arranged the furniture and the lighting. My lounge needed to be tidied, the seating arranged and the technology checked. Before my participant arrived, I arranged the necessary props and limited the chance for interruptions by turning the telephone off. I had a sense I was directing the encounter as I selected and established the physical boundaries for the experience.

Normally as friends at my house, we sit on the sofa to chat. This time we sat at the round dining table, which felt more business-like. It meant I could put my two recording devices on the table between us and also have a note-pad in case I needed to take a written record of our conversation. We had two wine glasses present on the table and kept re-filling them. I am used to sitting at the table when I work with visiting career counselling clients but it was probably the first time my friend had ever sat at the table rather than in an easy chair at my house. It was 8.15 in the evening when the interview began, the house was empty except for the two of us and there were no interruptions except from the prowling of a curious cat.

There are pros and cons to interviewing people known to us. This friend who had heard about my research volunteered to be a participant. She was a recently elected governor at an inner city state school for pupils with special needs. She would provide interesting material, and would be available over time to enable monitoring her changing perceptions about her own motivation. The drawback was that where there is already an established relationship it can feel awkward to back off from or undo it, in order to establish a 'new' researcher/research participant interaction which can start afresh from the beginning of a new topic of discussion (Andrews, 2007; Etherington, 2004).

When conducting narrative research, the stories we hear through our participants will often be dramatic. The word drama comes of course from the ancient Greek, meaning action or doing, now used more specifically for fiction represented in performance. Our research sometimes unearths tragic or comedic elements, certainly stories have emotional undertones. As noted below, there will be a cast of characters appearing through the telling and re-telling of each of the stories. The researcher acts as the primary audience, who then interprets and edits and re-tells the highlights, identifying key elements, akin to the theatre critic in his or her review. Our work could therefore be seen to be a type of theatrical collaboration with the research participant as the narrator and the researcher as audience as well as co-performer.

The use of dramatic metaphor for life is a sociological perspective that stems from a clear thread. Kenneth Burke, the American literary critic writing in the 1940s, delineated five essential dramatic elements which he saw could be usefully applied to human relations. He talked of a dramatic pentad comprising: act, scene, agent, agency and purpose, which were to be used to illustrate the elements of social interaction (Burke, 1966). These ideas can still be seen to be in use today in the 'what, where, who, how and when' which are frequently used as basic enquiry points for a meaningful analysis of interactions of all sorts.

Erving Goffman, the influential American sociologist, first explicitly adapted the idea of dramaturgy from the theatre through his work in 1959. He paid homage to the work of Burke, a contemporary. Goffman did not like to explain or justify his writing, preferring his words to speak for themselves. His major work, *The Presentation of Self in*

Everyday Life (Goffman, 1959) is an extraordinary book, written as a stream of descriptive explanation, and it is really an extended metaphor for life lived in dramatic and theatrical terms. Goffman goes far beyond talking of dramatic touches in life and picks up Burke's ideas of life itself being a drama where humans by nature see and interpret situations totally as dramatic interventions (Burke, 1966). Similarly, actors perform in role on the stage, relating in turn to other actors in their respective roles and, in doing so, relate in varied ways to diverse people at different times.

To Goffman we are all actors, changing the parts we play according to our audience and the roles we are inhabiting. In his book he does not claim to be presenting a theory to explain all human relations, merely suggesting a descriptive framework for analysing social interaction thus providing a useful lens through which to considering human behaviour rather than as a rationale for the causes of behaviour. Goffman explains in the preface:

> I mean this report to serve as a sort of handbook detailing one sociological perspective from which social life can be studied ... A set of features will be described which together form a framework that can be applied to any concrete social establishment. (Goffman, 1959: 9)

Interestingly, the word person in ancient Greek translates as "mask". Goffman cites Robert Park:

> It is probably no mere historical accident that the word person, in its first meaning, is a mask. It is rather a recognition of the fact that everyone is always and everywhere, more or less consciously, playing a role. ... It is in these roles that we know each other; it is in these roles that we know ourselves. (Park, 1950, cited in Goffman, 1959: 30)

Applying this analogy to auto/biographical narrative research, which involves just two protagonists, may seem slightly unusual. We may be more used to the multi-actor ensemble cast, or troupe of actors, working together to deliver a theatrical production. However, playwrights of course, have often used few actors, or even one, on the stage as an experimental device. It is in this dramatic form that conducting research interviews can most closely be aligned to. A noted example of a playwright using this kind of dramatic presentation is Samuel Beckett in several of his works such as *Happy Days* (Beckett, 1961). Beckett uses one or two main actors just talking to each other. The action is minimal and the story unfolds through speech. Any kind of recognisable plot appears only fleetingly and the talk is of relationships and memories and plans: any development takes place through the words that are spoken.

There seem to be many ways in which this theoretical framework could enhance our experience as auto/biographical narrative researchers. Having a fresh layer to impose over our first analysis of our work, can bring alive our perception and enhance our interest. My exploration of Goffman's ideas has increased my involvement with the interaction beyond the superficial level of the presented story. I have become much more aware of the manifold layers of interpretation which can help unearth different meanings. As an experienced interviewer in my professional role as a careers counsellor, I had previously been used to relying on my own immediate and direct interpretation of my clients' stories and issues.

However as researchers we are not merely the passive audience of the story being told. Through our choice of research, our questions, our voice, appearance and gestures, through our very beings we are influencing and affecting the story being told. We are part of the story in that sense. Accordingly we need to have the knowledge as researchers of our own influence in the story being told. Our directing of the interview; the relationship with the narrator and how that may affect the telling of the story; the act of (active) listening, reacting, responding and pausing; that of transcribing including choosing what to include, leave out and highlight; the annotations we make to scripts; the analysis we bring to bear on our interview; the theorising we employ; the lens through which we view the encounter – these are all changing and shaping the story differently (Merrill and West, 2009).

Salmon and Riessman tell us:

> All narratives are, in a fundamental sense, co-constructed. The audience, whether physically present or not, exerts a crucial influence on what can and cannot be said, how things should be expressed, what can be taken for granted, what needs explaining, and so on. (Salmon and Kohler Riessman, 2009: 80)

Re-interpreting our findings

Although we cannot objectify our role in the interchange, in the language of conventional science, it is important in the name of a more inclusive science to be able to 'see' ourselves in the interaction, and to be able to describe more clearly the nature of our role. In our efforts to stand apart from our work, this can give us a different view and therefore another more inclusive way of seeing what has occurred. If we adopt the tenet of dramaturgical thinking and see that life is indeed theatre and we are all acting towards, and in reaction to, each other, this can be applied to the work of the narrative researcher. Using the metaphor of theatre in relation to our enquiry, we can talk of ourselves as actors too, certainly involved with the production. We can consider which persona we inhabit in the production. How have we constructed our role? Which 'mask' or front are we projecting, whether consciously or not, in our dealings with our research partners?

My first interview presented some role confusion as my participant was previously known to me as a friend, although I was interviewing her as someone about whose experiences as a governor I knew very little. I had to switch from the role of friend to the role of researcher –moving from the familiar to the strange as I did so. An additional issue here may be the power relationship between researcher and the researched. Hydén discusses the need for an awareness of the subtle disparities that can be perceived between the two people in the research interaction and the impact this can have on the authenticity of the research outcomes. Allowing and making space, either in the physical or the permissive sense, for the telling of stories can be a significant factor in allowing people to speak for themselves (Hydén, 2009). As researchers we are players, experimenting with the elements involved. Seeing ourselves as actors too, (in ancient Greek, actor meant one who interprets), we can vary our styles of interrogation and enquiry to better fit the role.

Analysing my first research interview, questions arose of how my participant felt in terms of the power balance between us. I noticed that there had been nervous laughter during the interview. Underlying feelings are more apparent when we concentrate on the interplay between characters. My participant was concerned after the interview that she had not said anything to interest me. I meanwhile had been worried that she would find the encounter turgid and boring compared to our usual lively chats as friends. In different ways we were both feeling responsible for the satisfaction of the other person. These feelings and the nervous tensions they represented were manifesting themselves during our interview as slightly edgy laughter sporadically bubbling up and escaping.

I used the framework of dramaturgy to ask my research participant explicit questions about how she sees her role as a governor and the roles of others she works with as governors. I was interested to know how she perceives this aspect of her life with her feelings about other roles she inhabits: working woman, mother, housewife, partner or businesswoman. Dramaturgy has given me a language and a visual image to offer as a discussion point around issues of identity and sense of self. Even on the governing body there will be times when different roles are required. I have just moved from being chair of the governing body on which I sit. As chair my role could be described as being objective, bridge-building, responsible, calm and measured, and also a leading role whereas I am now more of 'a back-bencher' (someone who is no longer so prominent: the phrase back-bencher comes from the British parliamentary tradition, where you play a role physically distant from the main protagonists, who face each other across a space defined by the length of two swords!). Thus the role is less visible and I am more of a subsidiary member of the cast – a valued member of the chorus perhaps but certainly a more minor player, just one of the company.

Acting is of course, very physical. Actors do not just act with their facial expressions and read the words in different ways. They use voice, stance, expression, movement and gesture as expressive tools to convey meaning and nuance. When we record, transcribe and then fillet our research, how can we build in these aspects of the interaction to inform our analysis? Noting and *remembering* the physicalities/emotionalities/relationalities of the interview, including asking questions directly related to a participant's feelings, could bring these more embodied elements into the theatre of doing and theorising research.

Conclusion

West observes:

> Narratives, like experience itself, are never complete. There is always another perspective, an alternative way of creating meaning and intelligibility from the fragments of experience. (West, 1996)

Making links between the words expressed and the dramatic roles we inhabit in our research is illuminating for me and can be helpful to encourage further exploration and analysis (Reid, 2008). I was able to share my enquiries with my research participant. She agreed with the feelings I had ascribed to her and felt that it added an extra element of understanding to describe some of the underlying feelings and emotions during our encounter which had not been expressed in words. Our research activities conducted in different places would have made a difference to the nature and progress of the event. Using a dramatic overlay on my interview helped me appreciate some of the physical and environmental sensitivities at play. The challenge of narrative research is to define, locate and unearth the starting and finishing points, the themes and the meaning. Andrews concludes:

Listening involves risking one's self, exposing oneself to new possibilities and meaning. (Andrews, 2007: 15)

I started off as an interviewer with over 20 years' experience of working one-to-one with people, so I had no qualms about sitting across a table and asking people to talk to me, nor about getting them to open up to me. My work as a careers counsellor involves just that, meeting up with complete strangers and finding out from a standing start about their view of their life history, their current situation and their hopes and dreams for the future. But I had underestimated the layers of understanding that could be added by analysing the more embodied dimensions and representations during the encounter. Interviews as a formal device of telling a story can in fact stifle disclosure, which may be interesting in thinking about the other's story, and the dynamics at work, but we may lack any understanding of her lived experience. The direct question, the sense of being on show and performing, being scrutinised, the anxiety of saying the wrong thing, may only show one side of the story being explored. Taking the risk of being more adventurous and playful with our material and our research activities could bring us the rewards of more rounded narratives, as well as of more understanding of what inhibits or facilitates the play of storytelling.

Only connect! … Live in fragments no longer. (Forster, 1910)

References

Andrews, M. (2007). *"Shaping History"*. Cambridge: Cambridge University Press.

Atkinson, P. (2006). *Everyday Arias: an Operatic Ethnography*. Lanham, Maryland: AltaMira Press.

Beckett, S. (1961). *Happy Days*. New York: Grove Press.

Burke, K. (1966). *Language as Symbolic Action*. Los Angeles: University of California Press.

Damasio, A. (2000). *The Feeling of What Happens: Body, Emotion and the Making of Consciousness*. London: Vintage.

Etherington, K. (2004). *Becoming a Reflexive Researcher*. London: Jessica Kingsley Publishers.

Forster, E.M. (1910/1989). *Howards End*. London: Penguin.

Gibbs, R.W. (2006). *Embodiment and Cognitive Science*. Cambridge: Cambridge University Press.

Goffman, E. (1959). *The Presentation of Self in Everyday Life*. London: Penguin Books.

Holliday, A. (2007). *Doing and Writing Qualitative Research*. London: Sage.

Hydén, M. (2009). 'Narrating sensitive topics'. in M. Andrews, C. Squire & M. Tamboukou, *Doing Narrative Research*. London: Sage, pp.121-136.

Kohler Riessman, C. (2008). *Narrative Methods for the Human Sciences*. London: Sage.

Merrill, B and West, L. (2009). *Using Biographical Methods in Social Research*. London: Sage.

Mills, C. Wright. (1959/2000). *The Sociological Imagination*. Oxford: Oxford University Press.

Reid, H. (2008). *Placing self in the research activity* in Journal of Research into Professional Development. Vol 1 issue 1. Canterbury: Canterbury Christ Church University Publishing.

Richardson, L. (1997). *Fields of Play*. New Jersey: Rutgers University Press.

Salmon, P. and Kohler Riessman, (2009). Looking back on narrative research: an exchange. In M. Andrews, C. Squire & M. Tamboukou, *Doing Narrative Research*. London: Sage, pp.78-85.

School Governors One Stop Shop website, a government-backed charity to promote the recruitment of school governors www.sgoss.org.uk (accessed 1/3/2013).

West, L. (1996). *Beyond Fragments: Adults, Motivation and Higher Education*. London: Taylor and Francis.

Sheild of Tears

◊   NORA BATESON

Stories breathe life into the abstractions of philosophical pursuit. The machine that seems to swallow up our children at the age of 5 and spit them out again at 18 ready for the world (or at least ready for university), is traced deeply into our entire social system. Avoiding it, altering it, fighting it, and changing it are not easy mandates. But, surviving it intact is not easy either. The crisis we face now in education is not really about what is or isn't provided in the curriculum, its not about test scores or about which universities are the most prestigious. It is, in fact, not even about knowledge. The issue is more diffused. Simultaneously, it is more acute.

Though nearly invisible to most eyes, the problem lies at the level of thought patterns generated in our education systems, that are not conducive to the sort of thinking the young generations need to have access to. It is a question of delivering an obsolete form of inquiry that fails to engage with the dynamics of living complexity. The stakes are high, the survival of the human species, as well countless others is at hand. And yet, the lethargy around turning the Titanic of what we call school, is apparent in every curriculum.

Our entry into the conversation about education starts with the relationship between the generations; a sacred territory between present, future and past. My memories of school are largely haunted by a sucking sound, a giant vacuum that pulled the oxygen out of the room, out of me, out of science, out of art out of everything it could drain it out of…

leaving a lifeless shell of multiple choice, right and wrong answers, shame and the small thrill of counting the minutes until lunch.

Stories were relegated to fluff. The fractured dominant paradigm ruled the school. I watched as an outsider, noticing that some people were good at pleasing the ideological superstructure. These were the students who had learned the game. They could take in exactly the right bits of information and knew how to present it back to the establishment in tune with overture of the of cultural savvy. Others would not be tamed, they fought, they ignored, they hid themselves in the folds of labels like "bad-boy", or "learning challenged", or "athlete".

All too familiar is the bright child who has chosen not try to succeed at the game when failure is immanent anyway. There is, in fact, a certain nobility in keeping some form of dented self-respect. These students are punished accordingly, not only with poor grades and distraught parent-teacher conferencing, but also by the shadow cast across their lives of the university they didn't go to, the job they didn't get, the wealth they will never have because they refused to drink the cool-aid when they were 14 years old. Most rebels are eventually broken.

I was somewhere in between. Not willing to comply, not willing to fail. My education was marching me toward an indoctrinated, acclimated adulthood, but I was headed elsewhere. I had a secret weapon. I was lucky. Only now am I beginning to know how lucky. I had protection. I had the tears of my father.

My father would walk me to the bus stop, stand with me there until the bus came. He was vocally suspicious of how I might be contaminated by the school system. His gloom deepened as we waited for the bus together. Then, with a little British irony he joshed as he helped me climb aboard, "Use the brains you were born with." As the school bus rolled away I could see from my seat out the window that my father was weeping.

He said to my mother, "They are going to ruin her mind." But they didn't. For me, the contrast between home and school was extreme. To begin with, the dinner conversation protocol was premised on the notion that anyone, children included, were perfectly capable and even expected to make valuable contributions to the discussion. A sloppy thought was a sloppy thought no matter the age or notoriety of its purveyor. All of us were of the understanding that the objective of our interactions was not to prove anything, or to be stroked for being knowledgeable in a particular subject, but rather to learn something, perhaps even stumble together into a new understanding.

And what was a sloppy thought? One that was riddled with the traps of split thinking captured in the net of mechanical logic. Our household was a place where breakfast was fried eggs and fresh thoughts, a piece of music was a starting place for a day's inquiry, the encyclopedia Britannia took up most of the table, and the fish tank was a source of poetic counterpoint to the Balinese art on the wall. The world for me was delivered unseparated.

So, clearly, school was Hell. I could not make it make sense. The tasks and the language, the tests and the social structures were not within my realm of success. They were asking the wrong questions. Good questions don't have answers at all, let alone right or wrong ones. They are invocations to other ways of thinking. It's bad math. The world as it is, bubbling and swirling, unreasonable and uncertain, is a story fountain. The world as it was taught was starved of its harmonies, it was study in single notes.

My father was writing a letter to a colleague when he wrote the phrase, "Break the pattern that connects and you necessarily destroy all unity." This became what is now a well known quote from the introduction to his book, Mind and Nature: "What is the pattern that connects the crab to the lobster, the orchid to the primrose, and all the four of them to you and you to me..?." That's a good question. That question alone is grounds for an entire education. It calls for the formal details of living ecosystems to be seen in the larger context of pattern. It requires the differences to be described through specific study in order to examine the minutia and the structures of living things, while simultaneously it pulling into focus a larger vision of the the patterns and rhythms of life. How do the many details learn? How they interact? How are they organized, or rather "organizing", since the adjusting is incessant.

Research is process, and the study of process is the research. How does the context of our study shift when we imagine the stories of all living things? Can we begin to place our story inside that ever unfolding epic of evolutionary development in nature? This is a question that interlaces empathy in the recognition of the patterns we share with life itself. The slightest recognition between ourselves and the sea creatures, between each other, between our family communication systems and the way a rainforest's flora and fauna are interwoven is a peek, into the possibility that we share a story. A gateway to another kind of ethics, and a careful tending to the aesthetic.

This was why my father cried. He was mourning the loss of that precious capacity to integrate and function within the uncertainty of outcome and the verity of the interdependency. What my father did not know, was that the tears that he gave me formed a shield. They carried a meta message that resided below my conscious understanding, based in the clarity there was something important that could be lost, that my mind was in danger, and that I should not trust the institutional authority I would spend the next decades in communion with. I cannot say that his shield made it easier for me, in fact it kept me alert to the need to stretch across a paradox-- to ride on a pair of mustangs one foot the hypocrisy of the educations system the other on the pursuit of wisdom, and to let them make friends.

I am not sure exactly how to alter the educational system to incorporate a study of the overlapping patterns in life. Education is of course part of a larger context of culture, including economy, language, politics, science and so on. We are normalized into an unworkable imbalance, forever tearing the world into pieces, and reifying the need to grasp each 'answer', each "solution" and freeze it. This is of course wildly out of keeping with the dance of life. As Heraclitus illustrated with his famous statement, "you cannot step in to the same river twice." Never rest in certainty. And yet the ambiguity we need is unacceptable to the needs of notions such as "authority," "credibility," "expertise." A politician cannot build a campaign on the premise of acknowledging the problems we face right now are so big that it is not possible to actually "know" how to fix them. Likewise a teacher can hardly begin a class by stating a complete inadequacy in the subject being taught.

As parents, I have found that in the best of scenarios we have to model for the children a kind of communication that is open, vulnerable, and learning… but also we have to teach them that this relationship is not to be taken for granted. Kids have to know that most adults will expect them to be respectful without any inclination of reciprocating that respect. Grown ups often abuse their authority by presuming their right to be right, and believe they should not be questioned, doubted or proven wrong under any circumstances. It is unfortunate to have to teach the children to feign respect. But they have to know how to deal with those people. Their touchstone will be the adults who were willing to learn. Education.

What is the restorative? Is there a prototype or a structure for another education? Can we fix this? From my perspective I see that the coming generations will be faced with a translation task. They will carry two narratives that are seemingly at odds. The story of the broken, the binary and the disenfranchised is one thread of stories. The other is the clearing focus of a world of stories, woven and tangled in ever changing response to one another. Somehow they will find balance, and the foot holds of transaction that will fuel the transitions.

In our relationship between generations we will move through a mis-alignment with nature, that is setting a discordant toxicity lose into our way of living; our way of learning, our way of seeing, our way of know-ing. Together. We cannot teach them. They need skills we do not have to offer- advice we cannot give. They need elders they will not find amongst the living, that have a broad horizon to draw from. Elders that have met the source of the earth, but know the coda of the Wall Street machine. A sci-fi grandmother – wise with humanity and rich with intuition, but a warrior of the digital, and adept in urban professionalism.

Since we can cannot supply this for them, to the best of my knowl-edge, our secondary task is that we must simply get out of the way. Our job is to weep at the bus stop. We will have to find the strength to carry the heaviest of all burdens; an empty bag of tricks. We have to allow this generation to make mistakes we could not afford to make, to let them play with the edges of our frames while we leave a trail for them, planted with baskets of the most magnificent examples of humanity we can find. Reasons. Our gravest responsibility is to maintain for the children our enthusiasm for great art, incredible mathematics, beautiful science, heartbreaking poetry, tales of history's turning points, told from multiple perspectives.

Multiple perspectives, multiple perspectives…